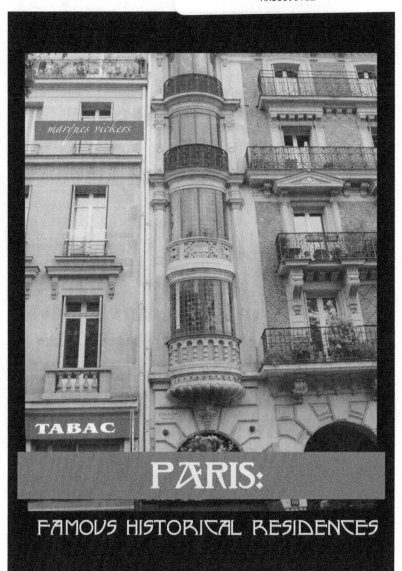

marques vickers

TABAC

PARIS:

FAMOUS HISTORICAL RESIDENCES

PARIS:

FAMOUS HISTORICAL RESIDENCES

By Marques Vickers

MARQUIS PUBLISHING
BAINBRIDGE ISLAND, WASHINGTON

Version 1.3

Published by Marquis Publishing
Bainbridge Island, Washington
TwistedTourGuides.com

Vickers, Marques, 1957

Editorial and Photographic Assistance: Caroline Vickers

PARIS: Famous Historical Residences

Dedication: To my daughters Charline and Caroline.

TABLE OF CONTENTS

Preface

HISTORICAL FIGURES:

Otto von Bismarck: A German Unifier At The Expense of France
Madame Claude: The Prostitution Industry Within Paris
Charles Parnell: An Irish Nationalist Leader Establishes His Foreign Headquarters
George Boulanger: The Populist Crusader Who Might Have Become King
Coco Chanel: High Couture and Questionable Wartime Affiliations
Karl Lagerfeld: A Chameleon of the Haute Fashion World
Jacques Verges: Terror's Advocate Representing Reprehensible Actors and Actions
Francois Mitterrand: Saving His Biggest Secret For The End of His Presidency

BONAPARTE ERA:
The Formative Years of Napoleon Bonaparte
Desiree Clary: The Desiree in Napoleon Bonaparte's Life
Empress Josephine Bonaparte: The Woman Behind Napoleon Bonaparte's Rise
Charles Maurice de Talleyrand: The Undeclared War Between The United States and France
James Monroe: The Diplomat Who Framed American Foreign Policy
Pauline Bonaparte: A Loyal, Lovely and Promiscuous Bonaparte
Louis Bonaparte: A Strong-Willed Rebellious Bonaparte Brother
Duke of Wellington: An Occupier As An Assassination Target

THINKERS/PHILOSOPHERS/WRITERS:
Rene Descartes: A Brilliant Philosophical Mind Felled By Barbaric Medical Practices
Blaise Pascal: A Mathematical Genius Tormented By His Religious Scruples
Jean-Jacques Rousseau: Mining Deeper Insight Through Recollection and Personal Examination

Voltaire: A Forerunner's Writings Spurring the French
Revolution
The Corruptible Legacy of the Notorious Marquis de Sade
Thomas Paine: A Writer Whose Idealism Permitted No Peace
Poet Andre Chenier's Dangerous Acquaintances and Ill
Timing
Vicomte de Chateaubriand: A Probable Fictitious Adventurer
and Statesman
Washington Irving: A Traveling American Author of
Accomplishment
Duke of Saint-Simon: Eavesdropping On Dysfunctional
Royalty
Stendhal: The Writer Who Adored Women
Honore de Balzac: Genius Inundated By Adversity That
Spurred Productivity
Alfred de Musset: A Celebrated and Sensitive But Ultimately
Wilted Prodigy
Heinrich Heine: A German Exile's Lost Illusions of Utopia
Alexis de Tocqueville: Democratic Moderation Portrayed
Through A Literary Observer
George Sand: A Romantic Writer Disdaining Society's
Restraints
Alexandre Dumas: The Tsunami Left By A Nineteenth
Century Literary Figure
Charles Dickens: An Authentic Witness Detailing Two
Familiar Cities
Charles Baudelaire: The First Modernist On The Paris
Literary Scene
Leo Tolstoy: The Madness Accompanying A Six-Week
Residence
Gustave Flaubert: A Writer Depicting Banality With Precision
Language
Theophile Gautier: A Master of Multiple Trades
Jules Verne: The Roundabout Journey Of France's Favorite
Travel Writer
Victor Hugo: Artistic Achievement and Political Ambition
Failure

PERFORMANCE ARTS:

Moliere Follows A Circuitous Exile To Sustain His Voice and Creative Expression

Pierre Beaumarchais: A Lifetime Of Contradictions Noteworthy By Classic Creations

Gioachino Rossini: The Pleasures Of Paris Terminate A Composer's Productivity

Frederick Chopin: A Delicate Bloom Flourishes and Prematurely Withers

Franz Liszt: The Reputed Greatest and Most Popular Pianist In Europe

Richard Wagner: A Maestro Fleeing Debts and Seeking Operatic Inspiration

Hector Berlioz: A Maestro Better Known For Conducting Than Composing

Jacques Offenbach: A Benevolent Composer of the Dance Parisian

Sarah Bernhardt: The Devine Goddess of International Theatre

George Bizet: Crowning A Career of Consistent Disappointment

Jean Sibelius: The Symphonic Musical Maestro of Finland

Isadora Duncan: A Blithe Spirit Capriciously Flittering Through Tragedies

Josephine Baker: Symbol of the Roaring Twenties and Civil Rights Activist

Edith Piaf: A Fragile Singing Sparrow Navigating The Brutalities of Life

Jean Renoir: Greatness Extending Beyond A Long Paternal Shadow

Jacques Tati: A Filmmaker's Glimpse Into A Sterile Future

Brigitte Bardot: Beauty, Animal Rights and Controversial Public Statements

Francois Truffaut: An Undisputed Crusader of French Cinema's New Wave

Jeanne Moreau: An Actress Who Helped Define The Film Industry *Nouvelle Vague*

Serge Gainsbourg: The Lasting Gainsbourg Mystique
Alain Delon: A Cinema Gangster and An Unsolved Contract Killing
George Moustaki: A Songwriter Eventually Discovers and Then Loses His Public Voice
The Decadent Decline of Doors' Lead Singer Jim Morrison
Dalida: A Songstress Who Reveled and Died Amidst Melodrama

VISUAL ARTS:
Jacques-Louis David: Genius Prized, Lost and Then Rediscovered
Eugene Delacroix: A Dramatic Action Painter Renowned For His Liberty
Honore Daumier: The Insightful and Illustrative Eyes of Nineteenth Century France
Gustave Dore: The Maestro Of The Book Illustration Trade
Jean Baptiste Corot: An Artist Lax On Enforcing Provenance
Gustave Moreau: A Painter Fleeing Fame and Recognition
Paul Gauguin: A Vision of French Polynesia That Launched An Artistic Legacy
Edgar Degas: A Solitary Intolerant Struggle to Depict Realism
Auguste Rodin: False Accusations of Life Casting And A Genius of Modern Sculpting
Camille Claudel: An Artist Who Devoured Herself and Her Finest Works
Theo van Gogh: The Supporting Force Behind Starry Nights
Henri Toulouse-Lautrec: A Ridiculed Appearance Masks Empathetic Portrayals
Claude Monet: The Consummate Impressionist Painter
Alphonse Mucha: An Artistic Prophet Nearly Ignored in His Homeland
The Towering and Enduring Art Legacy of Pablo Picasso
Henri Matisse: An Innovative Artist Until His Final Breath
Marc Chagall: A Creator of Vividly Whimsical Mysticism

Constantin Brancusi: The Patriarch of Modern Sculpture and His Open Studio

Amedeo Modigliani: A Tragic Bohemian Artist Recognized Posthumously

Marcel Duchamp: The Mystique Of An Art Influencer and Unproductive Icon

Man Ray: A Groundbreaking Mixed Media Maestro

Kiki de Montparnasse: A Celebrity Muse Whose Illumination Cruelly Dimmed

Joan Miro: Childlike Abstractive Compositions By A Mature Artist

Andre Masson: A Rebel Within The Surrealist Ranks

Yves Klein: Originality And Monopolizing Cobalt Blue

Alberto Giacometti: An Obsessive Recreation Of The Human Malaise

Frances Bacon: A Triumphant 1971 Painting Retrospective Darkened By Suicide

REVOLUTIONARIES:

Count Mirabeau: The Posthumously Disgraced Leader of the French Revolution

Jean-Paul Marat: A Nearly Discarded Revolutionary Voice Becomes A Martyr

Georges Danton: The Silenced Voice of the French Revolution

Camille Desmoulins: Drowning Out A Voice Urging Moderation

Maximilien Robespierre: The Bloodied Hands of A Pure Ideologue

Pierre-Joseph Prudhon: The Father Of A Movement Without A Patriarch

Karl Marx, Friedrich Engels, Vladimir Lenin, Leon Trotsky and Ho Chi Minh: The Refinement of Communist Philosophy

10

Sources and Archive Material Sourced:

LeftInParis.org, Memorable Paris Houses by Wilmot Harrison (1893), CNN.com, Devastating Disasters.com, TruCrimeDetective.co.uk, Wikipedia.org, NYPost.com, Webdoc.france24.com, Journal de Paris, VisitingParisByYourself.com, UnJourDePlusParis.com, TheGuardian.com, RFI.fr, The AmericanScholar.com, History.state.gov, Sas.upenn.edu, Britannica.com, Alijazeera.com, Maggielove.github.io, ElephantineBakery.com, Lumenlearning.com, Independent.co.uk, USAToday.com, CaveaudelaHuchette.fr, Rosicrucian.org, Refinery29.com, ParisByFoot.com, Jstor.org, WorldInParis.com, En.Parisinfo.com, TravelFranceOnline.com, Le Figaro, L'Aurore Newspaper, OperaDeParis.fr, HistoryToday.com, Shannonselin.com, FrenchMoments.eu, LifeOfWellington.co.uk, Fr.USEmbassy.gov, New York Herald Tribune, L'Express, The Daily Telegraph, TourEiffel.Paris.com, Parisianfields.com, Emmasu.org.uk, MTSU.edu, Ncronline.org, ParisMuseeCollections.paris.fr, Elysee.fr, Bookshelf.mml.ox.ac.uk, Le Monde Illustre, Gazette des Beaux Arts, Broadway.com, ElFaroDelCanal.com, PRCNO.org, DailyTelegraph.com.au, History.com, CitySeeker.com, Memoirs by Prince Talleyrand, Temple Bar: Volume 37, Napoleon.org, DeGruyter.com, TheGreatThinkers.org, TheParisReview.org. The News International, Le Figaro, BonjourParis.com, VanityFair.com, The Catholic Encyclopedia.com, LaVictoire.org, Haaretz.com, EntreeToBlackParis.com, Visual-Arts-Cork.com, NewYorkTimes.com, TravelFranceOnline.com, Le Canard Enchaine, Google.com, Le Journal de Debates, Parisology.net, AqrtandPopularCulture.com, Supervert.com, Maxims-shop.com, SnippetOfHistory.wordpress.com, IndianExpress.com, NumberOneLondon.net, FrenchMoments.eu, The IrishBookshop.com, Esquire.com, ImpressionistArts.com, ParisPerfect.com,

Messynessychic.com, Encyclopedie Larousse, Wikidata.org, SuchFriends.wprdpress.com, AmericanGirlsArtClubInParis.com , France-Voyage.com, ShakespeareAndCompany.com, UnJourDePlusAParis.com, Monticello.org, MTSU.edu, TheNewYorker.com, MillerCenter.org, WhiteHouseHistory.org, BBC.co.uk, ParisInsiderGuide.com, ArtNews.com, Tate.org.uk, LevineCenterArts.org, *Souvenirs* by Maxime du Camp, Trove.nla.gov.au, AlfonseMucha.org, En.ParisInfo.com, WTSP.com, CentrePompidou.fr, IrishTimes.com, HistoryIreland.com, Franceculture.fr, Montmartrefootsteps.com, Smithsonianmag.com, *The Life of Charles Dickens* by John Forster, FranceToday.com, ClaudeMonetGallery.org, BoundaryStones.weta.org, Golob-gm.si, *Directory of Authors* by Jerome Garcin, TheMorgan.org, ScottandZelda.org, France24.com, DarkLaneCreative.com, Musee-Rodin.fr, Paris Match, NMAAHC.si.edu, SeattleTimes.com, LeMonde.fr, NationalObserver.com, PBS.org, BonjourParis.com, BBC Financial Times, ParisResidencesJamesJoyce.com, Guggenheim.org, Archives.gov, ParisUnlocked.com, ParisPropertyGuide.com, Moma.org, News.Artnet.com, , ARussianAffair.wordpress.com, ArtNews.com, The ArtNewspaper.com, Wagner-Tuba.com, OperadeParis.fr, Canadian Encyclopedia and Dictionary of Canadian Biography,

Photography shot during 2022. Some of the locations may have or will alter with time and ownership changes. Many of the locations are still privately inhabited. Please don't disturb the residents.

PREFACE:

Consider this edition your personal Parisian address directory for the renowned that have historically shaped France and the world. This illustrated guide transports you geographically and photographically to famous residences formerly occupied by historical leaders, noteworthy figures, famous writers, performers, composers and visual artists. It is your map of the *stars* within Paris with profiles framing the unique impact and background of the occupants.

Known and unknown history, hidden delights and fascinating stories pervade the history of Paris. This kaleidoscope of discovery, personalities, egos, scandals, conflict framed by sheer beauty creates a vivid tapestry defining over two millenniums. You may imagine that you already know Paris, but that view is solely a prism of the whole. Many of the narratives defy believability, yet they are true.

This Famous Historic Guide is your alternative to conventional travel. It accommodates the restless visitor, tourist and resident seeking a unique and different perspective to traditional tourism. Paris remains one of the most beguiling, seductive and enchanting cities of the world. Its famed personalities are as statuesque and substantial as its iconic monuments.

Welcome to one on the most useful and enlightening introductions to the famed *City of Light*.

historical figures

A Peasant Girl That Inspired and Headed The French Army
Joan of Arc Gilded Equestrian Statue:
4 Place des Pyramids, 75001 Paris
Joan of Arc Bronze St. Augustine Statue:
Place Saint-Augustine, 75008 Paris

The legend of Jehanne d'Arc, better known as Joan of Arc is an integral part of French history. Her narrative still commands fascination. At the age of sixteen, she began hearing voices from three Christian saints, St. Michael, Catherine and Margaret. Her village of Domremy was located on the border between France and a consortium of English and Burgundy occupied territory.

In 1415, the Hundred Years War between England and France entered a significant stage when England's King Henry V invaded France. Seven years later following a series of decisive victories, the English controlled the majority of northern France including Paris.

In 1428, *Joan the Maid* as she called herself approached a captain of the French garrison in Vaucouleurs. She shared with him her vision of capturing occupied Reims and reinstalling the French throne there to Charles VII. The disheveled young peasant girl was promptly sent home, but returned the following year and was allowed an audience with the king.

Dressed in men's clothes and accompanied by six soldiers, she laid out her vision for France to expel the English invaders. Charles had her questioned by theologians at Poitiers. Given France's desperate military predicament, she was granted a small army in April 1429 to accompany her to Orleans. She led a military offensive against the English army who had besieged the city since the previous October.

Her will and uncompromising values inspired the French army to passionate resistance. They entered Orleans unopposed via the eastern gate. She personally led the charge in several battles and was wounded by an arrow to the shoulder on May 7 that was quickly treated. The following day, she returned to battlefield and the English retreated from Orleans.

There persist many myths regarding this improbable heroine. She never actually fought in battle or killed an opponent. She accompanied her soldiers for inspirational purposes waving a banner in lieu of weaponry. She was responsible for outlining military strategy, directing troop movements and enforcing discipline within the ranks. She berated knights for swearing, consorting with prostitutes, skipping Mass and/or dismissing her battle plans.

Medical experts have posthumously surmised that her visions and voices were the product of schizophrenia or another neurological condition. She exclusively credited divine inspiration. Her results where other leaders had failed were difficult to dispute.

Over the net five weeks, Joan and her French commanders continued a streak of victories over the English. They reached Reims on July 16 and Charles VII was crowned King of France within the gates of the city.

Paris remained in their sights. The army coordinated an attack against the city on September 8th. Joan rushed to the frontlines and the periphery of the fortress surrounding Paris at St. Honore Gate. The site is near where her gilded bronze statue is installed between the rue de Rivoli and rue Saint-Honore. Another patina bronze equestrian statue of her fronts Saint-Augustine Church.

At St. Honore Gate, she lifted her standard skyward and exhorted the Parisians to surrender the city to the king of France. She was shot during the ensuing battle by a crossbow in the thigh.

The French momentum faltered at the gates and Charles VII ordered an end to the unsuccessful siege. Despite their retreat, Joan would lead several more small campaigns. Along with her family, she became ennobled in December for her heroics. The honor peaked her successful thrust.

Her good fortune deserted her in May 1430 when she snuck into the city of Compiegne under darkness to campaign against the Burgundy army laying siege. On May 23rd, she led an unsuccessful attack and was captured. The Burgundians sold her to English. She was put on trial in March 1431 for heresy by ecclesiastical authorities in Rouen and condemned to death.

She might have been spared had Charles VII paid a ransom or intervened towards her release. He did nothing on her behalf.

Anxious to be rid of their military tormentor, the English secular authorities had her burned at stake in the Old Marketplace in Rouen on May 30, 1431. She was 19 years old. As the flames crept near to scorch her, she shouted out prayers loud enough for the gathered assemblage to hear.

Her sacrifice proved a continued source of military inspiration. By 1453, the English had been completely driven from France except in Calais. Five years later, the army secured the port city. The unworthy Charles VII would accept credit for the military conquests. The peasant girl from Domremy had however exhibited the purist courage and fidelity towards France. The Catholic Church recognized her as a Christian saint in 1920.

4 Place des Pyramids

Place Saint-Augustine

The Alchemist Legend and Contemporary Skepticism
Nicolas Flamel's Residence:
51 rue de Montmorency, 75003 Paris

Nicolas Flamel sought immortality through alchemy. Throughout the Middle Ages and Renaissance, chemists attempted to transmute baser metals into gold. The process was theorized that a universal solvent could become an elixir of extended life. Flamel reportedly reached the age of 88, seemingly immortal during his era. He was credited with discovering the philosopher's stone.

Two hundred years following his death, it was revealed that he learned his secrets from a Jewish convert to Catholicism on the road to Santiago de Compostela. During his lifetime, he operated two shops as a scribe and married favorably to Perenelle Flamel. The couple reportedly invested her wealth into real estate, churches, hostels and commissioned religious sculptures. Her fortune was derived from two previous marriages.

In 1410, Nicolas reportedly designed his own tombstone with the images of Christ, St. Peter, and St. Paul. He would die eight years later. The tombstone is preserved at the Musee de Cluny. One of his ancient residences remains, the oldest stone house in Paris. He is buried on the grounds of the Tour St. Jacques, a remnant of the former Church of Saint-Jacques de la Boucherie.

In today's more cynical culture, Flamel's achievements and reputation has been reduced to seventeenth century invention sourced from the book *Livres des Figures Hieroglyphiques*. His reputed wealth has also been called into question. Alchemy is no practiced as a means of reaching eternal life. The evidence is graveyards worldwide occupied by formerly wealthy individuals.

A Fatal Alchemy Potion That Reputedly Prolonged Youth
Diana de France's Hotel Lamoignon (Bibiotheque Historique):
24 rue Pavee, 75004 Paris

In 2009, French archeological experts dug up the remains of Diane de Poitiers from a mass grave. The intent was to return her body to the chapel at the Chateau d'Anet where she'd originally been buried before the French Revolution. She had lived there in comfortable obscurity and exile following the death of her patron and lover King Henry II.

During the Revolution, her original tomb had been opened, her corpse desecrated and her remains tossed into a mass grave. One of the notable findings during the exhumation process was the high concentration of gold in her hair. Experts concluded that the *drinkable gold* she regularly consumed to preserve youth might have ultimately killed her.

She was born on January 9, 1500 in the Chateau de Saint-Vallier in Drome. She was regarded as a beauty and dedicated athlete maintaining her figure by habitual riding and swimming. Her aristocratic upbringing enabled an education in humanism, Greek, Latin, rhetoric, etiquette, architecture and finance.

She was married at fifteen to Louis de Breze, the Grand Seneschal of Normandy, thirty-nine years her senior. Her reputation for intelligence and financial acumen distinguished her qualities. She became the lady-in-waiting to Queen Claude of France and then her mother following her daughter's death. Louis de Breze died in 1531 and she adopted the habit of wearing black and white for the rest of her life. The combination was considered permitted colors of mourning and the symbolic colors for both sides of the moon.

Three years after becoming a widow, she encountered Henry

II who at fifteen had married Catherine de Medici the year before. She was twenty years older than Henry, but became his longstanding mistress.

She cultivated a tenuous relationship with Catherine. She concluded that maintaining her as queen was in her own best interests. She reportedly encouraged Henry to procreate males with Catherine to preserve his dynastic lineage. This resulted in four sons with three living long enough to become kings. With Catherine, she became her nurse during one instance when she'd fallen gravely ill.

Henry would indulge in periodic affairs, but Diane remained his lifelong companion. For the next twenty-five years, she was considered one of the most powerful women in France. Her intellect, maturity and loyalty maintained his attachment towards her. She reputedly sustained her youthful beauty until her 50s. She was given charge over the education of his children and often gave direct orders to their governors.

Henry II's reign was notable by his employment of Michel de Nostradamus. The famed astrologer, physician and seer would become best known for his book *Les Propheties* published in 1555. Many of the passages have been interpreted to predict future events.

Diane de France, one of Henry's legitimized daughters with his young mistress Filippa Duci would leave one of the family remembrances within the Marais district. She began construction on the Hotel d'Angouleme in 1584, but was interrupted by the *Wars of Religion*. Later renamed the Hotel Lamoignon, it is considered one of the finest preserved architectural gems from that era. Following various transfers by succession, it would become in 1969 the home of the Bibiotheque Historique de la Ville de Paris.

Catherine de Medicis became frequently jealous of her rival's influence. She was powerless to alter the King's preferences as long as he lived. Diane de Poitiers was entrusted with the Crown Jewels of France and allowed to reside in the Chateau de Chenonceau, a royal property that Catherine craved. In 1555, Diane commissioned architect Philibert de l'Orme to construct the famed arch bridge joining the banks of the Cher River. She oversaw the planting of extensive gardens tastefully integrated with fruit trees.

Henry II would suffer a severe puncture during a jousting tournament inflicted by Gabriel de Montgomery, the captain of his Scottish Guard. He lingered ten days in delirium before succumbing to his wound. His injury and death immediately transformed the balance of power between Diane de Poitiers and Catherine de Medicis. Diane was restricted access to the royal chambers. Despite Henry repeatedly calling for her, she would not be admitted to his deathbed nor invited to his funeral.

Diane de Poitiers was obliged to return the crown jewels and depart the Chateau de Chenonceau. In exchange, she lived at the Chateau de Chaumont before relocating permanently to Chateau d'Anet. At 64, she suffered a fall from her horse that she never fully recovered from. She died from the lingering effects on April 25, 1566.

Hotel Lamoignon

A Navigator, Explorer and Colonial Governor of New France
Samuel de Champlain's Residence:
Maison Saintonge: 16 rue de Saintonge, 75003 Paris

During his lifetime, Samuel de Champlain sailed nearly thirty trips across the Atlantic Ocean from France to North America. He would be credited with founding Quebec and New France (Canada) on July 3, 1603.

He was born into a family of sailors and would earn distinction as a navigator, mapmaker, soldier, geographer and diplomat. He became the first European to describe the Great Lakes and his accurate coastal maps during his explorations founded various colonial settlements.

He formed lasting relationships with numerous Native American tribes and published accounts of their narratives and interactions. He learned and mastered their languages. He agreed to provide assistance to several tribes of the Ottawa River in the *Beaver Wars* against the Iroquois.

In 1619, he published an extensive book on his discoveries in New France. The following year, King Louis XIII ordered him to cease exploration, return to Quebec and concentrate on governing the territory. In that capacity, he would establish trading companies that exported goods, particularly fur, to France. He oversaw the expansion in the St. Lawrence River valley until his death from a severe stroke on Christmas Day, 1635.

16 rue de Saintonge

A Willful Queen Margot's Intrigues and Revenge
Marguerite de Valois' Residence (Hotel de Sens):
1 rue du Figuier, 75004 Paris

Marguerite de Valois, better known as Queen Margot of Navarre became famous for her licentious behavior, tell-all writings and revenge. Her authorship of *Memoires* published fourteen years following her death details her turbulent era through the perspective of a clear-sighted woman. Margot refused to become a victim and remained a force to be respected throughout her life.

Born on May 14, 1553, she was the daughter of King Henry II and Catherine de Medicis. She assumed her place in court in 1569, but shared strained relations with her brothers Charles IX and the Duc d'Anjou, the future Henry III. She confessed to an early sexual liaison with Henri, the Duke of Guise and the leader of the extremist Catholic party. Their relationship would prove useful to her later.

On August 18, 1572 she was married to the Protestant Henry de Bourbon of Navarre, who would become the future French King Henry IV. Their marriage was promoted as a conciliatory bridge between Catholics and Protestants. Instead, it became a magnet to lure the Protestant leadership to Paris. Five days later, they would be the victims of a widespread massacre on St. Bartholomew's Day.

Henry of Navarre escaped death during the massacre. Marguerite refused to annul the marriage and they remained together. Both parties kept separate lovers and she became renowned for her own intrigues and participation in conspiracies. Her brother, King Henry III banished her to the remote castle of Usson in the Auvergne region. With the assistance of her former lover, the Duke of Guise, she was able to assume control of the property and ultimately her fate.

She remained childless. Her husband's need to establish a dynastic heir created a potential outcome of an annulled marriage. She negotiated an arrangement favorable to her interests. She withheld her consent as long as Henry's mistress, Gabrielle d'Estrees remained alive. Upon her death, she released Henry to marry Marie de Medicis in 1600. She retained her royal title.

Five years later, she was given permission to settle in Paris. She lived in the Hotel de Sens constructed in 1500. The building had been the prior residence for the archbishops of Sens. Her stay in Paris was abbreviated. A discarded lover murdered her page and favorite Julian at the door of her carriage.

She swore that she would neither eat nor drink until she had avenged Julian's death. Two nights later, the killer would be captured and beheaded opposite her hotel before her presence. She departed Paris that same evening and never returned.

Hotel de Sens

France's Influential Statesman, Politician and Clergyman
Cardinal Richelieu's Residence (Palais Royal):
204 rue St. Honore, 75001 Paris
Cardinal Richelieu's Apartment:
21 place des Vosges, 75003 Paris

France's shrewdest and most ruthless statesman during the 17th century evolved from the ranks of the clergy. Cardinal Richelieu became recognized for his stealth, decisiveness and scrupulous planning. These traits endeared him to few, but ultimately established France as the strongest empire within Europe.

Born Armand-Jean du Plessis on September 9, 1585, his family was of marginal feudal rank. Through strategic marriages into the legal and administrative ranks, his father acquired the position of Seigneury Richelieu in Poitou. This post enabled him to become the chief magistrate to King Henry II. Armand's mother was the daughter of a councilor within the Parliament of Paris.

The potential advantages of his family's status vanished upon his father's death when Armand was five. Their estates had been financially mismanaged and teetered on ruin. The threat of poverty hovered precariously above his mother, two brothers and two sisters.

His eldest brother was designed to become heir to the seigneury. His second older brother became a monk. As the youngest son, Armand's path was orchestrated towards becoming a consecrated bishop as soon as possible. He welcomed the clarity and security of knowing his station. He would far surpass other's modest expectations of him simply remaining an isolated country priest.

He was thin, pale and often sickly, but he showed a

propensity towards learning and debating. He exhibited an enthusiasm towards order and manipulating other's lives. When he graduated from university, he was still younger than the canonical age for consecration. This rule required a papal dispensation to waive the age requirement. He traveled to Rome, charmed Pope Paul V and was ordained a priest at twenty-two. His first assignment was in Lucon.

Throughout his career, Richelieu remained ambitious, disciplined and obsessed with obtaining his decisive objectives. He expressed his own character succinctly with: *I undertake nothing save on full reflection. When once I have made up my mind, I change here, I abolish there, and my scarlet cassock covers all.*

France was on volatile terrain and the Catholic Church was wavering between necessary reforms and collapse. Henry IV had ended the *Wars of Religion* with his policy of tolerance for Protestants.

Henry's decree cost him his life and throne in 1610 via assassination leaving his spouse Marie de Medici and a nine-year-old heir. She would be appointed regent for the future Louis XIII intended until he reached the age for coronation. Corrupt advisers and a self-interested administrative system stymied her influence.

Richelieu harbored his own personal ambitions, yet focused his energies on supporting established royal authority. He played an important conciliatory role in the transition process. He was rewarded by being appointed chaplain to Louis XIII's new bride, Anne of Austria. This position enabled him entry into the royal council. Through negotiation with a dissenting faction of the court, he was appointed Secretary of State in 1616. He was 31 years old.

The honor arrived prematurely as he lacked experience with

international relations. War was declared between Spain (ruled by the Habsburg dynasty) and Venice (aligned with France). He remained in that position for less than a year. A palace revolution overthrew the regency of Marie de Medici. Richelieu was banished to Lucon and then exiled to the papal city of Avignon. His somber writings from that period suggested that he might never be granted an opportunity for redemption.

He was wrong.

The temporary setback would be rectified with Marie de Medici's recall to the palace and the king's nomination of Richelieu for a cardinal's position. Suddenly Richelieu had consolidated the status and power he sought personally. This redemptive reward would not be squandered.

He displayed a talent for unpredictability, compromise and outflanking his numerous enemies. His decisive decision-making often caught them unprepared. His perceived administration of justice did not contradict his personal moral principles. He believed that government and ethics were inseparable, even when the means appeared questionable. His intellectual capacity enabled him to sort through complicated political intrigues.

He was credited with some features of generosity and his promises could be relied upon. He was considered as ardent in serving his friends as in ruining his enemies.

Unlike most of his intolerant peers, he could compromise and moderate with his adversaries when the results furthered his longer range political ambition. His overriding policy goals were twofold. He focused on the centralization of power within France and to lessen the influence of the Habsburg dynasty within Europe. He shifted the previous religious conflicts between Protestant and Catholic interests towards nationalistic growth aimed at curbing the imposing dominance of the Habsburgs.

Richelieu consolidated centralized authority by suppressing the influence of the nobility and aristocratic class. He ordered all fortified castles razed, exempting only those needed to defend against invasion. His aim was to eliminate potential defense positions held by disgruntled princes, dukes and minor aristocrats in the event of a rebellion against the crown.

He targeted the peasant class with punitive taxation to fund his defense projects and restrained any attempts of their organizing. These policies made him a reviled target amongst both the nobility and lower classes.

His influence and regard deepened over time with Louis XIII. Richelieu had engineered a sound future for his successor. France emerged as the dominant military power within Europe eclipsing the influence of the Habsburg's. Richelieu's groundwork would elevate Louis XIV into the most powerful monarch of his era.

Richelieu would never serve under Louis XIV.

In June 1642, his secret service uncovered a plot against him organized by Henri Coiffier de Ruze, the Marquis of Cinq-Mars. The plot was particularly appalling because Richelieu had shielded the now 22-year old Marquis under his protection as a boy upon his father's death. Cinq-Mars had become the king's favorite and granted the title *Master of the Robes.*

The rise altered Cinq-Mars. His extravagance, arrogance and libertine behavior alarmed Richelieu. He decided to prevent him from gaining further royal political influence. Cinq-Mars decided to eliminate Richelieu by implementing a secret agreement in March with Spanish King Philip IV. France was at war with Spain, but Cinq-Mars promised to open the borders and aid their armies.

Upon Richelieu's secret service obtaining a copy of the document, Cinq-Mars was arrested two days later. He was convicted of treason and beheaded in Lyon.

Richelieu's health further deteriorated. He returned back to his Paris apartment inside a chamber hoisted on the shoulders of his guards. On his deathbed, he was composing five propositions regarding royal behavior towards ministers that he regarded as essential. He wouldn't survive the year, dying on December 4th. He would be buried in the chapel of the Sorbonne, a structure that he had financed.

Louis XIII died five months later from tuberculosis and was succeeded by his son Louis XIV. The potential clash of ego and will between a young Louis and Richelieu would never materialize.

Richelieu's lasting influence would far exceed his original ambition for France. His severe economic policies, however, would fracture the nation by the end of the subsequent century. A Revolutionary uprising by the peasant classes would ultimately decimate both the monarchy and aristocracy. During Richelieu's reign, he had suppressed and alienated the voices of the impoverished.

He was gifted the Palais-Royal for his own residence between 1633 until 1639. He would subsequently bequeath the Palais to Louis XIII. Upon his death, the complex was passed on to his son. During Louis XIV's reign and later relocation to Versailles, the property was given to his younger brother, the Duke of Orleans. Future inheritors made extensive alterations leaving only minimal remains from the original design. The Palais currently serves as the headquarters for the Ministry of

Culture and the central garden is a distinctive public park accompanied by arcade shops and residential apartments.

Palais Royale

21 place des Vosges

A Tale of Two King's Mistresses
Hotel d'Albret:
31 rue des Francs Bourgeois, 75004 Paris

Anne of Montmorency originally purchased the Hotel d'Albret for her son in 1563. The architect Vautrain modified the façade in 1744 giving the structure a unique appearance for the Marais neighborhood during the reign of King Louis XIV. The building is indistinguishable from similar stately mansions with courtyards. Two historical tenants however residing during Louis's era make the building more enticing. The two women would become the final acknowledged mistresses of the king.

Francoise-Athenais de Rochehouart, known as the Marquise de Montespan has been regarded as Louis most celebrated mistress bearing him seven children. The couple initially met amidst a dance at a ball hosted by the king's younger brother Philippe I, the Duke of Orleans at the Louvre Palace in 1667. Montespan's eventual influence would endure for over a decade. Her alleged involvement in a major poisoning murder involving witchcraft during the late 1670s doomed her status. She would unwittingly be responsible for the introduction of her replacement.

Francoise d'Aubigne would marry poet Paul Scarron, a favorite of King Louis XIII. He was twenty-five years older and their relationship evolved into her role as a caregiver. Following his death in 1660, she lived off his pension for six years before Louis XIV suspended it. As she was preparing to leave Paris to become a lady-in-waiting to the new queen of Portugal, she became acquainted with the Marquise de Montespan.

Montespan was so charmed by Francoise that she placed her second son by Louis into her care accompanied with a large income and staff of servants. Her new position as Royal

Governess brought her into close contact with the king. She was different from other women that he'd encountered. Initially she repelled him by her strong temper and fervent religious beliefs.

She evolved into one of the few individuals who were permitted to speak candidly with Louis XIV and on equal terms. He was charmed by her intelligence and they frequently discussed politics, economics and religion together. His wife Queen Marie-Therese confided to him that Francoise far better treated her in contrast with the rudest by Montespan.

Francoise claimed in her later memoirs that she didn't yield initially to the king's sexual advances. He would grant her the title of the Marquise de Maintenon incurring jealousy from her predecessor. Utterly discarded from the king's favor by then, the Marquise de Montespan's protests would be ignored.

Following the death of Queen Marie-Therese, Madame de Maintenon would become the king's primary mistress. Louis declared to confidants that *Madame de Maintenon knows how to love. There would be great pleasure in being loved by her.*

Louis would be granted his desire during an informal wedding ceremony on October 9, 1683. Due to their disparity in social rank, Maintenon would neither be publicly acknowledged as his wife or queen. Curiously one of the witnesses at the ceremony was the king's confessor, Pere la Chaise, the namesake of the famed Paris cemetery.

Maintenon would exert tremendous political influence with her privileged position. Observers equated her power as the equivalent of a prime minister. Her religious views affected the king's behavior by his no longer maintaining open mistresses and banning operas during Lent.

She promoted the careers of his children by Madame de Montespan for high positions at court and founded a school for girls of impoverished noble families. Her behind the scenes activities made her both respected and admired. Many have suggested her as an important early influence towards the feminist movement.

Louis XIV would die in 1715 at the age of 77. Madame de Montespan would retire afterwards to Saint-Cyr with a comfortable pension. She would follow his death four years later at the age of 83. One of her fondest admirers during her declining years was Tsar Peter the Great of Russia.

Her predecessor, the Marquise de Montespan would follow her public disgrace into retirement at the *Filles de Saint Joseph* Convent in Paris with a healthy pension. She donated large sums to hospitals and charities. She became a generous patron of the arts and befriended notable writers including Corneille, Racine and La Fontaine.

Despite her generosity, she lingered in guilt regarding her past indiscretion subjecting herself to penance habitually. She died on May 27, 1707 while bathing in a nearby resort's healing waters for an illness. She was 67. The king prohibited her children from wearing mourning clothes in her memory.

Hotel d'Albret

Commoner, Courtesan, King's Mistress and Revolution Victim
Madame du Barry Residence:
2 rue de la Juissienne, 75002 Paris

Jeanne Becu was the illegitimate daughter of Anne Becu, a 30-year-old seamstress. Speculation towards her father targeted a friar named Jean Jacques Gomard. He would never be confirmed. Jeanne was educated at the Convent de Saint Aurea until the age of fifteen.

Her beauty distinguished her early and posed both a blessing and a curse throughout her lifetime. She relocated to Paris carrying a box of trinkets for sale. She bounced around through various occupations until she became a milliner's assistant in a haberdashery shop. She was described as an attractive blond with thick golden ringlets and almond-shaped blue eyes.

Her beauty attracted the attention of Jean-Baptiste du Barry whose brother Count Guillaume du Barry owned a brothel and casino. Guillaume du Barry installed her into his operations and made her his own mistress. Under his tutelage, she became one of the most sought after courtesans within Parisian society.

Her large aristocratic clientele attracted the attention of King Louis XV's court. She became the mistress of several court ministers and captured the king's attention during a visit to Versailles in 1768. That same year his wife died and he assumed the role of *grieving* widower.

Becu could not qualify as a member of court unless she had a title. Given her modest background, a solution was arranged by her marriage to former lover and pimp Guillaume du Barry. A false birth certificate was created reducing her age by three years and establishing a fictitious noble descent.

The price of gilded slavery became immediate for the newly established Madame du Barry. She was installed in a set of luxurious rooms above the king's offices, but it was a lonely existence. She could not be officially presented to the court and few of the king's fawners made any discernible effort to associate with her. Her infamous commoner origins and past indiscretions tainted her palace existence. She was reportedly disliked intensely by Marie-Antoinette, the wife of successor Louis XVI.

Unlike her storied predecessor Madame de Pompadour, she exhibited little interest towards political affairs. She devoted enormous energy towards her appearance and cultivating extravagant tastes. She was constantly in debt despite a huge monthly income allocated to her by the king.

The declining years of Louis XV were dominated by his obsession with death and repentance. On April 26, 1774, he left for the Petit Trianon with Madame du Barry and several nobles from his entourage. The trip was intended as a hunting expedition, but he began feeling ill. Six physicians and six surgeons attended him. They bled him three separate times without effect.

Red eruption began to appear on his skin that was diagnosed as smallpox. There remained optimism for his survival since he had already contracted the disease previously. Over the next week, his condition worsened and he died ravaged by the outbreaks on May 10, 1774.

His most famous remark *After us...the deluge* would be taken out of context to represent his prediction towards the future of France following his death. The comment was actually made concerning the arrival of Halley's Comet twenty years earlier. At the time, commonly held church beliefs stressed that the comet preceded the Great Flood during Noah's era. His

39

remark was a flippant jest. Halley's Comet would pass the earth in April 1759 two years following its prediction. No flooding would accompany the event.

The fortunes of Louis XVI, Marie-Antoinette and Madame du Barry would become well documented following the king's death. Louis XVI would enjoy over two decades of rule before the French Revolution resulted in his abdication and execution.

Madame du Barry would be exiled by Louis XVI at the instigation of Marie-Antoinette to the Abbey du Pont-aux-Dames located on the Marne River. Two years later she purchased property and moved to the Louveciennes, a western suburb of Paris between Versailles and Saint-Germain-en-Laye.

She entered into two relationships during the following years. One was with Louis Hercule Timoleon de Cosse-Brissac. As the French Revolution bloodied the aristocratic landscape, Brissac was captured while visiting Paris and slaughtered by a mob. A drunken crowd approached her chateau and tossed a blood stained cloth below her window. It was wrapped around the severed head of Brissac.

Du Barry had kept her domestic household intact including her personal Bengali servant Zamor. He had been her faithful attendant since her palace residence and they had cultivated a perceived long-standing trust.

He became intimately involved during 1792 with the radical Jacobin club. Upon discovering his allegiance, she dismissed him with three days notice.

He immediately traveled to Paris to denounce her before the Revolutionary Tribunal. He accused her of financially assisting aristocrats fleeing France from persecution. In 1793, she would be arrested and charged with treason. She had no allies to save her and no public support to spare her. She was condemned to death.

She could not understand why that she had been singled out for punishment. She screamed for mercy and begged help from the unsympathetic and frothing spectators. She collapsed on her walk en route. Assisted to the elevated podium, she was dispatched, simply another victim of mob frenzy.

The First American Foreign Diplomat
Benjamin Franklin's Residences:
Hotel Valentinois (Demolished): 62-70 rue Raynouard, 75016 Paris
26 rue de Penthievre (Demolished):, 75008 Paris
Madame Helvetius Salon (Demolished):
59 rue D'Auteil, 75016 Paris

Benjamin Franklin did more to further the cause of American independence within France than any other personality, document or self-motivated treaty. He sailed for Paris months following his signing of the Declaration of Independence. The 70-year-old's mission was unclear to many upon his arrival. Some observers speculated that he'd landed to retire in Switzerland with his immense fortune. Recently widowed, he had left his three children behind in Philadelphia.

The British considered him a *dangerous rebel* and would later regret not intercepting his ship in the Atlantic and hanging him or tossing his body overboard. He was the most renowned American then known in the world for his scientific research and published works. He was greeted enthusiastically in France upon his arrival.

Franklin's true intention was to attract foreign nations and partners to assist in the American rebellion. France was the highest priority on that list due to their centuries long animosity towards England.

The average French citizen knew little about the American colonies and shared only marginal interest in their significance. Franklin was not any average American. He was well versed in the contemporary Enlightenment ideals of Voltaire and Rousseau. He leveraged his recognition to gain admittance into some of the most prestigious literary and philosophical salons within Paris.

His acceptance was not immediate. He spoke poor French laden with grammatical flaws. French and English spies followed him throughout the city. He frequently had his lodgings searched and pilfered for compromising documents.

During his initial years in Paris, he weathered morale discouraging reports of American military setbacks. He often downplayed their significance publicly, but became personally alarmed when the British occupied his hometown of Philadelphia in September 1777. The occupation would last until the following spring resulting in wartime shortages and suffering for those who'd remained. Franklin maintained public buoyancy, masking deeply troubled concerns.

His depression was uplifted shortly afterwards on October 17th. He received reports that British General Burgoyne had surrendered his entire regiment to surrounding American forces in Saratoga Springs, New York.

Franklin was informed of the news on December 4th via an American messenger. The surrender was regarded as a decisive military victory and changed the perception of Franklin's presence. Suddenly both French and British officials attempted to secure his favor. The French became the first country to sign a treaty of alliance without even the consent of their closet ally Spain.

Franklin delved into his duties with an industry and efficiency that French officials admired and acknowledged. These peers were charmed by his openness, hospitality and attempts to master the intricacies of the French language.

He would become the unanimous selection to become America's First Foreign Minister to France, serving from 1776 to 1778. He nearly remained permanently after proposing marriage to the widowed Madame Helvetius who'd organized a popular local salon. His other reputed love interest was Madame Brillon who was unfortunately married. Franklin had wed Deborah Read in Philadelphia during September 1730 with a common-law agreement. She had become an important printing business associate before her death in 1774, shortly before his departure.

Franklin universally enamored himself to nearly everyone during his Paris residence. The sole exception was prickly future President John Adams. He had sailed to Paris under the impression that he would be participating in French treaty negotiations and be offered the ambassador position. Neither occurred. He was finally given the First Ministry position in Britain where he would serve five years without distinction.

Franklin began requesting his own recall to America as early as 1783. His request was granted two years later and Thomas Jefferson would replace him in Paris. During the nine years that he'd been away, Philadelphia had become a metropolis and Franklin had become largely forgotten. Congress would barely acknowledge his contribution overseas. He had become a stranger to the very country that he had helped establish.

He died on April 17, 1790 at the age of 84 in Philadelphia and was buried at the Christ Church Cemetery. For the subsequent sixteen years, John Adams would marginalize his legacy and exploits. He would attempt to claim credit for activities that Franklin initiated. He criticized Franklin's *secrecy* and disregard towards him and his contributions.

Time and alternative perspectives would ultimately champion Franklin's perception. He has become acknowledged as the ideal individual to undertake such a delicate and sensitive assignment in France.

Site of 26 Rue de Penthieve

Site of 26 rue de Penthieve

The Treaty of Paris And The Public Slight of John Adams
Treaty Signing Location (Former Hotel Danemark):
56 rue Jacob 75006 Paris
John Adams Residence:
Hotel de Verrieres, 47 rue D'Auteil, 75016 Paris

The war for American Independence extended over eight years beginning in 1775 and officially ending in 1783. The signers of the Declaration of Independence took great risk in inking their names to the document. Had the American cause failed, they would have been signing their collective death warrants.

The defeat of Lord Cornwallis' forces at Yorktown, Virginia on October 19, 1781 effectively ended the Revolutionary War. The Treaty of Paris signed on September 3, 1783 formerly recognized the United States as an independent nation. That acknowledgement added the former British colonies into the ranks of the largest and most established prevailing world powers.

America sent John Adams, Benjamin Franklin and John Jay, three seasoned negotiators to sign the document. Adams and Franklin had previously resided in Paris and were well acquainted with the city. David Hartley represented Great Britain.

The treaty was crucial as it recognized American independence and the severing of boundaries that would later enable western expansion. There were three signed copies affixed with wax seals. Two are currently housed in the National Archives in Washington D.C.

The signing took place at the Hotel Danemark that would be the ignominious site of the February 13, 1777 arrest of the Marquis de Sade by Paris police inspector Louis Marais. De Sade would be transferred to the Vincennes fortress that evening where he would be imprisoned.

Future American President John Adams often considered himself the odd man out during negotiations with both France and England. In 1778 during the Revolutionary War, Adams had sailed to France to join Benjamin Franklin and Arthur Lee to negotiate an alliance with France. When he arrived, he discovered that Franklin had already signed a pact. He remained in Paris a year seething over the slight and Franklin's popularity with the French. Franklin would be asked to remain as America's sole minister. Adams returned to America without a new post being offered.

He alienated the French government in 1780 when he wrote a letter to French Foreign Minister Vergennes stating that France was not contributing enough towards the war effort. Vergennes was outraged and promptly severed communication with Adams. Franklin sided with the French Minister.

Adams was simultaneously seeking a loan from the Dutch government who had already been clandestinely supplying arms to the American cause. They delayed a commitment until news of the victory at Yorktown. Adams was able to secure a $2 million loan.

He returned a second time to Paris in 1783 for the treaty signing. He felt unappreciated by Congress as evidenced by some member's hesitancy to appoint him America's first minister to Great Britain. Their perception of Adams was that he was too independent and outspoken for the position.

He met strong resentment in London from the British government. They were reluctant to remove their troops from American soil and open their ports to American ships. During his five-year tenure, he was unable to accomplish many concrete results with the English king or government.

Upon his return, he envisioned living the balance of his life as a Quincy, Massachusetts farmer. Within a month of his return, he would shift objectives and run for the office of Vice-President. The most important half of his life was just commencing.

Former Hotel Danemark

An American Forefather Influenced Profoundly By Paris
Thomas Jefferson's Residential Sites:
Hotel de Langeac (Demolished): 92 avenue des Champs Elysees, 75008 Paris
Hotel Landron (Demolished): rue du Helder 75009 Paris

At the age of 41, Thomas Jefferson was appointed the American Minister to France replacing Benjamin Franklin. Jefferson was already an accomplished writer, lawyer, politician and was credited with being the primary author of the Declaration of Independence. He had served as a member of Congress, Virginia state legislator and governor.

Jefferson departed in July 1784 with his young daughter Patsy and two servants to Paris to join Franklin and future President John Adams. The trio was responsible for negotiating treaties of friendship and commerce with Great Britain and other nations.

During his five-year stint, his social horizons broadened significantly. He was introduced to the *enlightenment* philosophy, elegant social festivities, great thinkers in the salons, art, music, theatre, architecture and agricultural enhancements. The formerly rigid self-controlled Virginian evolved and became polished with this newfound classical education.

He became a regular companion of the Marquis de Lafayette, a hero from the American Revolutionary War. Jefferson was present during the storming of the Bastille and consulted regularly with Lafayette during his drafting of the *Declaration of the Rights of Man and of the Citizen.* Jefferson supported the French Revolution, but abhorred the violent elements and excesses. Jefferson was unable to attend the 1787 American Convention that supported the Constitution. He was particularly forceful in his advocacy of the Bill of Rights.

His relations with Britain were strained. During the summer of 1786, he and current English ambassador John Adams had secured a meeting with King George III. Still smarting from the loss of his invaluable colonies, the king turned his back on both men as a gesture of public insult. He had difficulty accepting this initial fragmentation of his empire. During the later stages of his life, he would suffer from reoccurring and ultimately permanent mental illness.

Jefferson's wife Martha had died two years before his departure to Paris. The couple had six children together. Two years following his arrival, he met and reportedly fell in love with married Maria Cosway, a 27-year-old Italian-English musician. They spent significant time together, but she returned to her husband in England. They maintained a lifelong correspondence.

In June 1787, he sent for his youngest daughter Polly who was accompanied on her voyage by a young slave form his plantation in Monticello named Sally Hemings. Her older brother James had traveled originally to Paris with Jefferson and was part of his domestic staff. Jefferson had him trained in preparing French cuisine.

Sally's son, Madison Hemings indicated that Jefferson impregnated her at sixteen. In France, slavery had been abolished, so she was re-classified a servant. She agreed to return to the United States only after Jefferson promised to free her children when they reached the age of majority. He concurred and the couple would have reportedly six children together. Their relationship was undisclosed to the public until two centuries later.

Many historians have credited Jefferson's broader worldview as a result of his five-year Parisian residence. He absorbed these lessons and observations into his personal lifestyle back at Monticello. He reportedly shipped 86 packing crates of European goods to his plantation. He would later employ many of the architectural and agricultural techniques he observed in France. These ranged from engineering prototypes to cultivating wine grapes.

Upon his return, he was anxious to implement his education into practical utilization. The American political scene dictated otherwise. He accepted President George Washington's invitation to serve as Secretary of State. Over the next two decades, he would become intimately entwined in the evolving American political legacy and landscape.

During Jefferson's presidency, he dealt with a range and diversity of issues that few successors have ever been challenged with and/or required to address. Ironically and fittingly, he died on July 4, 1825, eight months following a reunion with his long-term friend the Marquis de Lafayette. He had reconciled his political hostilities with political peer John Adams thirteen years before. Adams would die the same day several hours later.

Irony is often difficult to separate from a perception of divine intervention. Both men would leave their earthly existence precisely fifty years following the day of the signing of the landmark Declaration of Independence.

92 avenue des Champs Elysees

rue du Helder

A Genuine Hero On Two Continents
Marquis de Lafayette's Residences:
119 rue de Lille, 75007 Paris
202 rue de Rivoli, 75001 Paris
35, rue d'Anjou, 75008 Paris
8 rue d'Anjou, 75008 Paris (Death Location)

Without dispute, Marie-Joseph Roch Gilbert du Motier became the most famous French General in the United States. Known as the Marquis de La Fayette or simply Lafayette, he was an aristocrat from the Auvergne region, freemason and military officer who fought in the American Revolutionary War. He commanded troops in several battles, most noteworthy in the decisive siege of Yorktown.

Returning from America, his own nation was engaged in conflict raging into the French Revolution. Lafayette's success and renown in America propelled him to an immediate appointment to the Assembly of Notables in 1787. He helped author the *Declaration of the Rights of Man and of the Citizen* with the assistance of Thomas Jefferson. The work was modeled after the American Declaration of Independence.

Following the storming of the Bastille, he was appointed commander-in-chief of France's National Guard. With the ascension of radical factions into the government in August 1792, his moderate course of diplomacy was consisted an affront and archaic. He barely escaped the guillotine. His arrest was ordered and he fled into the Austrian controlled Netherlands.

No ally to France, Austrian troops captured and imprisoned him for five years. Napoleon Bonaparte secured his release in 1797 as a public relations gesture. Lafayette refused to participate in Bonaparte's government. Following the Bourbon Restoration in 1814, he became a liberal member of the Chamber of Deputies. He would maintain that position for the balance of his life.

Lafayette's perceived brilliance may have dimmed within France, but it never receded within the United States. In 1824, President James Monroe invited him to once again visit America. He consented traveling to all 24 existing states. He was adored and lionized at every public reception. Celebrity however never blinded his perspective.

His return to France was anti-climatic. He reportedly declined an offer to become a dictator during the July Revolution of 1830. Instead, he supported Louis-Philippe as king until the former became too autocratic.

Fidel to his democratic beliefs, he vehemently opposed slavery and maintained his democratic principles throughout his life. He died on May 20, 1834 and is buried in Picpus Cemetery.

202 rue de Rivoli

202 rue de Rivoli

119 rue de Lille

35 rue d'Anjou

8 rue d'Anjou

The Finance Minister Unable to Plug The Surging Waters of Discontent
Jacques Necker's Residence:
7 rue de la Chaussee d'Antin, 75009 Paris

Swiss born financier Jacques Necker understood a violent Revolution was nearing. He comprehended clearly that the excessive spending habits and taxation by the monarchy would ultimately result in their demise. He pursued the path of reformer as finance minister with the court of King Louis XVI, but to little avail.

In 1781, he took the unprecedented step of publicly revealing the country's budget. Previously with the absolute monarchy in existence, finances were kept publicly concealed. His goal was to establish a constitutional monarchy, but he met severe resistance from those in power. He would be dismissed from his position within a few months following the budget publication.

The French economy continued to stall and deteriorate following his dismissal. Spending discipline was non-existent and tax revenues to finance military campaigns depleted. All efforts to correct the off course ship proved futile. Economic theory could not feed the impoverished masses and declining tax revenues could not accommodate centuries of spending abuses, growing inflation and financial mismanagement.

Necker was recalled into royal service in 1788 as a desperation savior. His return was initially greeted with enthusiasm. The magnitude of the nation's financial crisis proved too severe for saving. He attempted austerity and tax reform measures, but both strategies were far too little and inadequate. His dismissal on July 11, 1789 became acknowledged as a factor in the attack and destruction of the Bastille three days later. The peasants had nearly given up hope for their future.

The King and the Constituent Assembly would recall him within two days. The news was greeted with great celebration throughout Paris. Continued opposition against his fiscal policies by the Assembly forced his resignation a year later. The ministers of War and the Navy were particularly hostile towards him. Vicious attacks against his character and dealings were published in Paris newspapers. He was no longer the dreamt for savior. This time, the gravity and escalation of economic woes elicited general indifference towards his departure.

Necker warned of the eminent bankruptcy of France and the dire collapse of the government. His attempted voice of reason was silenced. Following his final dismissal, he was arrested. On September 11, 1790, he would be allowed to leave France and re-settled in Geneva. The exile doubtlessly preserved his life.

His presence was not welcomed by his homeland due to a distrust of his motives. He continued his writings on political economy and law. He witnessed the French monarchy implode from afar. The government confiscated his remaining French estate. His doomsday economic forecasts were ignored. His wife's mental health sank deeply into delusional whimsy.

He would encounter Napoleon Bonaparte following the French invasion of Switzerland in 1798. Necker was treated with respect as soldiers marched past his mansion. Bonaparte confided in him his plans to reestablish a monarchy in France. Necker's final publication *Last Views on Politics and Finance* upset Bonaparte. He threatened to exile Necker's daughter, author Germaine de Stael from France.

Necker would die on April 9, 1804 at the age of 71. His legacy has remained lukewarm, shunned by both revolutionaries and monarchists. He shared a similar fate with Lafayette and Mirabeau. All three were briefly elevated to popularity, but then discarded by the French populace.

7 rue de la Chaussee d'Antin

A Popular Fortune Teller During the Revolution and Napoleonic Era
Marie Le Normand's Residence:
5 rue de Tournon, 75006 Paris

For over forty years, Marie Anne Le Normand held a distinctive power over the leaders of France. The accuracy of her fortune telling through the use of cards cultivated an impressive clientele. Several of the Revolution founders including Marat, Robespierre and St. Just were avid clients. All three met violent deaths, two by guillotine. Her readings remained in demand with the Empress Josephine and reportedly Tsar Alexander I of Russia.

She was born in Alencon, Normandy and orphaned at the age of five. She was educated in a convent school before departing to Paris at the age of twelve. In 1814 as Napoleon Bonaparte's reign concluded, she began publishing numerous texts. She would be imprisoned on multiple occasions but never for long stretches. Her popularity as a card reader made her a celebrity and wealthy. She died at the age of 71 on June 25, 1843. Her devoutly religious nephew became her sole heir. He burned all of her occult paraphernalia, but kept her sizable liquid assets.

5 rue de Toournon

The First Private Detective Emerging From A Shadowy Past
Eugene Vidocq Residence:
6 rue Vivienne #13, 75002 Paris

Eugene Francois Vidocq was born in Arras, located in northern France. He was the third son of a baker and corn dealer. His father was considered wealthy and well educated. Eugene shared a disdain for authority and was reputed to be idle. He took pleasure in stealing and developing a reputation as a formidable fencer. He was nicknamed *le Vautrin* (wild boar).

At thirteen, he stole his parents' silver plates only to be arrested three days later. His father had orchestrated the arrest with the police to teach him a lesson. He spent fourteen days incarcerated.

His wild streak would not be tamed. The following year, he stole a large amount of money from his father's cash box and left for Belgium. He attempted to travel to America, but was defrauded completely of his stolen proceeds. He joined a series of traveling entertainers portraying a Caribbean cannibal that ate raw meat. He flirted with the young wife of his employer and was sacked. Nearing his hometown, he returned to his parents seeking forgiveness. They obliged.

In 1792, Vidocq joined the military, but good fortune remained elusive with his impulsive entanglements and conflicts with superior officers. He gained a reputation as a womanizer with many of his seductions ending in duels.

He was imprisoned on multiple occasions, escaping frequently but was always captured. His final escape came on March 6, 1800 with the assistance of a prostitute.

He returned to Arras that same year. His father had died the year before. He hid inside his mother's house for nearly six months before being recognized. His life continued a predictable pattern of crime followed by jail time.

He decided following his latest arrest on July 1, 1809, to alter his direction. He sought to escape from the fringes of society. He offered his services to become an informant for the police. While incarcerated over the next two years, he spied on his contemporaries, reporting directly to the Police Chief of Paris, Jean Henry.

Vidocq was released on March 25, 1811 under the pretext of an escape. He continued to work as a secret agent for the Paris police, often employing disguises and other identities to fool criminals who began to suspect him.

He organized the initial police plainclothes unit, the *Brigade de la Surete* (Security Brigade). Napoleon Bonaparte incorporated the operation into the state security police force.

Vidocq became an integral part of local police investigations, distinguishing himself with his success and investigative innovation. Writer Honore de Balzac used him as a model for several law enforcement figures in his books.

His position within the police force frequently involved clashes with authority. His mentor police chief Henry retired and was succeeded by a pair of ambitious, but antagonistic heads. He finally felt that he'd had enough. On June 20, 1827, the 52-year-old Vidocq submitted his resignation. He would follow his decision by writing his memoirs with the assistance of a ghostwriter.

During his post-police years, be became an entrepreneur founding a paper factory. He employed primarily released convicts. His company dissolved within a year.

In 1833, Vidocq established a detective agency that also operated as a private police force. It is considered to be the first known detective agency. The operation flourished consisting of eleven detectives. Vidocq repeatedly had run-ins with the Paris Police Prefecture. Many of the conflicts were attributed to his hiring ex-convicts for employees and circumventing established police policies with his investigations.

By 1849, his credibility would be tested one final time. The overthrow of King Louis Philippe the year before had installed Alphonse de Lamartine as head of a transitional government. Vidocq was briefly incarcerated for fraud although the charges were later dropped. His finances would suffer severely from an unwise financial speculation. His health slowly deteriorated until he could no longer stand upright. On May 11, 1857, he died at his home at the age of 81.

His inheritance was predictably messy with his history of libertine behavior. Eleven women came forwards to claim interests in his will. He had no known children, but the son of his first wife attempted to become recognized as his. He even changed his surname to Vidocq to substantiate his claim. He failed when it was determined that Vidocq was jailed at the time of his conception. The remaining assets would be given to Anne-Heloise Lefevre, at whose house he had resided until the end of his life.

Many historians have credit Vidocq as the *father* of modern criminology. His unorthodox approach introduced undercover work, ballistics matching, plaster casting and a detailed record keeping system employed for criminal investigations. His contribution towards society ultimately superseded his criminal past.

6 rue Vivienne #13

A Vile Historical Murder and Subsequent Presidential Residence
Former Hotel Sebastiani
Elysee Palace:
55-57 rue Faubourg Saint-Honore, 75008 Paris

The Elysee Palace, the current residence for the French President was completed in 1722 for nobleman and army officer Louis Henri de La Tour d'Auvergne. He had been appointed governor for the Ile de France in 1719. Architect Armand-Claude Molet would design the mansion that required three years to construct. Before becoming the later residence of the President of the Republic, it had been the home for several dignitaries including Madame de Pompadour, King Louis XV's chief mistress and the Duke of Berry.

Adjacent to the structure was the Hotel Sebastiani whose gardens spilled out onto the Champs-Elysees. The owners were Theobald de Praslin and his wife Fanny Sebastiani. The couple had married in their teens. She was the daughter of Marshall Horace Sebastiani de La Porta. Fifteen years following their wedding, she had given birth to nine surviving children along with having a few miscarriages. She had become stout and obese as a result and her husband lost interest in her physically.

Fanny maintained a passionate love for her husband that frequently bordered on obsession. She reportedly wrote him several times daily expressing her longing for him. He remained distant and detached to her entreaties. He seethed inwardly during her emotional outbursts towards her children and household staff.

In 1841, the family hired Henriettte Deluzy as governess. She impressed outsiders with her charm and intelligence. She had formerly studied in the studio of Pierre Delorme, a noted historical painter. She remained with the family for six years. Duke de Praslin preferred her company and that of his children to his wife. The Duchesse de Praslin became increasingly jealous and presumed that Deluzy had become her husband's mistress. Her suspicions, never confirmed, became certain when her husband traveled to Italy with Deluzy and their children without her.

She terminated Deluzy's services in June 1847 and began divorce proceedings, intent on taking the children from their father. Deluzy found other employment, but sent letters to the family reiterating her sadness over her departure and current loneliness.

The Duke concluded that his wife's behavior had been excessive. On the evening of August 17, 1847, he determined that he had endured her conduct enough. The family was lodging overnight at the Hotel Sebastiani en route to their annual vacation excursion to Dieppe, Belgium.

Enraged, the Duke savagely attempted to slice his wife's throat open while she lay in her bed. She awoke and the pair struggled. He continued his assault with the butt of a pistol and then a candlestick. Her screams awoke the household. She collapsed and died from her wounds. He retreated to another room and attempted to burn his blood-saturated clothing in the fireplace.

The police investigator immediately recognized the inept murder dismissing any suspicion that the act was done by a professional thief. Abundant clues pointed towards de Praslin and he was placed under house arrest. He was transferred to the Luxembourg Palace pending his upcoming trial.

While in custody, he swallowed a large dose of laudanum. It was not determined if his suicide attempt was based on remorse or the certainty of his punishment. For six days, he endured merciless agony, refused to eat or answer questions regarding the charges. He denied all accusations claiming that an intruder was responsible. He would finally expire and the case was dismissed.

There was speculation that he had been offered the option of suicide by the authorities to avoid an embarrassing guilty verdict. The affair became one of the final scandals that undermined the monarchy of King Louis-Philippe. The 1848 Revolution the following year would result in his abdication and the creation of the Second Republic.

During the previous four years of Louis-Philippe's reign, the Elysee Palace building had been employed as a residence for foreign dignitaries visiting France.

The first French presidential election conducted during 1848 would modify its use. The Palace would become the home for the victor Louis Napoleon Bonaparte.

He soon afterwards initiated a renovation project for the palace grounds and surrounding neighborhood. Amongst the casualties of the redesign was the Hotel Sebastiani. The reconstruction would require several years and result in the present day layout.

During the renovation in 1852, Louis Napoleon Bonaparte would stage a coup d'etat and empower himself as Napoleon III. He relocated his residence to the Tuileries Palace.

Following the future abdication of Napoleon III and the establishment of the Third Republic, the Elysee Palace resumed its residential status. President Patrice de Mac Mahon became the first head of state to reside there in 1874. During World War II, the German appointed Vichy regime President abandoned the palace. Presidential functions resumed once again post war in 1947.

Elysee Palace

An Improbable Political Emergence From Exile
Louis Napoleon Residence and Campaign Headquarters
(Hotel du Rhin):
4-6 Place Vendome, 75001 Paris

Charles Louis Napoleon Bonaparte dreamed seemingly
irrationally of the Bonaparte name returning to govern
France. He would fulfill that ambition upon his election to the
presidency in 1848. The route to becoming a candidate
seemed improbable considering his obstacles.

He was a nephew of Napoleon Bonaparte, the son of Louis
Bonaparte and Hortense de Beauharnais. Following the
collapse of his uncle's regime, Louis Napoleon remained with
his mother in Switzerland. He enrolled in the Swiss Army and
trained to become an artillery officer. There, he cultivated a
political philosophy expressed through extensive writings.
His aim involved a resurgence of the Bonaparte name.

He was convinced that his destiny would eventually lead him
to the French throne. Poorly prepared, he mounted an aborted
coup from Strasbourg on October 29, 1836 against then
current King Louis-Philippe. The regiment he had assembled
fell apart quickly. Most of his men were arrested and he
retreated back to Switzerland.

The Swiss government resisted King Louis-Philippe's
demands to expel him. They countered that he'd become a
Swiss citizen and member of their military. Louis-Napoleon
voluntarily moved to London, next to Brazil and then the
United States. He was prevented from attending his mother's
funeral because he was forbidden to enter France.

He returned to London preserving his dream of eventually
seizing power. He lived in idle comfort. During the summer
of 1840, he attempted a second coup entering through the
French port of Boulogne. The fiasco and failure resulted in

71

his arrest, conviction and a sentence of life imprisonment in the fortress of Ham in the Somme department of Northern France.

His attempt was ridiculed in both the French and English press. He was dismissed as *insane* and *incompetent*. The French newspaper *Le Journal de Debates* skewered his attempt stating: *this surpasses comedy. One doesn't kill crazy people, one just locks them up.*

He might have remained a forgotten victim, but attitudes were shifting in France. The popularity of his uncle Napoleon Bonaparte was steady increasing. Huge crowds viewed the return of his remains from Saint Helena on December 15, 1840. Nostalgia towards the glory days of the French Republic became popular.

Louis Napoleon could only view these developments from a jail cell. His incarceration extended six years. He remained busy, but unhappy and impatient. He contributed articles to regional newspapers and cities throughout France. He refused to slip into obscurity. His books, poems and essays kept him in public viewing and began to establish his credibility as a potential leader. He proposed practical ideas for creating a banking and savings system aimed towards providing credit to the working class. His message was directed towards them. They were listening.

On May 25, 1846, he engineered as escape from his prison with the assistance of his doctor and outside allies. He disguised himself as a laborer carrying lumber. He simply strolled out of prison gates. An awaiting carriage drove him to the coast and a boat transferred him to England. A month later his father Louis would die making him the clearest heir to the Bonaparte dynasty. He expediently resumed his social position in London society. He became re-acquainted with celebrated personalities and continued his studies at the

British Museum.

He initiated two romantic and pivotal affairs. The first was with a famed French actress named Rachel while she was touring England. The second and more influential became the wealthy heiress Harriet Howard. They met in 1846 soon following his return and moved in together. She would finance his ambitions to return to Paris.

During 1848, a Revolution erupted forcing his arch political rival Louis-Philippe into abdication. Louis Napoleon departed London for Paris on February 27. Ironically, he left the identical day Louis-Philippe retreated for his own British exile.

His arrival in Paris was unwelcome by the Provisional government headed by Alphonse de Lamartine. He claimed to harbor no political ambitions. He consented to return to London upon de Lamartine's request until events calmed. His absence from Paris proved ideal timing.

In June 1848, a fresh uprising engulfed the city. Barricades littered the working-class neighborhoods. The Provisional government initiated a violent crackdown on the protests. Louis-Napoleon had distanced himself completely from their unpopular response and repression.

He decided to return in the autumn. He would be elected while traveling between London and Paris to the National Assembly receiving the most votes of any candidate. When he arrived on September 24th, his status had risen. Over the course of seven months he had shifted from exile to election as a highly visible National Assembly member. Within three months, he announced his candidacy for the first ever presidential election in the French Republic. He established his campaign headquarters and residence at the Hotel du Rhin under the shadow of the Vendome Column.

As a member of the National Assembly, he rarely gave speeches, voted or even attended sessions. His goal was not to establish a transparent democracy.

His Bonaparte name carried the election. He earned 74.2% of the popular vote. The results reflected a comeback once thought unimaginable. His triumph would ultimately leap giant steps backwards towards a centralization of power. Louis Napoleon would become Napoleon III, seize complete control of the government and ultimately become France's final monarch.

4-6 Place Vendome

The Best Kept Courtesan in 19th Century Paris
La Paiva's Residences:
28 Place Saint-George, 75009 Paris
25 avenue des Chaps-Elysees, 75008 Paris

Esther Lachmann was born into poverty in a Moscow, Russia ghetto to Polish parents. During her youth, she never forgot the humiliation of being pushed out of a cab on the Champs-Elysees by a hurried customer and injured. She vowed to one day construct a luxurious mansion on the famous boulevard. Lachmann was considered attractive, seductive and frequently calculating in her selection of lovers.

She married young to a tailor at seventeen, but never allowed the union to interfere with her larger objective of being one of Paris' most sought after courtesans. A Parisian Count and admirer crowned her *the queen of kept women, the sovereign of her race*.

Her sexual partners were numerous and often celebrated individuals. She acquired one of the foulest reputations within Europe for her dalliances. Two liaisons would prominently elevated her public station and regard within society. Each relationship resulted in marriage.

The first suitor was Albino Francisco de Araujo de Paiva of Portugal. He was an heir to two extensive wholesale fortunes in Macao based on the opium trade. He flaunted a fictitious title and Lachmann parlayed his deceit to become known as *La Paiva*.

The marriage lasted a single day. Following the ceremony, she dismissed him with a letter and kept their furnishings. She was awarded a significant stipend as specified in their marriage contract. Araujo reluctantly complied and returned to Portugal.

Her greatest conquest became a 22-year-old Prussian industrialist and mining magnate named Count Guido Henckel von Donnersmarck. They met at a party in 1852 hosted by the Prussian consul in Paris. She initially feigned indifference towards him exciting his curiosity. She managed to stalk him throughout various European cities by attending the same parties and social events. He became enraptured by her presence and pledged to share his wealth if she would become his mistress.

La Paiva was solely interested in his riches and his proposal suited her ambitions. In 1871, she obtained an annulment of her previous marriage to de Paiva and would marry Donnersmarck two months later. He lavished her with gifts, an extravagant annuity and the construction of her dreamed mansion on the Champs-Elysees. She spared no expense in furnishing the manor in opulence. Her former husband would commit suicide the following year.

Her sway over Donnersmarck prevailed even with the steady erosion of her beauty and charm. She hosted glittering parties and established a popular literary salon within Paris. She disdained and ignored gossip regarding her past vulgarity. Her re-invention had arrived full circle.

La Paiva would die on January 21, 1884 at the age of 64 inside the couple's German estate in Schloss Neudeck. Even in death, La Paiva possessed the garish ability to shock. A legend emerged that her husband embalmed her body, but did not bury it. Instead he stored it inside an attic on the property until his second wife accidentally discovered it.

A German Unifier At The Expense of France
Otto von Bismarck's Diplomatic Residence:
Hotel de Beauharnais, 78 rue de Lille, 75007 Paris

In May 1862, Otto von Bismarck relocated to Paris as Prussia's ambassador to the court of Napoleon III. Four months later, he would become Prussia's prime minister and foreign minister. Although his Parisian stint was brief, his residence was credited with altering his previous ultra conservative politics. His views evolved into an appreciation of the importance of an educated and propertied middle class.

Bismarck's background was military having spent the majority of his adult life in the army. His appointment was Emperor William I's desperate attempt to avoid parliamentary control over the military. At the time, a liberal legislative majority sought to rein in the king's influence and budget with reforms.

The monarchy could not have selected a more astute and adept leader to further their agenda. He was considered by many of his peers as a reactionary confrontational aristocrat *out of tune with his time*. Bismarck would accomplish a feat no predecessor could before. Through strategic warfare, diplomacy and sheer ruthlessness, he consolidated German nationalism into creating a united German Empire.

The unification of Germany would come at the expense of France and four independent southern German states. Napoleon III became indignant at the threat of an emerging Prussia. He became paranoid during 1869 of the Spanish throne being offered to Prussia fearing an encirclement of France.

Napoleon III demanded that Prussia immediately refuse any Spanish throne offer. Further he insisted that Prussia never consider the option in the future. Bismarck seeking to keep his options fluid declined Napoleon's demands.

The issue could have likely been resolved diplomatically. Napoleon III rashly declared war on Prussia on July 19, 1870. The French army was completely unprepared for such a conflict.

Following early battlefield losses, French forces on September 1-2 were completely annihilated at the *Battle of Sedan* in the Ardennes region of northeastern France. Over 104,000 men were taken prisoner including Napoleon III. Paris based government officials would immediately proclaim a *Government of National Defense* two days later and continue fighting. The Prussian forces streamed towards Paris.

During the conflict, Bismarck stirred up anti-French passions. The four formerly independent southern states joined the North German Confederation to create the German Empire.

German forces encircled Paris between September 19, 1870 until January 28, 1871. The encounter would be called the *Siege of Paris*. For four months, the city was bombarded by artillery and the population starved by blockades. The provisional French government continued urging resistance attempts to break through the blockade. Unsuccessful, the leaders agreed to a humiliating armistice that ceased hostilities.

The worst of the surrender treaty ceded the Alsace and Moselle department of Lorraine to Germany. This territory would remain a source of contention and dispute throughout World War I. In the aftermath, the territory would return to French possession.

The abdicated Napoleon III would be exiled to England where he died three years later. Bismarck would be lauded with honors and hailed as a triumphant national hero. For the next two decades, he would be credited with preserving the peace within Europe. Not everyone acknowledged his statesmanship.

In June 1888, Kaiser Wilhelm II ascended the throne of Germany following the death of his father after reigning only 99 days. His father was suffering from cancer of the larynx when he died at 56. He had previously professed hatred towards warfare and was praised for his humane conduct and intention to reform the German government. He was married to the eldest child of England's Queen Victoria.

Wilhelm II shared his father's distaste for Bismarck's policy of uniting Germany through force. The mysterious death of King Ludwig II of Bavaria in 1886 had only reinforced his distrust. In March 1890, he dismissed Bismarck and tilted the country away from a conciliatory position towards Europe.

He initiated an aggressive attempt to colonize foreign territories. His personality was perceived as impulsive and dismissive. His tactlessness and antagonistic posturing alienated world powers, especially former European allies.

Germany was left with only declining allies such as Austrian-Hungary and the Ottoman Empire. Wilhelm II would eventually provoke World War I. Upon Germany's defeat and his abdication, he would flee to the Netherlands. He remained in exile until his death in 1941 at the age of 82.

Otto von Bismarck retired to his estates an embittered man. For the next eight year until his death, he severely rebuked his successor. He was elected to the German Reichstag, but chose not to participate. In retirement, he wrote a popular selling memoir.

He was diagnosed with gangrene in his foot during 1896, but refused treatment. Within two years, he was confined to a wheelchair experiencing trouble breathing and suffering from chronic pain and fever. He died shortly after midnight on July 30, 1898 at the age of 83 on his estate in Friedrichsruh in northern Germany.

Hotel de Beauharnais

The Prostitution Industry Within Paris
La Grisette Sculpture:
Greenbelt Park Separating boulevard Jules Ferry, 75011 Paris
Belle-Époque Brothel:
36 rue Saint Sulpice 75006 Paris
Madame Claude Brothel:
18 rue de Marignan, 75008 Paris

Prostitution in Paris has consisted of periods alternating with tolerance and repression. Brothels have historically been an accepted institution, but sometimes a visible target for reformists. One of the earliest monuments to the poor working girls that turned to prostitution is found discreetly wedged inside a greenbelt park near the Canal Saint Martin. The sculpture is entitled *La Grisette* dating from 1830.

During the Belle Époque era of the late nineteenth century, there was an accentuated increase in sex workers due to governmental lenience and less restrictive laws. Women had to register at the prefecture to work at a brothel. They were taxed on their earnings and obligated to have a twice-weekly medical examination. Many avoided the check-ups.

Between 1871 and 1903, an estimated 155,000 women officially registered as prostitutes. During that same period, police statistics indicated that 725,000 others were stopped for clandestine prostitution. Many of the women were reportedly housewives and waitresses seeking a secondary income for themselves.

Artists and particularly impressionist painters glamorized the trade in their works. Many were active clients transforming the women into objects of desire and intrigue.

There was nothing glamorous regarding the sex worker trade. Violence administered by their clientele and pimps was commonplace. The stigma accompanying arrest and venereal disease were risks. The primary financial beneficiaries were the individuals who operated the brothels. Many Madames were former prostitutes who had saved their earnings and re-invested them into real estate and a trade they were intimately acquainted with.

During the two World Wars, prostitution was curtailed amongst Allied military forces. In occupied countries such as France, women were employed as entertainment diversions for the conquering officers and soldiers. Following the Second World War, many of the brothels were shuttered and outlawed.

For the wealthy, the option never slackened. During the 1960s, Fernande Grudet known as *Madame Claude* became the recognized head of a network of high-end call girls that specialized in dignitaries, criminal bosses and civil servants. Her clientele was an international *Who's Who* including reputedly the Shah of Iran, John F. Kennedy, Charles de Gaulle and George Pompidou.

Her own background was gauzy. In interviews, she indicated that she'd been interned in a Nazi concentration camp, worked as an agent for the French Resistance and began as a post-war prostitute before managing her own exclusive operation.

By the mid 1970s, her Paris based organization would become dismantled for tax evasion. She fled to Los Angeles in exile. She returned to France in 1986 to serve a four-month jail sentence. Upon her release, she attempted to resuscitate her business. She was arrested for procurement in 1992 and sentenced to a term in Fleury-Merogis Prison.

Her life or at least her version would be released in films, books and media interviews following her forced retirement.

She died on December 15, 2015 in Nice at the age of 92.

La Grisette

Belle Epoque Brothel

Madame Claude's Brothel

An Irish Nationalist Leader Establishes His Foreign Headquarters
Charles Tudor Stewart's Apartment:
122 avenue des Champs Elysees, 75008 Paris
Charles Parnell's Foreign Headquarters (Brighton Hotel):
218 rue de Rivoli, 75001 Paris

Charles Stewart Parnell is considered one of the most influential Irish nationalist politicians and orators of his era. He served as a Member of Parliament from 1875 to 1891. He was a spiritual leader of the Home Rule League movement followed by the head of the Irish Parliamentary Party between 1882 to 1891. At the peak of his domestic prowess, an adultery scandal eroded his reputation, base of support and dissipated his leadership influence.

Parnell's association initially with Paris began via his maternal uncle Charles Tudor Stewart, an American. Stewart leased an elegant apartment along the Champs Elysees between 1856 until 1873. Parnell's mother Delia frequently traveled with her ten children to visit him. During one of these visitations, Parnell encountered and became infatuated with Mary Woods, a wealthy young woman from Rhode Island.

Their union was not destined to flourish. Woods refused Parnell's romantic entreaties. Rejected, he then devoted himself exclusively into the Irish political movement. He made the Brighten Hotel his foreign headquarters. He utilized French banks and financial institutions to conceal gifts and cash donations from Irish-Americans away from the prying eyes of British authorities. Mary Woods would subsequently marry, but reportedly in an unhappy union.

Parnell would be arrested on October 13, 1881 together with his party lieutenants. They had vehemently protested the *Irish Land Act* promoted that same year. The legislation was an attempt by the Land Commission to institute land reform and lessen renter evictions.

While imprisoned, Parnell agreed to a compromise with the British government negotiated through another Member of Parliament Captain William O'Shea. Parnell agreed to moderate his militant rhetoric and renounce violent confrontation. His promise freed him from prison, but would entangle him into a far greater controversy.

Parnell's deepest crisis involved his advocate O'Shea with regard to the latter's wife Katherine. The couple had been separated since 1875, but O'Shea would not grant her a divorce as she was anticipating a substantial family inheritance. Parnell met her initially as an invited guest to a dinner party organized by the couple.

Katherine O'Shea captivated Parnell. The couple began to spend extended and soon intimate time together. Their relationship would culminate in three children in rapid succession. By July 1881, O'Shea had learned of their affair and challenged Parnell to a duel. Katherine prevented the armed conflict. O'Shea seethed silently viewing the three children he had not fathered.

O'Shea eventually filed for divorce on December 24, 1889 citing Parnell as the primary cause for the ruptured marriage. The contentious divorce resulted in headlines, scandal and condemnation by the clergy. The public repercussions immediately tarnished Parnell's moral reputation. His fragile political coalition splintered. O'Shea's divorce decree was granted on November 17, 1890 with Parnell's own two surviving children being place under O'Shea's custody.

Amidst the scandal, Parnell's health deteriorated from kidney disease and accumulating ailments. His vision of Irish unity fragmented into competing and combative factions. He would die in the arms of his beloved Katherine during October 1891 at the age of 45. Although his political strength had declined, his treasured memory and charisma would prompt forgiveness.

His funeral was conducted at the Irish National nondenominational Glasnevin Cemetery in Dublin. Over 200,000 people attended the service. A granite stone unhewn from the Wicklow region was erected in 1940 to adorn his grave. The inscription simply reads *Parnell*.

Brighton Hotel

The Populist Crusader Who Might Have Become King
Gare de Lyon Train Station:
Place Louis-Armand 75012 Paris

The Boulangisme movement was a far right radical cause resembling fascism. The beginnings as most populist campaigns were constructed upon hyperbole and general public discontent. In 1871, France had lost a bitter war with Prussia and endured a reactive Commune uprising afterwards. Public morale had plunged to extreme depths prompting the need for a savior amidst the malaise.

George Boulanger was a brigadier-general in 1880 and rose steadily within the upper ranks. His actual accomplishments were minor, but the public perception unveiled him as a dynamic leader.

During the undeclared Sino-French War from August 1884 to April 1885, he emerged as a hero. The French army and navy fought China to gain control in Tonkin (then Northern Vietnam).

The performance by the French army had proved lackluster ending in retreat. France's naval supremacy ultimately forced China to negotiate a peace settlement. The former nation of Annam (South and North Vietnam) was converted into a French protectorate. This agreement would become an enormous foreign policy catastrophe later in the 20th century.

Boulanger received adulation from a starved public and press for the perceived victory and colonial addition. He was appointed Minister of War under Prime Minister Charles de Freycinet's tenure. The choice was oddly determined based on the presumption that he was a liberal republican since he didn't attend mass. In fact, he was a conservative and advocated the return of the monarchy.

As Minister of War, he was credited with quelling a worker's strike and creating major reforms to the military. Most of these *improvements* were superficial including allowing soldiers to grow beards (he wore one). He lathered in positive publicity.

What Boulanger clearly understood was that the French populace dreamed of an alternative outcome to their humiliating defeat to Prussia. In his capacity, Boulanger repeatedly goaded the newly consolidated Imperial Germany. His ultimate declared ambition was to reclaim the Alsace-Lorraine region *stolen* from the 1871 defeat.

His provocations included constructing military facilities in the border region of Belfort, banning the export of horses to Germany and instituting a prohibition of performing Richard Wagner's *Lohengrin*. His war rattling provoked German government calls to arms, but military conflict was averted.

Boulanger's bombastic rhetoric and theatrics were well received domestically. He became an embarrassment and risk to President Rene Goblet's administration. When Goblet was voted out of office in May 1887, his successor Maurice Rouyvier immediately sacked Boulanger.

He would be appointed commander of the troops stationed in Clermont-Ferrand. The change was intended to remove him from Paris. His positive press was steadily building him a political constituency. He earned 100,000 votes during an election in the Seine department without even declaring a candidacy for the position.

When his train bound south for Clermont-Ferrand departed on July 8th, an estimated crowd of 10,000 swarmed the Gare de Lyon station in support of him. They covered his train with posters showering affection and encouraging his return. Several partisans blocked the railway tracks but eventually he was smuggled out.

By January 1889, George Boulanger posed the greatest political threat to the reigning Third Republic government. His base of support derived from the working class districts of Paris and other cities, plus traditionalist Catholics and royalists. He promoted aggressive nationalism and calls for revenge against Germany.

Political observers viewed his surging popularity as a groundswell for a coup d'etat. Boulanger procrastinated. Instead of leading a popular revolt that may have elevated him to power, he vanished to spend time with his mistress. Marguerite Brouzel, the Vicomtesse of Bonnemains had developed an enormous influence bordering on obsession with him. His supporters were unable to locate him. The moment and opportunity passed.

When he resurfaced, he determined that the better option for him was to contest the upcoming general election and take power legally. The months leading up to the election enabled his opponents to seize ammunition and strategize against him.

The election of September 1889 decisively lowered the brakes on his movement. His party was soundly defeated principally due to changes in electoral laws preventing Boulanger from running in multiple constituencies. Shortly afterwards, the still paranoid government issued an arrest warrant for Boulanger citing *conspiracy* and *treasonable* activity.

Rather than address and combat the charges, he opted to flee, traveling initially to Brussels and then London. The French Senate condemned him for treason and sentenced him to deportation and confinement in absentia.

A clearer image of the disgraced Boulanger emerged. The media reversed their earlier reverence towards him. He became regarded *as lacking coolness, consistency and decisiveness. He was a mediocre leader who lacked vision and courage.*

His dependence, devotion and relationship with Marguerite Brouzel ultimately sealed his fate. She had relocated to Brussels amidst the election turmoil. She became ill there and died in his arms in July 1891. The melodrama could only conclude in a single manner. While visiting her grave on September 30, 1891, a bereaved Boulanger raised a pistol to his temple and pulled the trigger.

Gare de Lyon Train Station

High Couture and Questionable Wartime Affiliations
Coco Chanel Headquarters Boutique:
21 rue Cambon, 75001 Paris
Coco Chanel Apartment:
31 rue Cambon, 75001 Paris
Coco Chanel Suite Residence (Ritz Hotel, Room 302):
15 place Vendome, 75001 Paris

Gabrielle Bonheur *Coco* Chanel became one of the world's most celebrated French fashion designers and businesswomen. She founded her namesake Chanel brand and revolutionized post-World War I era styling. She popularized a sporty, casual chic that captivated and simplified women's fashion. Her designs were easier to wear, more comfortable and less expensive than her competitors without compromising elegance.

She parlayed her clothing success into design involving jewelry, handbags and fragrance. Chanel No. 5 became her signature iconic scent. Her famed interlocking CC monogram was introduced during the 1920s.

Chanel was born into poverty during 1883 in Saumur, France. Her mother was a laundrywoman in a charity hospital and her father an itinerant street vendor. She and her two sisters did not attend school and were housed at the convent of Aubazine that operated an orphanage. Her first employment was as a seamstress. She sang in a nearby cabaret frequented by cavalry officers. She reputedly earned her nickname *Coco* from her cabaret gigs, but preferred to confide publicly that her father gave her the nickname.

Chanel recognized by 1906 that her prospects were limited as an entertainer. She drifted between the resort town of Vichy and Moulins until she met a young ex-cavalry officer and textile heir, Etienne Balsan. She soon became his mistress and lived with him inside his chateau Royallieu near

Compiegne.

Balsan and his circle of friends introduced her into a life of extravagance, indulgence and decadence. The chronology of her life and professional ascent is often considered more self-promotional than precise. Whether true or modified, Chanel crafted an existence that would prevent her from ever returning to her impoverished roots. She steadily cultivated a friendship base of French and English aristocrats, literary and cultural elites and politically prominent individuals including Winston Churchill and Edward the Prince of Wales.

Her creative intensity, innovation, marketing skills, and profound work ethic established her as an international success story and icon brand. Rumors and speculation regarding her political sympathies and later alliances clouded her personal reputation.

Her couture house closed in 1939 upon the outbreak of World War II. Chanel remained in Paris and was accused of collaborating with the German occupiers and the French Vichy puppet government. One of her infamous liaisons was with a German diplomat, Baron Hans Gunther von Dincklage. Post-war, she was interrogated about her relationship with von Dincklage. She evaded charges of collaboration reportedly due to her friend English Prime Minister Winston Churchill's intervention.

She moved to Switzerland to avoid criminal espionage charges. Archival documents released by the French intelligence service implicated her as an agent for the German military intelligence. She would never face legal accountability if indeed this role was legitimate. The stigma clouded her legacy domestically. Posthumous efforts to honor her fashion contributions with memorials have often been shelved.

She wouldn't return to Paris until the 1954 season to revive her fashion house. Her professional re-emergence was viewed as a *breakthrough* in the American and British fashion press. She continued her operations and seasonal catalogues, expanded her headquarters and client base. Fashion trends and designs began to shift away from major couture houses. Most of her competitor icons would profit handsomely by selling their goodwill, name recognition and intellectual properties to mass-market clothing distributors.

By 1971 at the age of 87, most of her friends had died and her own health had deteriorated. Following an extended afternoon drive on Saturday, January 9, 1971, she felt ill and went to bed early.

She reportedly confided to her maid: *You see, this is how you die.*

The memory of her possible wartime improprieties has been consigned to public amnesia. Her professional legacy dominates the majority of favorable writings about her. Subsequent biographical films have blurred the darkened edges and softened a harsher scrutiny of her past.

Channel Headquarters

A Chameleon of the Haute Fashion World
Karl Lagerfeld's Residences:
17 quai Voltaire, 75007 Paris
6 Place Saint-Sulpice, 75006 Paris
Hotel Pozzo di Borgo: 51, rue de l'Universite, 75007 Paris

Karl Lagerfeld began his process of personal reinvention shortly following his entrance into the public limelight. He started by claiming a younger age of five years and insinuating noble birth. In truth, he was born on September 10, 1933 in Hamburg, Germany. His father owned a company producing and importing evaporated milk. His mother was a lingerie saleswoman from Berlin. They had married in 1930.

From an early age, Lagerfeld became absorbed with art and design. He gravitated towards Paris in 1953 attending the Lycee Montaigne. He won prestigious fashion design competitions prompting the Fendi Company to hire him to modernize their fur line of clothing. Throughout the 1970s, he became increasingly recognized as an influential fashion designer, shifting his styling and themes as trends dictated.

In the early 1980s, the Chanel Company hired him. Founder Coco Chanel had been dead for over a decade and the luster of the brand was floundering. Heading their couture department in 1983, he resurrected the label by revamping its ready-to-wear fashion line. In 1984, he established his own Karl Lagerfeld fashion line to broaden his individual appeal. Throughout his career, he collaborated with numerous designers and fashion houses.

His designs and collections would remain popular during the first two decades of the new century. During that period, he cultivated a personal style appearance consisting of white hair, black sunglasses, fingerless gloves and high, starched detachable collars. His personal lifestyle and rumored relationships remained clouded. He reputedly amassed one of the largest personal book libraries in the world.

As his public profile expanded, he would court controversy with statements regarding fur, women's weight, Islam and the *Me Too* Movement. Whether this persona and commentary were genuine or simply a sniping charade remained debatable. Despite his attempts to confound the fashion industry and his public following, he was unable to evade the consequences of aging and disease.

Throughout January 2019, he suffered from the effects of pancreatic cancer. On February 18, he was admitted to the American Hospital of Paris located in Neuilly-sur-Seine. He died the following morning from complications of the disease at the suspected age of 85. His body would be cremated and his ashes spread at various undisclosed locations.

17 Quai Voltaire

Terror's Advocate Representing Reprehensible Actors and Actions
Jacques Verges' Residence:
27 Quai Voltaire, 75007 Paris
Jacques Verges' Law Practice
20 rue Vintimille, 75009 Paris

Attorney Jacques Verges claimed to be a fighter in the French Resistance during World War II. Following the war's conclusion, he earned a law degree at the University of Paris. His initial public notoriety arrived with his defense in the 1950s of FLN militants during the Algerian War of Independence. He represented Algerian guerrilla Djamila Bouhired on murder charges for planting a bomb inside an Algiers café that killed eleven people upon detonation.

His defense rationale was that the bombing was a military action staged by an opposition soldier. She was convicted and sentenced to death. She was later pardoned and freed following public pressure stimulated by Verges. He would later marry and then abandon Bouhired completely.

Verges took international ambulance chasing to storied heights. He represented some of the most reprehensible clients, many convicted of crimes against humanity. Amongst his notable roster included Klaus Barbie, Saddam Hussein, the Khmer Rouge, Ilich Ramirez Sanchez (Carlos the Jackal), Idi Amin, the German Baader-Meinhof gang, Slobodan Milosevic and numerous undesirable personalities and unpopular causes.

None of these clients would be acquitted. His primary motivation appeared to be a public forum to espouse their respective causes or simply defend their right to representation. The irony that so many of his clients were responsible for the collective deaths of thousands seemed lost amidst his judicial pleas for leniency or mercy. Many observers simply concluded that his role was self-serving to publicize himself and his law practice, absent of principles.

His personal life was most noteworthy for an eight-year absence between February 1970 until 1978. He refused to offer an explanation for his whereabouts that led to significant speculation. His death on August 15, 2013 at the age of 88 was ironically inside the same residence as the 18th century writer Voltaire. The wit, wisdom and satire of the controversial Voltaire remains lacking and missed in contemporary society. The warped hatred ideology represented by Jacques Verges, an advocate for terror is not.

27 Quai Voltaire

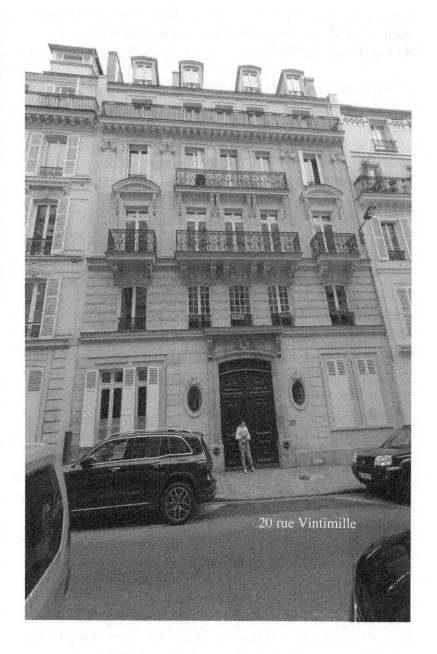

20 rue Vintimille

**Saving His Biggest Secret For The End of His Presidency
Anne and Mazarine Pingeot Former Residence:
40 rue Jacob, 75006 Paris**

Francois Mitterrand became the first left-wing politician to become President of France. He remained the longest serving president in the history of the country between May 1981-1995. His reign was noteworthy for elevating the Socialist Party to prominence at the expense of the Communist Party.

Mitterrand was man of secrets and discretion. Throughout much of his tenure, he suffered from terminal prostate cancer that he was able to successfully conceal from the public.

His biggest secret however, he saved until the closing of his administration. He had been engaged in a long-term extramarital affair for many years with Anne Pingeot. She was an art historian specializing in 19th century French sculpture and curator of the sculptural department at the Louvre and Musee d'Orsay. Together they had a daughter named Mazarine in December 1974. Mitterrand would publicly reveal her existence.

French Presidents with mistresses are not particularly novel. Many have been rumored to engage in extracurricular trysts, none before Mitterrand ever revealed any resulting offspring. The French public ultimately shrugged off the news whereas during the same time as his public introduction of his daughter, American President Bill Clinton was commencing his own sexual scandal with Monica Lewinsky.

The reaction towards Clinton's actions once exposed became radically different. Clinton was impeached from office by the U.S. House of Representatives, but ultimately kept his position prevailing in a close U. S. Senate conviction vote.

Mitterrand would die eight months following the end of his presidency on January 8, 1996 at the age of 79. Once the original novelty of his announcement subsided, Mazarine would carry on with her life. She completed her Parisian university studies and then professionally became a writer, journalist and professor. She would have one son and two daughters with her former partner Mohamed Ulad-Mohand, a film director.

40 rue Jacob

bonaparte era

The Formative Years of Napoleon Bonaparte
Napoleon Bonaparte Residences:
19 rue de la Michodiere, 75002 Paris
13 Quai Conti, 75006 Paris

The rise of Napoleon Bonaparte to the supremacy of France is the equivalent of tracking a streaking meteor across the sky. His paternal ancestors descended from minor Tuscan nobility. They immigrated to Corsica in the 16th century. He was fourth child and third son born on August 15, 1769 in Ajaccio, Corsica.

The island was part of the kingdom of France, but distinctive in language, mannerisms and customs. Corsican was Bonaparte's first language and Italian his second. He began learning French at the age of ten and although he developed fluency, retained his Corsican accent throughout his life. His spelling in French would always remain suspect.

During his youth, he supported Corsican independence, but a career in the French military became his sole career option. He trained to become an artillery officer completing the course in one year instead of two due to a drastically reduced allowance from his family. He became the first Corsican to graduate from the French Ecole Militaire.

He was commissioned as a second lieutenant in an artillery regiment based in Valence and Auxonne. When the French Revolution first erupted in 1789, he was assigned to Corsica to fight in a complex struggle amongst French royalists, revolutionaries and Corsican nationalists. He became a supporter of the Jacobin revolutionary movement terminating his loyalty towards the Corsican independence movement. This decision alienated him from their leader and his former mentor Pasquale Paoli.

The perceived betrayal marked the ascendancy of Bonaparte as a self-interested individual. He published a pro-Republican pamphlet entitled *Supper at Beaucaire* that earned him the support of Augustin Robespierre, the younger brother of revolutionary leader Maximilien Robespierre.

He would be appointed a senior gunner and artillery commander during the September 8, 1793 siege of Toulon against British forces. He distinguished himself with his unconventional strategy and success as the French captured the city. He was wounded in the thigh during the battle. The Paris Committee of Public Safety designated him in charge of France's Army in Italy. He was promoted from the rank of colonel to brigadier general at the age of 24.

By 1795, he had returned to Paris to further his career prospects. He lived frugally along the Seine River in a fifth story apartment. His prospects for advancement had stalled. He was impatiently awaiting the next chapter of his life. During his residence on the rue de la Michodiere, he received elocution lessons from his friend Talma. He also reportedly lodged on the top level of another apartment building located adjacent to the Seine at Quai Conti. It would be later renamed the *Eagle's Nest*.

Bonaparte became engaged to Desiree Clary whose sister had married his eldest brother Joseph. He refused a commission in April 1795 to fight in the War in the Vendee, a region in west-central France on the Atlantic Ocean. This post as infantry commander would be a demotion from artillery general. His refusal to serve isolated him into professional limbo. He was removed from the list of generals in regular service. By September, he faced a bleak financial situation and significantly reduced career prospects. He broke off his engagement to Clary.

The professional trajectory of Napoleon Bonaparte appeared to have flatlined at that stage. The events of 13 Vendemiare, Year 4 would alter everything by the end of the following month. The rise of Bonaparte would subsequently dominate French and European history for the subsequent two decades until his death at the age of 51 on May 5, 1821.

13 quai Conti

The Desiree in Napoleon Bonaparte's Life
Desiree Clary's Residence:
28, rue d'Anjou, 75008 Paris

Before there was the Empress Josephine in Napoleon Bonaparte's life, there was Desiree Clary. She was born in Marseille into an affluent family with a brother and sister. Her father was a silk manufacturer and merchant. Her mother was his second wife. Desiree was educated initially in a convent common with the upper class. Upon the spread of the French Revolution, all convents were closed. She returned to her parent's residence and was home schooled.

In 1794, Desiree's father died and her brother Etienne became the head of the household and her legal guardian. Revolutionary forces would arrest him due to his aristocratic status. She would successfully appeal his release. She encountered Joseph Bonaparte during the appeal process and invited him to their home.

Joseph soon became engaged to her older sister Julie whom he would marry. Desiree would follow with her own engagement to Joseph's younger brother Napoleon on April 21, 1795. Her fiancé's prospects temporarily dimmed during that summer. By September, Napoleon's future became more secure with the Revolutionary Council and he had met a more desirable companion. He broke off their engagement.

His lead role in the attack of 13 Vendemiare on October 5 would preserve the existing ruling body. Freed from his own marriage engagement, Bonaparte openly courted the widow Josephine de Beauharnais. Her husband, Alexandre had been guillotined during the *Reign of Terror* the year previously. She had since been engaged in affairs with several leading political figures, but saw more promise in Bonaparte, six years younger.

De Beauharnais was a better fit for his evolving ambitions and rise to power with her social contacts and popular artistic salon. The couple would marry in 1796.

In 1797, Desiree moved to Rome to live with her sister and brother-in-law, who had been appointed the French ambassador to the Papal States. She was briefly engaged to General Mathurin-Leonard Duphot during her stay. Many observers presumed their introduction was arranged by Napoleon as compensation for his own withdrawal. Duphot agreed to the marriage primarily due to her dowry and the status of her brother-in-law. He reportedly already had an existing relationship and a son from another woman. Their union would end abruptly on the eve of their ceremony. Duphot was killed during an anti-French riot outside of his residence, the Palazzo Corsini in Rome. Clary would deny in later years that she was ever was engaged to Duphot.

She would return to Paris resuming her residence within the Bonaparte family circle. She refused another proposal of marriage from General Jean Junot. She finally consented to marry a Bonaparte General, Jean Baptiste Bernadotte in August 1798. In the marriage contract, she was given economic independence. On July 4, 1799, she gave birth to their only son Oscar.

Her marriage with Bernadotte was frequently long distance. They shared marginal time together, but remained on good terms. She was described as *pretty, pleasing* and *a skillful dancer*. Her presence however was described as *anonymous*. During the turbulent reign of Bonaparte, her husband ascended in rank and position. She rarely opted to visit him outside of France. In August 1810, General Bernadotte was elected as heir to the throne of Sweden. She preferred to remain in Paris for the majority of time before and immediately after he assumed the throne. In 1818, he officially became king. During this interim period, she was rumored to have fallen in love with the French Prime Minister, the Duc of Richelieu. Her affection was not returned.

Eventually she settled reluctantly into the Swedish court as Queen Desideria. She was disinterested in politics. She pined for her former life and society in Paris. She complained about the frigid Swedish winters, her royal status and limited entertainment options. She lived indifferently towards the behavioral expectations of royalty.

She never learned Swedish and never earned the affection of the populace. She kept erratic late hours pursuing frivolity. She was habitually late and considered eccentric. Her husband Bernadotte, now titled King Charles XIV John understood her anguish, but forbade her to return to Paris.

She would outlive him and their son, King Oscar I. As queen mother, she was allowed to continue living in the Royal Palace inside the queen's quarters. Despite her diminished status, her son and grandson (King Charles XV) allowed her to maintain her lifestyle and keep her entire court staff. On December 17, 1860 she collapsed inside her carriage returning from a performance of the Royal Swedish Opera. She died before reaching her apartment at the age of 83.

28 rue d'Anjou

The Woman Behind Napoleon Bonaparte's Rise
Josephine de Beauharnais' Residences:
**6 rue de la Victoire (Formerly Rue Chantereine), 75009
Paris**
60 rue de la Victoire (Demolished), 75009 Paris
**Pentemont Abbey (Destroyed), 106 rue de Grenelle, 75007
Paris**

On March 2, 1794, the Committee of General Security
ordered the arrest of General Alexandre de Beauharnais for
his poor defense of Mainz during the siege in 1793. His
aristocratic birth made his status suspect amongst the radical
elements of the Committee. His wife Rose was jailed in the
same Carmes prison on April 21, 1794. The couple had
shared two children together.

He would be guillotined during the *Reign of Terror* in July at
the age of 34. The timing of his execution proved particularly
poor as his accuser, Maximilien Robespierre would be
arrested and beheaded only five days after him. Beauharnais'
wife Rose would be released afterwards.

Her liberation would influence the future of France. Her
formation made that prospect seemingly remote.

The newly widowed Rose's birth location has been disputed
as either the island of St. Lucia or Martinique in 1763. Her
wealthy French family owned a sugarcane plantation that was
decimated by a hurricane three years later. In October 1779,
she accompanied her father to Paris for an arranged marriage
with Beauharnais in December.

The marriage was a complete disaster. Despite fathering two
children, Alexandre continued to frequent brothels. He
abandoned his family for an entire year during a tryst. Rose
was granted a legal separation before his arrest. She resided
in the Pentemont Abbey during her separation while her case

against Beauharnais was being heard. Upon his death, she discarded his surname.

Following her release, she engaged in brief affairs with several prominent political figures. In 1795, she met Napoleon Bonaparte who was six years younger and then engaged to Desiree Clary. He broke off the engagement and she became his mistress. He preferred to call her Josephine. For the remainder of her life, she kept that name.

Bonaparte was thoroughly intoxicated by Josephine. She was polished and refined as contrasted to his clumsy unsophisticated Corsican background. Her renowned Parisian salon hosted the most elevated minds, artists and performers of the era. His own family felt awkward and resentful in her presence and criticized him relentlessly for marrying an older women with two children.

The couple would be wed on March 9, 1796. Two days later, Bonaparte left Paris to lead an army into Italy. During their separation, he composed frequent passionate love letters. She responded rarely with cold and detached correspondences.

It became common speculation that she shared significantly less passion towards him. Left behind, she initiated an affair with a Hussar lieutenant. Bonaparte became enraged upon hearing the news and altered the intensity and tone of his passion. He began his own numerous affairs during his military campaigns. He was quoted in 1804 as confessing: *Power is my mistress.*

While in Paris during December 1800, the couple was nearly killed by a bomb attempt of their separate passing carriages heading to the opera. The bomb detonated just after Josephine's had passed killing several bystanders.

Bonaparte was elected Emperor of France in 1804, making

his wife Josephine the new Empress. Their legendary coronation ceremony took place at Notre Dame Cathedral and was officiated by Pope Pius VII. Bonaparte first crowned himself and then placed the crown atop Josephine's head. The act was symbolic to declare a relegation of the clergy's supremacy over Europe.

Over time, Bonaparte and Josephine grew increasingly closer in affection and intimacy. Her inability to produce an heir doomed the marriage. When it became apparent that she could no longer have children, they agreed to divorce so that he might father a future emperor. Their divorce ceremony was conducted on January 10, 1810 at the Louvre. Each read a statement of devotion and continued friendship to the other.

Bonaparte insisted that Josephine retain the title of Empress and created a fresh designation for her as the Duchess of Navarre. He remarried in April 1810 to Marie-Louise of Austria and she delivered his desired son in March 1811. He was christened Napoleon II and given the title of King of Rome. Two years later, Napoleon introduced him to Josephine.

She would witness the initial fall of Bonaparte in 1814 begging Emperor Alexander I of Russia to allow her to join him in exile on the island of Elba. Her request was denied. Shortly afterwards on May 29, 1814, she died of pneumonia at the age of 50.

Bonaparte plunged into intense grief upon hearing the news of her death. During his second exile on Saint Helena, he confessed that he had truly loved her, but *did not respect her*. He reportedly uttered her name amidst his final words on his deathbed.

His second wife Marie-Louise did not follow Bonaparte to either exile destination. The 1814 Treaty of Fontainebleau provided her with the Duchies of Parma, Piacenza and Guastalla that she ruled until her own death in December 1847 at the age of 56. Following Bonaparte's death, she would remarry twice to men considered below her social status. She bore three additional children with the first husband.

Her son with Bonaparte, Napoleon II would live an abbreviated life of 21 years in Austria under the title, Franz, Duke of Reichstadt. He was educated by a staff of military tutors and became a cadet in the Austrian Army. Franz would grow distant from his mother often belittling her as *kind but weak*.

In 1831, he was given the command of an Austrian battalion. He would never have the opportunity to prove his capabilities. In 1832, he caught pneumonia and remained bedridden for several months. On July 22, he died from tuberculosis inside Vienna's Schonbrunn Palace. He was initially buried in Vienna, but in December 1940, Adolph Hitler ordered his remains to be transferred to Les Invalides.

Site of 60 rue de la Victoire

6 rue de la Victoire

The Undeclared War Between The United States and France
Talleyrand Hotel (Hotel Infantado):
2 rue Saint-Florentin, 75001 Paris
Talleyrand Residences:
24 rue Taitbout, 75009 Paris (Demolished)
57 rue de Varenne, 75007 Paris

Charles Maurice de Talleyrand-Perigord is considered France's most renowned and successful Foreign Minister. As the nation's chief diplomat, he parlayed his background in theology into operating at the highest echelon of French governments including Louis XVI, the Revolutionary Directory, Napoleon Bonaparte, Louis XVIII and Louis-Philippe.

Such dexterity and cunning often bred distrust amongst those he served. Each profited handsomely from his negotiating skills, calculations, and usefulness. Scholarly opinion views Talleyrand with mixed regard. He was accused of often elevating personal gain for national interests. His corruption was well documented.

In the aftermath of the American Revolution, relations between America and France were cordial. American independence from England provided France with a welcomed military distraction against their historical foe. The government following the French Revolution stiffened relations with the United States. During France's military engagements with Britain and Europe, President George Washington maintained strict American neutrality.

Sustaining impartiality became problematic in trade and commercial interests for the United States. France and Great Britain were the two dominant naval powers and trading partners. Each habitually seized cargo ships of neutral countries including the United States for trading with their enemies.

The American government reached a compromise with Britain, but the French Navy stepped up efforts to completely eliminate trade. By the conclusion of Washington's term, the interruption of seafaring commerce had reached a crisis stage.

In late May 1797, American President John Adams appointed a special commission to approach France and negotiate a similar treaty as they had with Britain. A contentious five-member Directory operated France's executive branch. They had chosen Talleyrand as their foreign minister and hardened their concern towards American interests. Talleyrand did not welcome diplomatic relations between America and Britain. He slowed down negotiations with the American delegation using an unconventional tactic.

Through informal channels and agents, Talleyrand demanded bribes and a loan before he would diplomatically recognize the American delegation's credentials. His request was commonly practiced towards countries that he considered insignificant. The American delegation composed of Charles Pinckney, John Marshall and Elbridge Gerry were deeply appalled and refused his brazen request. Pinckney and Marshall returned immediately to the United States.

Gerry lingered for several months hoping to bridge reconciliation. Instead, Talleyrand hoping to strike an independent agreement apart from the other delegation members manipulated him. Talleyrand never softened on his bribe demands, but dropped the request for a loan. Gerry ultimately refused to engage in substantive negotiations with him. Upon his return, his own Federalist political Party would discredit him.

The French Directory eventually became aware of Talleyrand's duplicity. They summoned him to appear before them for an explanation. He denied all accusations against him.

Reaction towards the commission's failure to negotiate a treaty with France became surly within American political circles. Adams had initially suppressed revealing Talleyrand's bribery demands. His conservative Federalist Party who controlled Congress forced him to release the delegations written dispatches. Adams substituted the letters X (Jean-Conrad Hottinguer), Y (Pierre Bellamy) and Z (Lucien Hauteval) for the identities of the participating French diplomats. The intrigue would be labeled the XYZ Affair.

The revelation of Talleyrand's impropriety prompted immediate outrage and demands for war. The crisis resulted in an expansion of American military forces. Adams sagely resisted declaring formal war. On July 7, 1798, Congress nullified the 1778 Treaty with France and authorized attacks on French warships. For the next two years, the countries would engage in military skirmishes on the open seas staged primarily within the Caribbean.

Talleyrand was obliged to retreat from his original proposal. He realized that that he'd badly miscalculated the American response and willingness to engage French forces. He should have been savvier having lived previously in New York City for two years as Aaron Burr's houseguest. Burr would subsequently become President Thomas Jefferson's political opponent and future Vice President.

The French government officially initiated diplomatic overtures to cease the hostilities. The United States sent Secretary of State James Marshall to negotiate the Treaty of Mortefontaine in September 1800. A new French government would ratify that agreement the same year. First Consul Napoleon Bonaparte represented France. He had overthrown the ruling Directory in November 1799. Any incidental quarrel with the United States became an unwelcome distraction. His ultimate ambitions were elevated to subjugating Russia, England and the rest of Europe.

For Talleyrand, the diplomatic embarrassment did nothing to diminish his professional longevity. His skills continued to be employed, even if his ethics remained perpetually suspect.

Talleyrand and Bonaparte shared a long history together and his house on rue Taitbout (now demolished) played an intriguing role in Bonaparte's rise to central authority. A few days before his intended Coup d'Etat called *Brumaire 18*, Bonaparte visited him discreetly at his residence situated on the upper first floor. They were discussing Bonaparte's plan to overthrow the ruling Directory.

As the two men conversed in the drawing room lit by a few candles, there was a great commotion in the street below at 1:00 a.m. The noise sounded like the riding of carriages and trampling of horses, resembling a cavalry brigade. A horse halted abruptly in front of Talleyrand's house. Both men feared the ruling Directory had come to arrest them.

Talleyrand blew out the candle and crept to the front window overlooking the sidewalks. The noise had originated from numerous horse-drawn cabs that nightly collected and transferred gaming table proceeds. Gendarmes were escorting the party to the proprietor's house. One of the lead cabs had met with an accident in front of Talleyrand's front door prompting the others to halt abruptly. The hasty repairs required fifteen minutes as both men spied upon the fiasco silently. Their panic slowly receded and turned to laughter.

Days later, Bonaparte would solely control the government of France.

Talleyrand incurred the wrath and admiration of many

notable contemporaries. French writer and diplomat Francois-Rene de Chateaubriand recalled him as a *handsome man* during his youth that evolved into the very image of a *death's head*.

A sketch in *Temple Bar* labeled him *greedy of renown, more greedy still of riches, loving women with his senses, not with his heart, calm in critical positions, haughty to the great, suave to the humble, neither vindictive nor wicked*.

In 1816, Lady Morgan called him *cold, immovable, neither absent not reflective, but impassable; no colour varying the livid pallor of his face*.

Writer Victor Hugo epitomized Talleyrand best as *one of noble descent like Machiavelli, a priest like Gondi* (Cardinal of Retz), *unfrocked like Fouche* (Bonaparte's Minister of Police), *witty like Voltaire*, and *lame like the devil* (he suffered from a birth deformity and limped). *In his palace, like a spider in his web, he allured and caught in succession, heroes, thinkers, great men, conquerors, kings, princes and emperors...all the gilded and glittering flies who buzz through the history of the last forty years*.

2 rue Saint-Florentin

24 rue Taitbout

The Diplomat Who Framed American Foreign Policy
James Monroe Residence Site (Mansion Demolished)
95 rue Richelieu, 75002 Paris
Signing of the Louisiana Purchase (Hotel Tubeuf):
8 rue des Petits Champs, 75002 Paris

President George Washington sent James Monroe to Paris initially in 1794 as the U.S. Minister to France. His two-year appointment proved turbulent following the signing of the Jay Treaty with Great Britain. America had opted for strict neutrality amidst the ongoing French-English War. The French government felt the treaty favored England and their disappointment in Monroe doomed his tenure.

One of his most successful negotiations involved securing the release of writer Thomas Paine, supporter of the American Revolution. Paine had been jailed for his outspoken criticism over the execution of King Louis XVI. Once Paine was released, he was allowed to reside with Monroe's family in the American ministry mansion.

Monroe fought during the American Revolution initially in the Virginia infantry. He became an officer in the Continental Army joining George Washington in New York. He fought with distinction in several major battles suffering a near fatal wound to his shoulder as he led a charge against enemy cannon fire. By the end of his military service, he had risen to the rank of major.

He returned to his native Virginia and studied law taking Thomas Jefferson as his mentor. He was elected to the Virginia Assembly and lost by 300 votes to James Madison for a seat in the U.S. House of Representatives. He married Elizabeth Kortright in 1783, the daughter of a former wealthy Virginia merchant. He was 26, but she was only 16.

When Thomas Jefferson won the presidency in 1800, Monroe

would become involved in his administration. In 1803, Monroe was sent to Paris as an envoy to negotiate the Louisiana Purchase.

The Louisiana Purchase became the largest land acquisition sale in history. For $15 million, the United States acquired sovereignty across the Mississippi River Valley nearly doubling the territorial size of the country. The most desirable acquisition was the city of New Orleans. At the time of the purchase, only 60,000 non-native inhabitants lived within the territory. Half were enslaved Africans. France only controlled a small fraction of the area. The United States bought the *preemptive* right to obtain Native American lands.

As frontier history evolved during the 19th century, that *right* would evolve into a literal steal of the lands incrementally by treaty. Warfare with Spain and Britain early in the century would ultimate define the territory boundaries to the west and north.

The purchase was strongly derided by Jefferson's opposition Federalist Party. The negotiations between France and the American purchasing delegation wavered over price and French foreign minister Talleyrand's disapproval. Napoleon Bonaparte overruled Talleyrand. He needed the funds for his planned invasion of England and likely envisioned retaking the territory once he had conquered and secured Europe.

The signing of the Louisiana Purchase Treaty took place at the Hotel Tubeuf on April 30, 1803. Months later, the Cabildo, New Orlean's city hall became the transfer site of the territory finalizing the acquisition.

Monroe served as U.S. Minster to Britain from 1803 to 1807. This period included a brief stint as a special envoy to Spain in 1805. His diplomatic skills became increasingly respected within international circles. He was nominated by dissident Republicans to oppose James Madison in the 1808 presidential election. Madison won easily and Monroe returned to Virginia where he was elected governor three years later.

Madison would name him secretary of state shortly afterwards. He presided over the initially disastrous War of 1812 with Britain as hastily appointed Secretary of War. The ill-equipped and unprepared American military forces were defeated in early conflicts. Eventually, the American forces would prevail.

By 1816, Monroe's popularity elevated him to receive the Democratic-Republican Party nomination for President. He would serve two terms as the fifth American president. His most enduring legacy was the Monroe Doctrine. This landmark opposed any European intervention with recently independent countries of the Americas. Monroe's Parisian residence, called the *Folie de Bouexiere* was demolished long ago. The Hotel Mercure Paris Opera Louvre currently operates on the site.

95 rue Richelieu

8 rue des Petits Champs

A Loyal, Lovely and Promiscuous Bonaparte
Hotel de Charost (Currently British Embassy):
35-37 rue du Faubourg St. Honore, 75008 Paris

Few within the Bonaparte family clan proved loyal and generous to Napoleon following his 1814 defeat at the Battle of Leipzig and subsequent abdication. Upon his exile to Elba, his favorite and younger sister Pauline proved the most. She would sell her residence, the sumptuous Hotel de Charost to the British Government. The proceeds from liquidating the property and all her assets would be given to her brother upon his own failed fortune.

She was reputedly fond of pleasure and hosted a popular salon during her brief residence. She was the only Bonaparte to visit him during his exile on his principality island of Elba.

The mansion was originally erected in 1725 and designed by architect Antoine Mazin, who died the year of its completion. The initial owner was the Duke of Charost. In 1803, Pauline Bonaparte purchased the mansion following the death of her husband General Charles Leclerc the year before. He died from yellow fever in Haiti where he was Governor-General. She was able to acquire the property due to a generous inheritance from the Leclerc estate.

Soon afterwards her brothers Napoleon, Joseph and Lucien induced her to marry Camillo Borghese, a titled Italian prince. The match became literally a business transaction with exchanged dowries and titles. The marriage was an attempt to strengthen ties between France and occupied Italy. Her apathy towards Borghese turned into hatred. Their only son died following a violent fever and convulsions in childhood.

The Hotel de Charost sale proved ironic as the mansion was converted into the British Embassy. The first English

126

ambassador to inhabit the property was the Duke of Wellington, Bonaparte's military nemesis. When he left his exile from Elba and attempted to regain the French throne, it was Wellington who headed the opposition forces. Bonaparte's army was soundly defeated at Waterloo and his leadership ambitions permanently thwarted.

Pauline's health had always been fragile. In Haiti she declined measurably. She reportedly could not longer walk due to bouts with yellow fever and was compelled to a reclining position for several hours daily. Curiously some of these reclining periods involved liaisons with several of her husband's soldiers. This pattern would repeat during her second marriage. Both Pauline and Borghese engaged in repeated extramarital affairs while predominantly living apart.

Pauline would barely outlive Napoleon. She died in her Florence villa at the age of 44 on June 9, 1825 from a cancerous tumor on her stomach.

35-37 rue du Faubourg St. Honore

A Strong-Willed Rebellious Bonaparte Brother
Louis Bonaparte's Residence:
52 rue de la Victoire, 75009 Paris

Louis Bonaparte became the most independent and rebellious of Napoleon's siblings. The younger brother was born and raised in Corsica before following his brother's footsteps in the military. He accompanied Napoleon's expedition to Egypt where he was made Aide de Camp. By the age of 25, he was promoted to a General, a position he felt was unmerited.

Louis returned with his brother to France where he became intimately involved with his coup d'etat to overthrow the ruling Directory. After becoming First Consul, Napoleon arranged a marriage between he and Hortense de Beauharnais, the daughter of Empress Josephine his wife. Hortense opposed the union initially, but agreed to the match for the sake of the family. The couple never got along, pursued other dalliances and ultimately avoided each other's company. She would precede him in death at the age of 35.

As Napoleon's military victories and rise to power continued, he determined the northern Batavian Republic had become too defiant to his liking. He renamed the country the Kingdom of Holland on June 5, 1806 and placed Louis on the throne. He envisioned simply a subservient extension of France.

Louis differed in his attitude towards Holland. His goal was to create an independent nation. He preferred autonomy from Napoleon's control and strove to become a responsible and independent ruler. He attempted to learn the Dutch language, forced his court ministers to speak Dutch and even renounce their French citizenship. He adopted the Dutch name *Lodewijk I*. His efforts to induce his wife to speak the language were stonewalled with absolute refusal.

128

His sincere effort was greeted with a mixture of respect and ridicule. His language and pronunciation skills were so poor that many subjects hearing him speak laughed behind his back at his unintentional malaprops.

His capriciousness was often labeled as mental illness. He could never decide on the location for Holland's capital city. He chose over a dozen cities. One time following a visit to a wealthy Dutch merchant, he evicted the owner so that he could assume residence. Seven weeks later, he decided upon another location. His court remained in upheaval following him with each change. The European diplomatic court petitioned him to remain in a single location.

Hortense bore him two sons while she was in Paris and he in Holland. Louis requested their return to Holland. She refused and Napoleon sided with her keeping them in France.

Napoleon recognized his error in appointing Louis. He had requested Dutch troops for his militia to invade Russia. Louis refused. The English landed an army of 40,000 in 1809 with the intent to capture control of Antwerp and Flushing. Louis was unable to defend the territory requiring Napoleon to send 80,000 soldiers to repel the invasion. Following their success, he suggested to his brother that it was time to leave. On July 1, 1810, he reluctantly abdicated and settled in Graz, Austria. Napoleon annexed Holland to France the following week.

While in Graz, he began writing and composing poetry. He attempted to revisit Holland, but replacement King William I repeatedly denied him permission. His son William II allowed him a visit during 1840 under an assumed name. A group of citizens discovered his identity and gathered under the window of his hotel room. Their cheering and applause visually moved him. Despite his brief rein, he had earned the affectionate title of *Louis the Good*.

Upon the death of his eldest brother Joseph in 1844, Louis was view by Bonapartists as the rightful Emperor of France. He took no further action to pursue the claim. His son was imprisoned in France at that time having attempted his own personal coup d'etat. His efforts would later be rewarded by his election as President in 1848 and scizure of the throne three years later as Napoleon III. Louis would die on July 25, 1846 in Livorno, Italy with his remains transferred for burial at Saint-Leu-la-Foret in France.

52 rue de la Victoire

An Occupier As An Assassination Target
Duke of Wellington's Residences:
2 avenue Gabriel, 75008 Paris
39 rue du Faubourg St. Honore, 75008 Paris
1 rue Boissy d'Anglais, 75008 Paris
24 rue Boissy d'Anglas, 75008 Paris

Arthur Wellesley, better known as the first Duke of Wellington proved a permanent obstacle to Napoleon Bonaparte's conquest ambitions. During the Napoleonic Wars, he led the British and allied forces to victory at the Battle of Vitoria in 1813. During Bonaparte's exile in 1814, he served as the British Ambassador to France.

He returned to battle during Bonaparte's *Hundred Days* resurgence in 1815. He commanded an allied army with Prussian Field Marshal Gebhard von Blucher to victory at Waterloo. He spared Bonaparte's execution when he was captured on the battlefield. Wellington was credited with participating in over sixty battles during his military career.

Concerned regarding the political stability of France and the maintenance of peace within Europe, a multinational army occupied the country between 1815-1818. The intent was to prevent an uprising or insurgency against the newly crowned King Louis XVIII. Wellington was placed in charge of the occupation forces.

From the outset, he understood the collective dangers to him posed by supporters of the Revolution (Jacobins) and Bonapartists. They despised the restored monarchy and his role in defeating Bonaparte.

Two plots directly against him would be exposed publicly during his Paris residency. The first occurred on June 25, 1816 during a ball he gave at the British embassy. The rooms were crowded with attending guests when an alarm was

131

sounded that the mansion was on fire.

A barrel of oil had been placed in a cellar with an opened window facing the street. Wood shavings were scattered on the floor along with bottles filled with gunpowder. The shavings were ignited and the blaze soon spread. There were no reported fatalities resulting from the attempted arson.

A much closer instance occurred on the evening of February 10, 1818 when a shooter appeared from behind a sentry box as Wellington was returning home from a party. A well-dressed man reportedly fired his pistol at Wellington's carriage window from close range. Wellington saw the flash of the gunfire, but the shot missed both he and his carriage. The potential assassin escaped into the darkness. When the Paris police arrived to search the surrounding area, no trace of a bullet was found. Local newspapers mocked the incident.

Wellington had been warned about the impending attempt earlier, but disregarded the threat. A further investigation isolated two probable suspects. The men were arrested but later released due to insufficient evidence.

Marie-Andre-Nicolas Cantillon was identified as the shooter. He had been a sub-lieutenant in the French army. The accompanying notoriety would demote him to sergeant. Bonaparte, however, did not forget him. Upon his death on May 5, 1821, he bequeathed Cantillon 10,000 francs in his will.

Bonaparte shared no affinity or respect towards Wellington. He had conveniently forgotten that the latter had ordered his troops to spare his life at Waterloo. Bonaparte concluded that Cantillon's action was justified as an act of war. Wellington reacted to the news by merely expressing regret that Bonaparte had lowered himself in such a manner.

In 1830, King Louis Philippe would appoint Cantillon as a gamekeeper at the Palace of Fontainebleau. His name later surfaced as a grocer in Brussels.

In November 1818, the allied occupation of Paris ended and the Duke of Wellington would return to England. He would become Britain's Prime Minister between 1928-1934 and remained Commander-in-Chief of the Army until his death in 1852 at 83.

24 rue Boissy d'Anglais

writers

A Brilliant Philosophical Mind Felled By Barbaric Medical Practices
Rene Descartes' Residence:
14 rue Rollin, 75005 Paris

Rene Descartes is considered an important contributor to modern philosophy and science. His rational process of deductive reasoning became his signature contribution to humanity. His philosophical statement *cogito, ergo sum* (I think therefore I am) is still widely repeated, frequently with comic intonations.

Descartes was born on March 31, 1596 in the Touraine region. His mother died the following year after giving birth to a stillborn sibling. His father was a member of the Parliament of the Brittany located in Rennes. Rene earned a degree in canon and civil law from the University of Poitiers in 1616. Afterwards he moved to Paris.

He became a professional military officer two years later enlisting as a mercenary in the protestant Dutch Army. During his service, he began formative studies on analytic geometry. He determined by the conclusion of his military stint that he would devote his life to mathematical theory in the pursuit of philosophy. He reasoned that discovering a fundamental truth and proceeding with logic would eventually open the way to all science.

Upon leaving the army in 1620, he visited various European countries before returning to Paris. He relocated permanently to the Dutch Republic in 1628. Once settled, he joined the University of Franeker. He would commit the majority of his remaining life to researching, publishing and working in Holland. He became globally recognized as a central intellectual within the Dutch Golden Age.

His philosophical and scientific system would ultimately be

called *Cartesianism.* The popularity of his theories and notable writings would influence European opinion during the remainder of the 17th century leading up to the Enlightenment. As Descartes' fame and reputation spread, enticing commissions, opportunities and appointments became available.

In 1650, he agreed to give lessons in philosophy to Queen Christina of Sweden following her birthday. Their relationship and study interests soon proved incompatible. Lodging during winter within the confines of her frigid castle, he contracted pneumonia.

He initially refused to allow the Queen's physician to bleed him as a potential cure. As his fever heightened, he consented to be bled three times daily. His condition worsened. He would expire ten days later on January 15, 1650 inside the household of the French ambassador Chanut. Medieval quackery could not rescue one of the most brilliant thinkers of his era.

14 rue Rollin

A Mathematical Genius Tormented By His Religious Scruples
Blaise Pascal's Residence:
2 rue Rollin (Replacement Structure), 75005 Paris

Blaise Pascal led a tormented life of only thirty-nine years. During that period, the child prodigy and mathematical genius pioneered significant discoveries in economics, social science, mechanical calculators, natural and applied sciences.

He wasn't afraid to contradict accepted theories by previous philosophers including Aristotle and Descartes. He made important contributions to the study of fluids, and the clarification of pressure and vacuum.

Despite his accomplishments, he lived a humble and submissive existence. From the age of twenty, he devoted himself to a life of meditation and prayer. He renounced all pleasures reportedly wearing an iron girdle full of points next to the skin. Any idle or superficial thought would trigger a self-flagellation.

In 1646, he and his sister Jacqueline would become ardent members of a sect within Catholicism known as *Jansenism*. His writings broadened into a religious vein often widening the gap between his sect and the Jesuits. His two most famous works included *Lettres Provinciales* and *Pensees*, published seventeen years following his death.

He suffered from frail health throughout his life and died inside his home (formerly 8, rue St. Etienne du Mont) on August 19, 1662. The house was razed and replaced by the present structure. It would become the residence of his biographer and sister, Marguerite Perier until her death.

2 rue Rollin

Mining Deeper Insight Through Recollection and Personal Examination
Denis Diderot Residence (Death Site):
39 rue Richelieu, 75001 Paris
Jean-Jacques Rousseau's Residences:
2 rue Jean Jacques Rousseau, 2nd Floor (Birthplace) 75001 Paris
58 rue St. Denis, 4th Floor (Death Site), 75001 Paris

Jean-Jacques Rousseau made his own life the subject for many of his celebrated writings. He was born in Geneva in 1712 and raised by his father, a clockmaker. His mother died days following his birth. His father introduced him to classical Greek and Roman literature. He would be apprenticed to become an engraver.

Two major events prompted his eventual move to Paris. His father was compelled to leave Geneva while he was still young. At sixteen, Jean-Jacques left Geneva for Annecy. There he met Francoise-Louise de Warens who evolved from being his benefactor to mistress.

For the next decade, he scraped together a livelihood as an engraver and music teacher. He renounced his Calvinist beliefs and converted to Catholicism.

He arrived into Paris during 1742 to pursue a musical performance and composition career. He befriended an important influence in Denis Diderot who would earn his own fame for publication of the *Encylopedie*. Diderot commissioned Rousseau to write the articles on musical subjects. His professional trajectory continued to rise with his appointment as Secretary to the French ambassador in Venice from 1743 to 1744.

Over the next twenty years, he devoted himself to popular writings, essays and musings on philosophical discourse. His work became elevated as one of the important illuminations of the Age of Enlightenment.

During the peak of his productivity, he transgressed in the eyes of the clergy by questioning the relevancy and validity of Christianity. His public popularity and prior successes could not spare him from their condemnation. Two of his books, *On the Social Contract* and *Emile* were singled out for public burnings. The French government ordered his arrest. He fled for asylum to the Swiss frontier city of Neuchatel.

For the subsequent eight years, he wandered around Switzerland, England and the French provinces in exile. Dispirited, he plunged into depths of paranoia and depression. He endured increasingly hostile attacks from leading writers and lesser talents. He irrationally convinced himself that he had become universally despised. The professional attacks weighed down his spirit. The humiliation stimulated one of his greatest writings, the autobiographical *Confessions*.

He would return to Paris in 1770 as one of the most famous men in Europe, yet repeatedly stated his indifference towards fame. He claimed that he no longer was concerned about his reputation. He resided quietly with his companion Therese in a modest apartment near the Palais-Royal.

Over the next ten years, he embraced the virtue of contemplation, self-sufficiency and solitude within his writings. Some friends described him as generally *mild, modest, gentle and good-humoured.* Others less complimentary found him *rarely affable and never open-hearted. Timid distrust was evidently visible. He observed everything with a suspicious attention.*

He authored an intimate account of ten walks throughout Paris called *Reveries of a Solitary Walker*. The edition would become his final published work two years before his death.

The confessional series became his purist attempt to process the impressions he'd accumulated throughout his life. His readers shared a voyage of discovery through the eyes of a talent whose own turbulent existence had experienced the peaks of acclaim and weathered the distain of contempt and rejection.

Rousseau died unexpectedly on July 2, 1778. Many of his collected works would be published posthumously four years later. Freed from the judgmental constraints of public and critical approval, his works would become even further appreciated with time. In 1794, his ashes would be relocated to the Pantheon.

2 rue Jean Jacques Rousseau, 2nd Floor

A Forerunner's Writings Spurring the French Revolution
Voltaire's Residences:
2 rue St. Louis en L'ile, 75004 Paris
25 rue Moliere, 75001 Paris
27 Quai Voltaire (Death Site), 75007 Paris

Francois-Marie Arouet, better known as Voltaire became an illuminating voice during the French Enlightenment. Voltaire remains relevant even in contemporary times with his passionate advocacy of free speech and maintaining distinct separation between church and state.

His barbed wit often overshadowed the unpopularity of his criticisms towards the Catholic Church and slavery, controversial issues during his era. He continually battled against the strict censorship policies of the Catholic French monarchy.

His prolific writings elevated him professionally into a distinguished niche. He wrote plays, poems, novels, essays, histories, and scientific expositions. He is credited with writing in excess of 20,000 letters and 2,000 books and pamphlets. His longevity and the sheer volume of his production made him one of the first authors to become internationally successful.

He spent fifteen years living with Madame du Chatelet inside a 17th century palace on the northeastern periphery of the l'ile Saint-Louis. The mansion was originally constructed for President Lambert de Thorigny. Their cohabitation was considered an *improper* liaison and *whimsical*, but primarily described as a *steady friendship between two individuals of corresponding tastes*. Voltaire slaved over his writings like a devoted monk. Passion between the couple reportedly intervened infrequently. He began the composition of his *Henriade* while living at this residence.

His next home on the rue Moliere was shared with tragic actor Henri Lekain. His move was prompted by the death of his companion Madame du Chatelet. Voltaire served as a mentor and liberal protector for the aspiring performer at the Comedie Francaise. Despite his acknowledged ugliness and harsh voice, Lekain cultivated an admiring audience including Louis XV. During his career, he would amass a considerable fortune.

Voltaire's acclaim prompted frequent confrontation with religious and literary authorities. Over time, he maintained a habit of avoiding open public confrontation to concentrate on his writings. In mid 1750, he moved to Prussia at the invitation of King Frederick The Great, a passionate admirer of his work. Their relationship would soon sour following a series of misunderstandings with Frederick's agents. He would continue his travels through Mainz and the Alsace region.

In January 1754, Louis XV banned Voltaire from Paris. He relocated to Geneva where he purchased a large estate. Soon afterwards, he bought an even more expansive estate in Ferney on the French side of the Franco-Swiss border. In early 1759, he published *Candide,* a satire on a prevalent philosophy of optimistic determinism. This work would become his most famous. While residing in Ferney over the subsequent twenty years, he would entertain frequently and champion numerous causes and individuals he felt unjustly persecuted.

His celebrated return to Paris came amidst the twilight of his life in February 1778. The house where he stayed was the residence of the Marquis de Villette, a gay friend, philosopher and writer. Voltaire dressed in a habitual costume of dressing gown and nightcap. Crowds gathered around the house hoping to catch a glimpse of the distinguished visitor.

A steady stream of notable celebrities in literature, theatre and art paid homage to Voltaire with visitations. Villette received each and announced their respective names. Voltaire lasted seven weeks before his death on May 30th at the age of 84. His end was reportedly accelerated by the fatigue from rehearsals involving his final production of *Irene*. His strength was reportedly sapped by the constant visitations. His intake of black coffee as a stimulant and the ingestion of laudanum, a pain medication containing 10% powdered opium did little to ease his suffering.

Voltaire was denied a Christian burial in Paris, but friends and relations managed to bury his body secretly at the Abbey of Scellieres in the Champagne region where his niece's brother was abbot. On July 11, 1791, the National Assembly of France had his remains returned to Paris and enshrined in the Pantheon. Assembly members regarded his influence and writings as the forerunner of French Revolution doctrine. His works strongly influenced American writers of the period advocating independence from Britain.

The nephew of the Marquis de Villette and the subsequent apartment owner, Madame de Montmorency sealed Voltaire's apartment for nearly 47 years after his death.

During the World War II occupation, the building became a site for clandestine French Resistance gatherings. Infamous attorney Jacques Verges would eventually purchase the building and die from a heart attack inside his bedroom on August 15, 2013 at the age of 88.

2 rue St. Louis en L'ile

25 rue Moliere

27 Quai Voltaire

The Corruptible Legacy of the Notorious Marquis de Sade

Marquis de Sade Residences:

Conde Mansion (Demolished):
Rue de Conde, 75006 Paris
20, rue des-Mathurins, 75009 Paris

Secured Prostitutes:
Rue Mouffetard, 75005 Paris

Arrest: (Former Hotel Danemark)
56 rue Jacob 75006 Paris

Imprisonment:

(Conciergerie) Palais de la Cite:
2 Boulevard du Palais, 75001 Paris

Bastille:
Place de la Bastille, 75011 Paris

Chateau de Vincennes
Avenue de Paris, 94300 Vincennes

Wife's Residence During His Imprisonment (Convent de Saint-Aure):
16-20 rue Tournefort, 75005 Paris

Mother's Death:

Carmelite Convent: (Saint-Joseph-des-Carmes):
70 rue de Vaugirard, 75006 Paris

Sexual depravity and sadism found a welcoming quill amongst the writings of the Marquis de Sade. Debatably, no man has ever suffered more to pursue obsessive sexual perversity. His reputation and appetite for debauchery appeared insatiable. His era during the corrupt reign of Louis XV was an ideal accompaniment.

He was born on June 2, 1740 in the Conde mansion (since destroyed) to the Count and Countess of Sade. Their titles were legitimate and long standing. He was christened by accident with the name Donatien-Alphone-Francois instead of the intended first name Louis. His parents and godparents were absent for his baptismal the day following his birth at

Saint Suplice Church. Instead two appointed members of the household replaced them.

An uncle, the abbot of the Saint-Leger d'Ebreuil monastery was entrusted with his early education. At ten, he returned to Paris and attended the Louis le Grande College, a Jesuit school. He was assigned a personal tutor. During his teenage years, he was commissioned as an officer in an infantry regiment at the rank of captain.

There were no records or behavioral observations then suggesting what triggered his descent into sexual depravity.

At twenty-three, his life began a tumultuous trajectory that would worsen as he aged. He became engaged with two young women simultaneously. Despite his father's preference for the wealthier bride's family, Sade convinced him to accept Laure de Lauris to whom he was *wildly in love with*.

In May, the King and royal family give their consent for the marriage and the wedding ceremony was celebrated at Saint-Roch Church. Marital bliss and fidelity was short-lived. Sade routinely hired prostitutes on the Rue Mouffetard for carnal experimentation. By October, he would be imprisoned for the initial time. He was convicted for excesses committed in a brothel that he had frequented during the previous month.

He would be released two weeks later, but ordered by the king to remain at Echauffour Manor located in northwestern France. A police report would later surface indicating that a prohibition had been issued against providing Sade with girls to go into any private chambers with him.

Sade would continue a predictable pattern of recruiting sex partners, plunging into debt and impregnating his wife. They would have four children together, but he spent little time with the family.

He inherited his father's estate and titles at twenty-seven and was promoted to the rank of Captain Commander for the Mestre Regiment. His mother would die when he was thirty-six at the Carmelite Convent of Saint-Joseph-des-Carmes in Paris.

The following year, one of his prostitute partners lodged a complaint against him for sexual abuse. She cited being unwillingly bound and flogged. She was able to escape via a second-floor window after being abandoned. Her deposition became his first public scandal. She disappeared after receiving a payoff.

Sade would be incarcerated at the Pierre-Encise Prison near Lyon before being transferred to the Conciergerie in Paris. His wife remained in Lyon during his incarceration. At thirty-one, he was elevated to the rank of Colonel after his petition to a superior.

His family would gather at the Chateau de Lacoste, located in Provence. In January, he authored his first comedic play in Marseille at the Theatre La Coste.

Trouble would continue during his stay. He instructed his manservant to secure four women for their entertainment pleasure. He offered each woman aniseed sweets laced with Spanish fly extracts. The group would commence an orgy that extended until morning.

The women become violently ill with intestinal pain. They pressed charges against Sade for poisoning them and committing *homosexual sodomy*. He escaped and while a fugitive, eventually returned to Paris. His pattern of libertine sexuality, arrest and literary work would define his future and legacy.

He became know for his erotic writings depicting sexual fantasies with an emphasis on violence. His work stressed absolute freedom unrestrained by conventional morality, religion or law. Many were published anonymously due to the infamy attached with his name. The majority of his works were written during his periods of incarceration. He would be jailed in prisons and insane asylums for thirty-two years of his life.

During a brief stretch of freedom, he was elected to the French National Convention in 1790. He represented a group called the *Piques*, notorious for radical liberalism. He reportedly suffered abuse by his revolutionary peers due to his aristocratic background. One son would desert from his military service in 1792, prompting Sade to disavow him.

The French Revolution became a revolving door for Sade. He supported Jean-Paul Marat and wrote an admiring eulogy upon his death. He publicly criticized Maximilien Robespierre and the *Reign of Terror*. He was removed from his political office and imprisoned once again. He was released following the conclusion of the terror.

Napoleon Bonaparte was disgusted by Sade's writings. He had him arrested and declared insane. By then, Sade was in a pitiful state, broke and divorced. His ex-wife and children had agreed to pay his pension.

In 1803, he was transferred to the Charenton Asylum. The progressive director of the institution, Abbe de Coulmier allowed Sade to stage several of his plays with inmates as actors before the Paris public. The action was widely criticized. Six years later, Sade would be placed in solitary confinement and deprived of pens and paper. He died incarcerated on December 2, 1814 at the age of seventy-four.

152

Posthumously, the pornographic chronology of his life and content of his works were considered a scandal demanding repression. In the mid-twentieth century, his works resurfaced and were re-examined as censorship laws became relaxed. The sexual revolution of the 1960s made Sade's work even more accessible and acceptable in some quarters. He remains a divisive figure of both fascination and revulsion.

56 rue Jacob

20 rue des Mathurins

Convent de Saint-Aure

Rue Mouffetard

Carmelite Convent

A Writer Whose Idealism Permitted No Peace
Thomas Paine's Residences:
1 rue des Petits Peres, 75002 Paris
7 Passage des Petits Peres, 75002 Paris
10 rue de l'Odeon, 75006 Paris

Thomas Paine is best remembered for writing *Common Sense* in 1776. The 46-page pamphlet became enormously popular critiquing King George III rule in the American colonies concluding with a call for independence. This highly influential writing stressed the justification for the colonists' separation from England. Paine outlined a government that would be guided by a written charter emphasizing liberty and freedom of religion.

Paine was born in 1737 to a Quaker father and Anglican mother in Thetford, England. He labored as a corset-maker, tax collector, seaman and shopkeeper. His wanderlust prompted his departure for the American colonies in 1774. He traveled with only a letter of introduction from fellow Quaker Benjamin Franklin.

His timing proved fortuitous as he was hired as the editor for *The Philadelphia Magazine*. Paine's text bridged the gap between the wealthy political elite and colonial working class. *Common Sense* was published nine months following the battles of Lexington and Concord. Paine would remain to see the conclusion of the Revolutionary War, but depart the United States for Europe in 1787.

As with many progressive thinkers, his writing also cultivated enemies within America. His opposition to slavery and support for women's rights provoked animosity. His travel to Europe was planned as fundraising expedition for an iron bridge design that he had previously patented.

Amidst his travels between England and France, Paine

responded to writer Edmund Burke's criticism of the French Revolution. Paine's *Rights of Man* critique faced enormous hostile `criticism and a major seditious libel suit initiated by English authorities.

He escaped to France to avoid arrest where he was initially feted as a national hero. He was elected as a representative to the National Convention, but soon fell out of favor. His opposition to the death penalty for Louis XVI prompted his arrest for treason.

He was tried in absentia on December 26, 1793 and convicted. He narrowly escaped the guillotine. He was interned in Luxembourg Prison formerly a palace. He was detained in a large room with two windows and locked up solely at night. His meals were catered from the outside and servants were even permitted. He didn't take advantage of that option.

Paine's imprisonment prompted outrage within the United States. Diplomat and future American President James Monroe employed his connections to secure his release in November 1794.

Paine's final two publications created a legion of supporters, but primarily detractors. His *Age of Reason* (1794) criticized Christianity and religion. A second work, *Agrarian Justice* (1797) established the precepts for the labor movement and welfare state.

Paine's idealism and uncompromising views consigned his status as a citizen of the world, but a man without a country. He reportedly came to despise the United States and the sustained criticism over his final works ruined his reputation. The man of ideals would die impoverished in 1809 in New York. Only six mourners attended his funeral.

1 rue des Petits Peres

Poet Andre Chenier's Dangerous Acquaintances and Ill Timing
Andre Chenier Residence:
97 rue de Clery, 75002 Paris

Poet Andre Chenier had perhaps the worst luck of any victim of the French Revolution. His sensual and emotional verse ranks him as an important member of the poetic Romantic Movement. His fate became entangled amidst the chaos during the *Reign of Terror* orchestrated by Maximillen Robespierre. He was described as more feminine than masculine. Although not conventionally handsome, his large eyes and round forehead gave extreme expression to his features.

In 1783, Chenier enlisted in a French military corps at Strasbourg. He tired of the regimentation and returned to his family in Paris within a year. Until 1787, his work had not been published. He took advantage of a family friend's offer to relocate to London. The Chevalier de la Luzerne had been appointed the French ambassador to England and Chenier would become his secretary.

He returned to France upon the outbreak of the Revolution in 1789 and concentrated his writings on political satires. His barbed texts antagonized certain members of the ruling leadership. The works remained relatively tame in comparison with more seditious works by critics.

On March 7, 1794, he was arrested along with everyone else in the proximity of a home owned by an acquaintance Madame Piscatory in Passy. She had already fled France to evade arrest. Chenier was presumed to be a fellow aristocrat. He was taken to Luxembourg Prison and then transferred to the Prison Saint-Lazare. During his confinement of 140 days, he wrote some of his most descriptive and later famous works denouncing the Revolutionary Convention. The painter

Joseph-Benoit Suvee completed a well-regarded portrait of him ten days before his trial.

Robespierre's status with the Revolutionary Council was tenuous. Lacking concrete evidence against Chenier, he personally denounced his writings as *venomous* in the *Journal de Paris*. The tribunal sentenced Chenier to death. Two days afterwards, Robespierre would be seized, condemned and executed.

Chenier would become one of the final individuals sentenced by Robespierre. On July 25, 1794, he was transferred to the square now named *Place de la Nation*. He would be executed at sundown along with two others on charges of conspiracy. Robespierre would be guillotined three days later at the Place de la Revolution (later Concorde).

The timing and senselessness of Chenier's death at only thirty-one elevated his posthumous regard. Many of his writings would prove difficult to publish as they had been smuggled out page by page from prison. His love of nature and political freedom would be compared later with several great English poets including Percy Bysshe Shelley and John Keats.

A Probable Fictitious Adventurer and Statesman
Francois Auguste, Vicomte de Chateaubriand's
Residences:
21 rue Denfert Rochereau, 75014 Paris
94 rue du St. Honore, 75001 Paris
88 Place de Beauveau, 75008 Paris-
25 rue de l'Universite, 75007 Paris
120 rue du Bac, 75007 Paris

Francois-Rene de Chateaubriand lived an extraordinary lifetime of adventure, travel and literary output. His contemporaries suggested that he considered himself the *greatest* lover, writer and philosopher of his age. His detractors maintained that many of his exploits were simply personal invention. Arguably, he was considered the dominant voice of the French literary scene during the first half of the nineteenth century.

He was born in Saint-Malo on September 4, 1768, the last of ten children to Rene de Chateaubriand, a sea captain, ship owner and slave trader. The Brittany region darkened Francois-Rene's outlook with its savage coastal landscape and accompanying severely depressive solitude. His own impulsiveness once prompted a suicide attempt with a hunting rifle. The weapon failed to discharge.

Chateaubriand became a political royalist that put him at odds with the prevalent Revolutionary movement.

His sole option to imprisonment and execution became exile. He departed France on a voyage of discovery to North America in July 1791. He would later write a popular book in 1826 of his extensive travels. His accounts detailed living with Native American tribes, viewing raids along the Ohio and Mississippi Rivers and conducting an interview with George Washington. Many of his stories would be dismissed as fiction.

The following year he would return to France and participate in the *Siege of Thionville*, a military clash between Royalist troops and the French Revolutionary Army. He barely survived the conflict and was transported to the island of Jersey. He would remain in London afterwards. His poverty was barely supplemented by offering French lessons and doing translation work. His familiarity with the English language and literature would deeply influence his later writings.

During his eight-year exile, he would profoundly examine the causes behind the French Revolution and his own religious beliefs. They would become important subject material. He converted back to his boyhood Catholicism, although his behavior did not necessarily reflect his freshly embraced faith.

He took advantage of the May 1800 amnesty issued to French exiles and returned to Paris. As intellectuals during the Revolution had turned against the church, he authored *Genie du Chiristianisme* (Genius of Christianity) in 1802, a defense of Catholicism. His timing proved ideal. A religious revival started shortly afterwards throughout France. His publication appealed to Emperor Napoleon Bonaparte, anxious to reconcile with the Catholic Church.

Bonaparte appointed Chateaubriand secretary of the legation to the Holy See in the Vatican. He quarreled with the existing French Cardinal Fesch and was re-appointed minister to the Republic of Valais. He would resign abruptly following Bonaparte's execution in 1804 of Louis XVI's cousin. His absence of employment left him dependent on revenue from his literary output. Chateaubriand experienced unforeseen good fortune when the wife of Tsar Alexander I bequeathed him a large sum of money for his earlier published defense of Christianity.

He would use this newfound wealth to travel through Greece, Turkey, Asia Minor, North Africa and Spain. He wrote epic prose chronicling the Roman persecution of early Christianity.

Upon his return to France, he brazenly published a severe criticism of Bonaparte, comparing him to Rome's Nero. Bonaparte threatened to have him stabbed to death on the steps of the Tuileries Palace. Instead, he merely banished him from Paris.

Following Bonaparte's two major defeats and abdications, Chateaubriand would emerge as a major political force. His capricious nature and ego would shift his regard in and out of political favor. He continued his popular writings. His descriptions of nature and analysis of emotions made him a favored model for generations of Romantic writers. Despised or espoused, Chateaubriand's influence would not be ignored.

During his final years, he became a recluse within Paris leaving his apartment only to pay visits to close friends and engage in periodic strolls. He died on July 4, 1848 amidst yet another Paris revolution in the arms of his dearest friend Juliette Recamier at the age of 79. He would be buried on the tidal island Grand Be near Saint-Malo, accessible only when the tide is out.

TWISTED TOUR GUIDES.com

A Traveling American Author of Accomplishment
Washington Irving Residence:
4 rue du Mont Thabor, 75001 Paris

Washington Irving is considered one of the first American writers to earn acclaim in Europe and substantiate writing as a legitimate profession. He was raised in Manhattan and cultivated a career as a short-story writer, essayist, biographer, historian and diplomat. His best known works include *Rip Van Winkle* and *The Legend of Sleepy Hollow*.

Following the publication of *The Sketch Book of Geoffrey Crayon*, he arrived in Paris to lodge at the age of 38. His building was located next door to French dramatist and novelist Alfred de Musset. He would spend seventeen years abroad continuing his writings until returning to New York in 1832.

President John Tyler would appoint Irving as Minister to Spain in February 1842 following an endorsement from Secretary of State Daniel Webster. Spain was in the midst of political upheaval throughout his four-year term. He returned homesick and suffering from a crippling skin condition.

He resumed his writings and collected numerous honors while living in Sunnyside, New York. He frequently visited Washington D.C. and Mount Vernon for research purposes. He suffered a fatal heart attack at the age of 76 on November 28, 1859. Eight months earlier, he had completed the final volume of his biography of George Washington. He would be buried under a simple headstone at the Sleepy Hollow Cemetery in New York.

4 rue du Mont Thabor

Eavesdropping On Dysfunctional Royalty
Duke of Saint-Simon's Residence:
17 rue du Cherche Midi, 75006 Paris

Louis de Rouvroy, better known as the Duke of Saint-Simon was an eavesdropping fly on the wall insider of King Louis XIV's court. His extensive posthumous memoirs provided an expansive and lively account of the court of Versailles during Louis XIV's reign and the Regency at the beginning of his great grandson's Louis XV rule.

His father, Charles de Rouvroy was a French soldier and courtier and one of the favorite hunting companions of King Louis XIII. Their relationship, later strained, resulted in him being gifted lands, the title of Duke of Saint-Simon and a peerage in France. He had his sole son Louis at the age of 68. Louis became the complete opposite of his father. He was shorter, garrulous and preferred life indoors.

He failed to distinguish himself militarily or politically and barely maintained his position. He immersed himself in court intrigue at Versailles cultivating a collection of informants including servants and other titled members. He wrote incessantly, but discreetly. He was exposed to an extraordinary amount of privileged information and gossip that would be published nearly seventy years following his death.

De Rouvroy's personality and petty divisiveness cultivated various enemies at court on a minor scale. He shared a grandiose vision of establishing the French peerage designation into a *Great Council of the Nation* based on merit. His own inclusion would have been doubtful. The death of the king and his role in the transitional Regency stimulated his aspirations for greater involvement with the throne. He was appointed *ambassador extraordinary* to Spain in 1721 during a stretch prior to the proposed marriage of Louis XV with Mariana Victoria of Spain.

The marriage was never consummated. De Rouvroy contracted small pox and upon his return to France became gradually forgotten. He would live an additional thirty years in obscurity, accumulating debt and unable to bear a successor to his title. He died in Paris on March 2, 1755 at 80 having outlived his own generation and exhausted his family's wealth.

All of his possessions including his writings were confiscated by the state upon his death. That same year marked the birth of Louis XVI. His manuscript *Memoirs* was kept under sequestration and probably the reason it survived.

His death might have concluded an inconsequential legacy. Instead, the existence of the manuscript circulated through private copies and excerpts.

His heirs would receive the manuscript in 1828 and they would become widely published. Saint-Simon's *Memoires* became a classic of French literature due to the writer's skill for narrative and inventive dialogue. His portrayals, petty bias and sheer volume of material provided insight to a gilded age of scheming, ambitious and character-flawed participants. Ferreting the truth from his subjective ramblings would prove a monumental commission in itself.

17 rue du Cherche Midi

The Writer Who Adored Women
Stendhal's Residence:
61 rue Richelieu , 75002 Paris

Marie-Henri Beyle better known by his pen name *Stendhal* blazed a writing style of realism that delved deeply into his character's psyche. He published under various pen names before settling upon Stendhal, the German birthplace of Johann Winckelmann, a noted mid-18th century art historian and archeologist.

Stendhal would earn his literary fame as the author of *Le Rouge et le Noir* (The Red and the Black) in 1830 and *The Charterhouse of Parma* in 1839.

Le Rouge et le Noir is a historical novel originally published in two volumes that chronicles the attempts of Julien Sorel to rise socially beyond his modest origins. The intimate portrait of Sorel reflects a complex combination of hard work, talent and deception. The analytic satire is staged amidst the Bourbon Restoration. Sorel's passions ultimately betray him.

The Charterhouse of Parma is an equally complex work relating the history of an Italian nobleman during the Napoleonic era. Protagonist Fabrice del Dongo's turbulent lifestyle follows a dissolute youth, military service, doomed romantic liaisons, political plots, betrayals and his ultimate retirement into a monastery. Stendhal borrowed liberally from his own personal experiences establishing legitimacy to the narrative.

Stendhal's unhappy formation began in Grenoble. He deeply resented his unimaginative father and desperately missed his mother who died when he was seven. That mourning resulted in distinctive depictions of women within his writings. Rather than traditionally depicting them as idyllic and desirable icons or rigid caricatures, he was capable of fleshing out empathetic and genuine portrayals of often rebellious heroines.

Throughout his lifetime, he was characterized as an obsessive womanizer. His fixation with women resulted in valuable insight, but also a painful and premature death.

During the Napoleonic era, he was named an auditor with the State Department. He took part in Bonaparte's administration including battlefield experience in Italy and Russia. He witnessed the burning of Moscow from the periphery of the city and labored through the disastrous retreat. Following Bonaparte's abdication, he would settle in Milan. He was appointed as French consul in Triest and Civitavecchia, maintaining affection for Italian culture the remainder of his life.

Stendhal suffered crippling physical disabilities from syphilis that he reportedly contracted in December 1808. The potassium and quicksilver he ingested to treat his sexual disease often left him with worse degenerative side effects. He sought the best available treatments for his condition in Paris, Vienna and Rome. He died on March 23, 1842 at 59 followed a seizure on the streets of Paris hours before. He was buried in Montmartre Cemetery.

61 rue Richelieu

Genius Inundated By Adversity That Spurred Productivity

Honore de Balzac's Residences:
9 rue Lesdiguieres, 75004 Paris
2 rue de Tournon, 75006 Paris
47 rue des Martyrs, 75009 Paris
3 rue Cassini, 75014 Paris
33 rue Reynouard (Formerly rue de Basse), 75016 Paris
47 rue Raynouard, 75016 Paris

Writer Honore de Balzac suffered throughout his adult life with health issues and financial troubles. One of his most regarded works, *La Comedie Humaine* (The Human Comedy) mirrored his own struggles with adaptation and compounding difficulties.

He is considered one of the founders of the *Realism* movement in European literature. He excelled in flushing out three-dimensional personalities and complexities in his characters. His work strongly influenced some of the most well regarded writers of his era.

Balzac insatiable curiosity and independent thinking prompted problems during his formative years. His willful nature and weariness of banality resulted in his failure as a lawyer, publisher, businessman, critic and politician.

These failures stimulated his true genius. His financial debts forced him into prolific writing spans, often detrimental to his health. His legendary work schedule usually began from 1 a.m. until 8 a.m. each day, sometimes extending longer in the morning.

He wrote rapidly with a quill pen reportedly at a pace comparable to thirty words per minute. His routine included a light meal in the late afternoon. He then slept until midnight before repeating his regime.

He spent limited time in Parisian salons and clubs habitually avoiding society. He was reluctant to appear outside during daylight hours for fear of arrest due to his existing debts.

His stated goal was to depict individuals as *real* people, complete with imperfections. He stressed extensive detailing that included their surroundings. He was known for squandering funds to create the precise room environments of the characters that he was portraying. He became obsessive regardless of expense.

He made acquaintances with notable contemporary writers who kept him informed regarding current events. He revised his work obsessively altering his finished version significantly from the original written text.

His romantic life and liaisons were predictably messy. His greatest passion was simply his writing and siphoning his fertile imagination into his characters. This pursuit left him minimal leisure opportunities.

He was linked with an intrigue to writer Maria du Frenay. She was ten year younger. The couple conceived a daughter. He began a written correspondence in 1833 with married Polish Countess Ewelina Hanska, a fervent admirer of his work. When her husband, Marshall Hanski died in 1841, he visited her in St. Petersburg two years later.

His hoped-for stability never materialized. The couple was finally given permission to marry by Tsar Nicholas I. By the time of his wedding date on March 14, 1850, his health was already in steep decline. Their return by coach to Paris nearly killed him.

Five months later on Sunday, August 18, 1850 he died in the presence of his mother. Writer Victor Hugo had visited him earlier in the day and his wife had already gone to bed. He was only fifty-one and in the process of completing several additional book projects.

The tributes from mourning contemporaries soon followed. Every credible writer and artist in Paris attended his funeral. He would be lionized with tributes and memorials. Adversity had forged his genius yet ultimately extinguished his continued contribution.

9 rue Lesdiguierres

47 rue des Martyrs

TWISTED TOUR GUIDES.com

A Celebrated and Sensitive But Ultimately Wilted Prodigy
Alfred de Musset Residences:
23 Quai Voltaire, 75007 Paris
6 rue du Mont Thabor (Death Site), 75001 Paris

Alfred de Musset became a celebrated French poet, dramatist and novelist. His most famous novel was the autobiographical *The Confessions of a Child of the Century*.

De Musset was born in Paris into a family well connected with governmental and social contacts, but skirting financial ruin. His father withheld him money that ultimately prompted him to become a flagrant spendthrift.

From the age of nine, Alfred became a recognized creative prodigy. After unsuccessful attempts at medicine, law, drawing and piano, he found his niche as a *Romantic* writer. At the age of twenty, he was already recognized as a literary talent. He became the librarian of the French Ministry of the Interior under the liberal monarchy of Louis Philippe. His politics likewise leaned left and he remained on good terms with the king's family.

De Musset was described by author Michael Sadler *(An Englishman in Paris)* as *having a tall and slim figure, auburn wavy hair and beard, blue eyes and finely shaped mouth and nose. He gave one the impression of a dandy cavalry officer.*

At the age of twenty-three, he became romantically involved with writer George Sand (Aurore Dupin de Francueil), six years his senior. Their affair was last two years. He elaborated upon their relationship primarily through his writings. He would describe in intimate detail the emotional upheaval of his love for Sand from early despair to final resignation. He has been speculated to be the anonymous author of *Two Nights of Excess* written in 1833, a lesbian erotic novel modeled on Sand.

Frugal and economical older brother Paul kept him from financial ruin. Alfred was a frequent patron in brothels. He developed a rumored unhealthy obsession towards beating and humiliating one courtesan named Celeste de Chabrillan.

He was troubled and conflicted emotionally, yet touted by writer Victor Hugo as the most gifted man in his generation. He was labeled the *Lord Byron of France*, but without the accompanying splendor or prestige as the original.

De Musset would receive the *Legion d'Honneur* in April 1845 at the same time as writer Honore de Balzac. He was dismissed from his librarian post in 1848 following the revolution and abdication of Louis Philippe. He was elected to the Academie Francaise in 1852 following two failed attempts. He would be appointed librarian of the Ministry of Public Instruction in 1853.

He aged poorly according to French writer Maxime Du Camp. By the age of forty-four, *he retained only the attractiveness of his light glossy hair*. His face was described a being *long, thin, and wrinkled. The forehead was fine with the under lip weak and effeminate.*

His health suffered severely from his alcoholism and a heart defect. His head would begin bobbing as the result of the amplification of his pulse. He died in his sleep at his Paris residence in 1857 at the age of 47. He would be buried in Pere Lachaise Cemetery. His poetry would become popular lyrics for numerous French music composers during the 19th and early 20th century.

23 Quai Voltaire

6 rue de Mont Thabor

TWISTED TOUR ᴳUIDES.com

A German Exile's Lost Illusions of Utopia
3 Cite Bergere, 75009 Paris
65 rue du Faubourg Poissonniere, 75009 Paris
50 rue d'Amsterdam (Demolished), 75009 Paris
82 rue de Passy, 75016 Paris
82 rue Vital, 75016 Paris
3 avenue Matignon (Death Site), 75008 Paris

One of the resulting consequences from the July Revolution of 1830 that elevated King Louis-Philippe to power was the immigration of German poet, writer and critic Heinrich Heine to Paris. He arrived with enthusiasm that the *Citizen King* had the potential to overturn the conservative political order in Europe.

Heine was attracted by the freedom from German censorship and a utopian philosophy called *Saint-Simoniansm* based on merit replacing hereditary distinctions in wealth and rank. The movement also stressed female emancipation.

Heine was welcomed as a celebrity based on his earlier lyrical poetry that was integrated into works by German composers including Robert Schumann and Franz Schubert. Heine's retelling of the legend of *The Flying Dutchman* was Richard Wagner's source of inspiration for his epic opera. Heine was christened the *Voltaire of Germany* for his freethinking, lively wit and repartee.

Life in Paris consigned him to the role of outsider, although he cultivated famous acquaintances. He had no interest in French literature, religion and continued to compose exclusively in German. He earned a livelihood as the French correspondent for the German newspaper *Allgemeine Zeitung* and lived frugally.

In 1834, he made the acquaintance of a 19-year-old Parisian shopgirl, Crescence Eugenie Mirat and began a reluctant relationship. She was illiterate, shared no interest in intellectual or cultural matters, and spoke no German. She moved in with him two years later. In 1841, he narrowly escaped death in a duel with the husband of Jeanette Wohl, a German radical he had attacked in print. His adversary's bullet grazed his lip. He married Mirat afterwards to safeguard her future. She would remain with him throughout his life.

In October 1843, Heine's distant relative Karl Marx and his wife arrived into Paris after the Prussian government had suppressed his radical newspaper. Marx was an admirer of Heine and his early writings reflected Heine's influence. Both men respected and liked the other, but their political philosophies ultimately became incompatible. Both shared negativity towards the upper class, but Heine could not embrace Marx's radicalism. His own personal vision of an earthly utopia had vanished amidst his personal financial hardships and disappointment in the French ruling leadership.

Heine's skepticism pervaded his later writings and his health worsened leaving him bedridden. He died in 1856 at the age of 57 from a fit of indigestion. The sole condition of his will was that all religious solemnities be dispensed with at his funeral.

Despite his acclaim, writers Theophile Gautier and Alexandre Dumas were the sole eminents that attended his funeral. His epitaph stressed that *he had many admirers but few friends.*

50 rue d'Amsterdam

Democratic Moderation Portrayed Through A Literary Observer
Alexis de Tocqueville's Residences:
46 rue des Mathurins, 75008 Paris
8 rue Pasquier (Death Site), 75008 Paris

Alexis de Tocqueville became a literary eyewitness to the American democratic experience. He was an aristocrat, diplomat, historian and political philosopher. His two-volume work *Democracy in America* was published in 1835 and 1840 and surveyed the living standards, prison conditions and social conditions of individuals. The works were published following his travels to the United States and Canada.

In 1841 and 1846, he traveled to the French colony of Algeria. He became skeptical towards the extremes of democracy. He advocated an abolition of slavery and criticized the French model of colonization.

He became active in French politics during the reign of King Louis Philippe and the French Second Republic. He retired from political life following Napoleon III's coup in December 1851.

He spent his final decade writing *The Old Regime and the Revolution*, published three years before his death. His writings argued that the Revolution was essential to continuing the modernization and centralizing of the French government. He cited the failure of the Revolution was due to the inexperience of the deputies too inflexible by abstract ideals.

Tocqueville was labeled a classical liberal who advocated parliamentary government and moderation. His complex thinking and detailed writings classified him as an early proponent of sociology and political science. He professed his religion as Roman Catholicism, but strongly felt that a

185

division between religion and politics was imperative. He suffered from bouts of tuberculosis and finally expired from the disease on April 16, 1859 at the age of 53.

9 rue Pasquier

A Romantic Writer Disdaining Society's Restraints
George Sand's Residences:
3 rue Racine, 75006 Paris
31 rue de Seine, 75006 Paris

Aurore Dupin de Francueil navigated Parisian society better in men's clothing. Writing under the pen name George Sand, readers were obliged to evaluate her works on their merit rather than their perceptions of gender capabilities.

She was born on July 1, 1804 into a wealthy and titled family in Paris. She was raised for the majority of her childhood by her grandmother in the village of Nohant, in the province of Berry. She inherited the house at seventeen upon the death of her grandmother. The residence would be used later as the setting for many of her novels.

At the age of twenty-seven, she chose her pseudonym George Sand based purposely on confusing her identity and increasing her publication chances in a predominately male literary world.

In 1800, Paris police issued an order requiring women to apply for a permit to wear male clothing. Sand ignored the law and claimed that men's outfits were more comfortable. Her male attire enabled her to circulate more freely in Paris than her female contemporaries giving her access to venues that forbade them.

At the age of eighteen, she married Casimir Dudevant and the couple had two children, Maurice and Solange. They would remain together for a decade before she launched into a *five-year romantic rebellion*. The couple never legally divorced.

Sand would be associated with numerous high-profile lovers of both genders. The three most renowned included dramatist Alfred de Musset, actress Marie Dorval and pianist Frederick

Chopin. The relationship with Chopin would gain wide exposure in 1838 when they spent a winter together in the formerly abandoned Carthusian monastery of Valdemossa in Mallorca, Spain. Chopin was already ill with tuberculosis that would ultimately shorten his life.

The couple spent numerous summers together at Sand's country manor in Nohant. He composed many of his most famous works there. They had a falling out regarding issues involving her children. They would separate two years before his death. He was never invited back to Nohant after the separation and she would be absent at his funeral during 1849.

Sand had a prolific literary career that made her one of the most popular writers in Europe. She became associated as one of the most notable writers of the European Romantic era. Her first efforts were collaborations with writer and lover Jules Sandeau. Their published works were under the name Jules Sand.

Her first independent novel, *Indiana* was released in 1832. During her extended career, she was credited with 70 novels and 50 volumes of various works including tales, plays and political texts. She stood up for women's rights, against arranged marriages and prejudices stemming from a conservative society. She wrote for the theatre due to financial difficulties. Her fame enabled her to remain in France despite her tenuous relations with the regimes of Louis Philippe and Napoleon III. She was appalled by the violence generated from the 1871 Paris Commune.

She died at her country home on June 8, 1876 at the age of 71. During her lifetime, she was widely respected by the literary and cultural elite within France. Victor Hugo gave her eulogy at her funeral.

3 rue Racine

31 rue de Seine

The Tsunami Left By A Nineteenth Century Literary Figure
Alexandre Dumas' Residences:
107 boulevard Malesherbes, 75008 Paris
77 rue d'Amsterdam (Demolished), 75009 Paris
120 avenue Wagram (Death Site), 75017 Paris

Writer Alexandre Dumas blazed recklessly through existence as a celebrated tsunami. He became one of the most widely read French authors. He was credited with composing more than 1,200 volumes. Some of his works were rumored to be written by his numerous collaborators with only the final touches applied by Dumas.

His prodigious spending habits and affording the entourage that trailed his every public footstep necessitated his literary production factory.

Dumas' father was born in the French colony of Saint-Domingue (Haiti) to a French aristocrat and African slave. He was taken to France at fourteen and raised in a military academy. He would join the service afterwards rising to the rank of general in Napoleon Bonaparte's army. Austrian troops nicknamed him the *Black Devil* for his military prowess and fierceness.

He would accompany Bonaparte on his Egyptian expedition during 1798 as commander of the French cavalry forces. He clashed verbally with Bonaparte on a march from Alexandria to Cairo. In March 1799, he left Egypt on an unsound vessel that ran aground in Naples. He was taken captive and languished in a dungeon there until his liberation in Spring 1801.

Upon his release, he returned to France, but was not awarded a general's pension. The family struggled financially. He and his wife bore Alexandre in 1802 in Villers-Cotterets. He would die three years later of stomach cancer at the age of 43. Although, he had only scant memories and third-person accounts, his father's exploits would inspire many of his future literary characters.

Dumas's grandfather's aristocratic rank enabled him to acquire employment under King Louis Philippe. His prolific published writings soon elevated him into celebrity status. Dumas was described by contemporaries as *generous, big-hearted, amusing* and *egotistical*. He loved to talk about himself and brag about his exploits even if the truth veered towards the exaggerated.

Many of his historical adventure novels were originally published as newspaper serials. Amongst his most famous works include the *Three Musketeers* trilogy, *The Count of Monte Cristo* and *The Man in the Iron Mask*. He also wrote plays, magazine articles and travel books.

His reputation fell out of favor in 1851 with the election of President Louis-Napoleon Bonaparte. Dumas departed France for Belgium for several years before relocating to Russia. He continued onto Italy where he founded and published a newspaper espousing Italian unification. His literary productivity never slackened,

He returned to Paris in 1864 and resumed his chaotic, widely exposed and sometimes scandalous lifestyle. Along with several prominent writers of his era, he was a member of the *Club des Hashischins* that met monthly in a Paris hotel to consume hashish.

Dumas' African origins, facial features and flamboyantly bushy hair set him apart from his contemporaries. He married in 1840, but had countless affairs resulting in between a reported four to seven illegitimate children. One of sons would become a renowned author and playwright composing under the writing identity *Alexandre Dumas fils* (son).

Dumas' final scandal resulted from widely circulated photographs in 1866 displaying his latest lover, American Adah Isaacs Menken. She was half his age and then the highest earning actress internationally. She had arrived from San Francisco intending to perform in Paris and London. Her signature role was in the hippodrama *Mazeppa* climaxed by her riding a horse off the stage in a body stocking seemingly nude.

Their affair invoked scandal and ended badly. She left for London to continue production of *Mazeppa*. The novelty of the play soon fizzled with declining attendance. She became violently ill and soon after was obliged to cease performing.

During that year of extreme hardship, she collapsed during a rehearsal. She would expire weeks later from reportedly peritonitis or tuberculosis at the age of 33. Her body was returned to Paris and she was buried in Montparnasse Cemetery.

Dumas would be lavishly honored during his lifetime and posthumously. He was completing a novel entitled *The Knight of Sainte-Hermine* when he died from a probable heart attack on December 5, 1870. His death was overshadowed by the unfolding events of the Franco-Prussian War. He was initially buried in his hometown before a 2002 national ceremony re-interred his ashes inside the mausoleum of the Pantheon.

77 rue d'Amsterdam

TWISTED TOUR GUIDES.com

An Authentic Witness Detailing Two Familiar Cities
Charles Dickens's Residence:
38 rue de Courcelles, 75008 Paris

Writer Charles Dickens first visited France during 1837. He would regularly travel to the seaside retreat of Boulogne-sur-Mer with his family. He reportedly resided within the country on six separate occasions. His first exposure to Paris during 1844 created an immense impression. The characters and individuals that he encountered provided him with fresh material for his novels. His fellow writers offered him fraternal companionship. His closest intimates included Victor Hugo, Theophile Gautier, Alexandre Dumas and poet Alphonse de Lamartine.

Dickens described Paris as *wicked and detestable, though wonderfully attractive*. This contrast paralleled his themes of good and evil that were interlaced throughout his novels. Dickens was a humanist that found poverty disturbing. He blamed political injustice and the unfair distribution of wealth as its roots. The Paris that he encountered was in the midst of massive redevelopment. Baron Haussmann's transformation of the city had razed many of the former slums, although poverty and misery still existed.

He described his Paris residence that he lived in during the close of 1846 as: *the most ridiculous, extraordinary, unparalleled, and preposterous in the world: being something between a baby house, a shades, a haunted castle and new kind of clock. One room is a tent; another room is a grove and another room a scene at the Victoria Theatre.* Many of his short stories referenced familiar Parisian sites. One of his most popular classics, A Tale of Two Cities was begun in March 1859. His familiarity with the East London poverty and discontent twinned with an intimate knowledge of Paris added to his credibility in depicting the story's setting prior and during the French Revolution.

The First Modernist On The Paris Literary Scene
Charles Baudelaire's Residence:
Hotel Pimodan, 17 quai d'Anjou (also known as the Hotel de Lauzun), 75004 Paris

Charles Baudelaire's reckless, wanton lifestyle and controversial verse set him apart from contemporary writers. His most famous work *Les Fleurs du Mal* (The Flowers of Evil) expressed the changing nature of beauty in an era of industrialized Paris. He coined the term *modernity* to designate fleeting, ephemeral urban experiences. He emphasized in his work the role of artists to encapsulate that sensation.

His work might exalt imagination, but never strayed far from a depiction expressing real life and its accompanying trauma. He was unable to sustain constancy with his own life, relationships and finances constantly living on the periphery of despair.

Baudelaire is considered one of the major innovators in French literature. His work then was often considered scandalous and provocative. He wrote on a variety of subject matter and with a penetrating candor. The reaction often attracted criticism and outrage. He generally refused to tone down or follow a diplomatic approach with his critiques, even with colleagues. He stressed the importance of maintaining artistic integrity and credibility.

Amongst his circle of friends included prominent artists Gustave Courbet, Honore Daumier, Franz Liszt, Victor Hugo, Gustave Flaubet, Edouard Manet and Honore de Balzac. He translated American writer Edgar Allan Poe's short stories. Writer Theophile Gautier lived in his same building. The pair established the *Club des Hashischins* where they experimented with hashish.

The novelty of his subject matter and uncompromising values influenced numerous subsequent writers including Arthur Rimbaud, Paul Verlaine and Marcel Proust.

Baudelaire suffered from a variety of health maladies throughout his life. He dependence on laudanum, alcohol and opium failed to lessen his burdens of stress and poverty. He would suffer a massive stroke in 1866 followed by paralysis. His final year was spent in Brussels and Parisian nursing homes. He died on August 31, 1867 at the age of forty-six.

17 Quai d'Anjou

The Madness Accompanying A Six-Week Residence
Leo Tolstoy Residence:
Hotel Wagram, 206-208 rue de Rivoli, 75001 Paris

Russian writer Leon Tolstoy resided in Paris for only six weeks, but the stay impacted him permanently. It is unknown how long that he intended to initially remain. He arrived into the city on February 9, 1857 via a train at the Gare du Nord. Writers Ivan Turgenev and Nikolay Nekrasov received him. The trio was well acquainted but not intimate friends.

The initial night he stayed at the Hotel Meurice, but rented a furnished apartment nearby the following day. The evening of his arrival, Turgenev reportedly escorted him to a costumed ball at the Opera. His appraisal of the event was summarized by a single word penned in his diary: *Madness*.

Tolstoy maintained a hectic pace while in Paris attending lectures at the Sorbonne, visiting tourist sites, concerts and enjoying evenings of wine and conversation with his countrymen. He declined to meet acclaimed French writers and was disappointed by the various homages paid to Napoleon Bonaparte citywide.

His relationship with Turgenev and Nekrasov became strained, but his ultimate disgust was reserved upon attending an execution by guillotine. The experience traumatized and revolted him. He couldn't sleep. Finally, unable to come to terms with the memory of the spectacle, he left Paris to never return.

206-208 rue de Rivoli

A Writer Depicting Banality With Precision Language
Gustave Flaubert's Residences:
21 rue de l'Odeon, 75006 Paris
240 rue du Faubourg St. Honore, 75008 Paris
42 boulevard du Temple, 75011 Paris

Gustave Flaubert's debut novel *Madame Bovary* published in 1857 vaulted him into literary eminence. He was considered a leading exponent of *literary realism* during his era. The movement stressed the values of style as an objective method of presenting reality.

The character of Emma Bovary is trapped in a boring provincial marriage that she worsens by excessive spending and conducting dead ended extramarital affairs. Her indulgences, debts and desperation lead her to a premature and agonizing suicide by swallowing arsenic. Her husband is completely devoted to her despite her indifference towards him and his dullard universe.

Flaubert serialized the work in *Revue de Paris* beginning in October 1856. He chose the plot setting near Rouen where he was born and raised. He understood the social mores of provincial life well. He was less familiar with marital existence having never wed nor fathered children. He reportedly began a relationship with poet Louise Colet from 1846 to 1854. His letters to her have survived. It was reputedly his only serious romantic union.

Flaubert preferred brothels to conventional relationships. He was very open about his bisexual relationships with prostitutes, particularly during his travels in the Middle East. He contracted syphilis in Beirut, which would torment his health the balance of his life.

His politics he confessed were that of an *enraged liberal* against all despotism and supporting *every protest of the individual against power and monopolies.* He once described himself as *a romantic and liberal old dunce.*

Flaubert spent six years in Paris during his twenties studying law. He was an indifferent student and found urban life distasteful. Following an attack of epilepsy, he abandoned law and Paris. During his residence, he became acquainted with Victor Hugo. He would return periodically to visit future literary acquaintances such as George Sand, Emile Zola, Alphonse Daudet and Ivan Turgenev.

He was diligent with his writing work ethic. He was a perfectionist with employing precise language and avoiding clichés. He attempts to craft his prose with harmonious sentence structures.

The 1870s became a difficult period for him as Prussian soldiers occupied his house during their occupation of northern France in the 1870 war. His finances dipped precariously and the residuals effects of his venereal disease diminished his health. He died from a brain hemorrhage in 1880 at the age of 58. He would be interned at the family vault in the Rouen cemetery.

21 rue de l'Odeon

A Master of Multiple Trades
Theophile Gautier's Residences:
Hotel Pimodan 17 quai d'Anjou, 75004 Paris
24 rue Grange Bateliere, 75009 Paris
14 rue de Navarin, 75009 Paris
8 Place des Vosges, 75004 Paris
60 rue de Longchamps, 75016 Paris

Theophile Gautier compressed sixty-one years of living into a single lifetime. He maintained his finger prominently on the pulse of France's Romantic, Aestheticism and Naturalism writing periods throughout the 19th century. He was born in Tarbes on August 31, 1811, but lived the majority of his existence in Paris.

He is not an easy artist to classify. He was poet, novelist, critic and journalist who could effortless blend into seemingly conflicting disciplines.

The young Gautier's appearance was considered flamboyant crowned by long flowing hair and a scarlet waistcoat. He was described as dashing, athletic, amorous and mercurial. He radiated a stately figure and strongly marked face lit up by majestic eyes.

He studied painting, but felt his primary strength was in poetry. He was an integral component of Parisian warring cultural factions. He disregarded traditional morality and even the exaltation of beauty. His journalistic work frequently estranged and entangled him. His reckless lifestyle burdened him financially with supporting himself, two mistresses, two sisters, and three children.

He concluded that journalism drained his creativity, but paid his lifestyle expenses. His literary output was enormous, but his reputation was earned primarily by his drama criticism and keen insight into quality performance. His contemporaries respected his multiple roles as commentator, poet, playwright and storyteller.

During the Franco-Prussian War in 1870, Gautier returned to Paris upon hearing that Prussian troops were closing in upon the capitol. He remained with his family throughout the military conflict and subsequent Commune protest the following year.

During his final residence in Paris, artist Gustave Dore would dine at his home every Thursday when in town. The evenings were described as *a curious blendings of seriousness and fun, reckless gaiety and simple recreation. Some of the after dinner amusement were acting, charades and private theatricals.*

Gautier would die from a longstanding heart ailment at sixty-one on October 23, 1872. It is easily imaginable that a smile of mirth traced his lips during his final breath.

17 Quai d'Anjou

The Roundabout Journey Of France's Favorite Travel Writer
Jules Vernes's Residences:
24 rue de l'Ancienne-Comedie, 75006 Paris
2 rue Therese, 75001 Paris
Hotel Scribe: 1 rue Scribe, 75009 Paris
6 rue Jean-Jacques-Rousseau, 75001 Paris

Jules Verne would become the most translated French author in the world by the late twentieth century. His best selling novels feature travel and adventure to an extent that was distinctive during the era they were published.

His characters became intimately accessible to readers although initially his celebrated travel writings were dismissed as children's tales. Over time, his literary reputation became expanded to a broader readership appreciation. Verne would lament the exclusion during his lifetime of being considered a serious French author worthy of academic study.

His voluminous writings included plays, short stories, autobiographical works, poetry, songs and artistic studies. His works have remained relevant for adaptation into film, television, theatre, opera, music and even video games. His most popular adventure novels remain *Journey to the Center of the Earth* (1864), *Twenty Thousand Leagues Under the Seas* (1870) and *Around the World in Eighty Days* (1872).

Verne's father, a provincial attorney near Nantes disapproved of his son's career decision. He envisioned him inheriting his legal practice and sent him to Paris to complete his law studies. The move was also intended to distance him temporarily from Nantes and a prospective love interest. In 1848, he arrived into Paris for his second year of studies amidst a revolution that would depose King Louis Philippe.

Using his family connections, Verne was introduced into Paris society and literary salons. Victor Hugo initially influenced his writings. He had yet to discover his own literary voice and direction. He would cultivate friendships with writer Alexandre Dumas and particularly his son. Together they revised a stage comedy entitled *Les Pailles Rompues* (The Broken Straws) that opened in June 1850 at the Theatre Historique.

He continued writing profusely and spending time in the literary salons. He earned his law degree in January 1851 creating a major career crossroad heading into alternative directions. His father insisted that he terminate his writings and concentrate on developing a law practice. Verne sensed that a more successful and happier future was possible as a writer. Up to that point, any sustained readership or theatre outlets had largely ignored his works and plays.

Despite the obstacles, he opted to follow the path of his instinct. Still pursuing his literary niche, he ventured into writing about travel and geography without ever having strayed from France. One of his important influences evolved from a friendship with renowned geographer and explorer Jacques Arago. The pair had met during one of Verne's innumerable research visits inside the Bibiotheque National. Arago had lost his sight two decades earlier, but continued to travel. His innovative and humorous accounts of his experiences mesmerized and fueled the imagination of Verne.

While attending Amiens to be the best man at the wedding of a friend, he fell in love with the bride's sister. Honorine Ann Hebee Morel was a 26-year old widow with two children. He lodged with her family during the proceedings and ingratiated himself with the household. He eagerly accepted her brother's offer to become an associate with his brokerage firm at the Paris Stock Exchange. When his financial situation finally appearing promising, he married Honorine.

Verne launched into his business profession with enthusiasm. He awoke early to enable writing time. Two complimentary opportunities to travel outside of France resulted in manuscripts recreating his voyages to Great Britain and Scandinavia. His stop in Denmark was abruptly shortened by the birth of his only son Michel in August 1861 and hasty return to Paris. Travel became his obsession, but not simply for touristic amusement.

The components towards his literary success were piecing together. He was given an introduction to magazine publisher Pierre-Jules Hetzel. The timing proved impeccable. Hetzel was in the process of establishing a bi-monthly magazine slanted towards education and recreation. He was prominently situated within the French literary world representing well-known authors Honore de Balzac, Victor Hugo and George Sand.

Verne and Hetzel established their first collaboration in 1863 based on Verne's manuscript *Five Weeks in a Balloon,* a story of travel across Africa. Over the next decade, the pair's recognition would flourish with a formula series called *Voyages Extraordinaire* (Extraordinary Journeys). Verne's writings would be introduced as serials in Hetzel's magazine and then published as novels when the series concluded stimulating immediate demand.

Hetzel influenced many of Verne's storylines. Initially, Verne readily accepted his suggestions. In 1869 the pair quarreled over one of the character in *Twenty Thousand Leagues Under the Seas*. Following their poorly resolved conflict, their relationship soured. Verne still considered Hetzel's story suggestion ideas, but more frequently rejected them. Verne limited his manuscripts with Hetzel to only two annually.

Verne's own family relations turned volatile despite his

success. His only son Michel married an actress against his father's consent, fathered two children with an underage mistress and became immersed in debt. His 26-year-old nephew Gaston shot at Verne twice with a pistol in March 1886 as he returned home. One bullet struck him in the left leg burdening him with a permanent limp. The affair was publicly hushed, but his nephew spent the rest of his life in a mental institution.

Hetzel's death the same year altered the course of Verne's life. The theme of his writings became darker. He moved to Amiens and entered politics. He would be elected town councilor and serve for the next fifteen years until his death in 1905 at the age of 77. His works would continue to be published following his death with his son Michel making extensive editorial changes.

A manuscript *Paris in the Twentieth Century* was later discovered by his great-grandson and published in 1994. Hetzel had dismissed the manuscript over a century earlier as being too pessimistic towards the future. Verne's clairvoyant insight into society and future innovations has been credited as a major influence on the science fiction genre.

1 rue Scribe

Artistic Achievement and Political Ambition Failure
Victor Hugo's Residences:
30 rue du Dragon, 75006 Paris
9 rue Jean Goujon (Demolished), 75008 Paris
21 rue de Clichy, 75009 Paris
6 place des Vosges, 75004 Paris
37 rue de La Tour d'Auvergne, 75009 Paris
124 avenue Victor Hugo (Death Site), 75116 Paris

Victor Hugo ascended the mountaintop of artistic achievement during a literary career that exceeded sixty years. He wrote in a variety of genres and is best known for his poetry and classics *The Hunchback of Notre-Dame* and *Les Miserables*. He produced more than 4,000 drawings and became renowned for his involvement with important political causes.

Mixing political ambitions with artistic achievement has seldom resulted in alchemy. In 1845, Victor Hugo was nominated by King Louis Philippe to the Upper Chamber of Parliament. He spoke tirelessly against the death penalty and social injustice. He advocated freedom of the press and self-government for Poland. Three year later, he was elected to the National Assembly as a conservative.

He broke ranks with the conservatives when he gave a noteworthy speech calling for the end of misery and poverty. Later public speeches advocated universal suffrage and free education for all children. He may have aspired eventually towards France's presidency, but the events of 1851 altered his course irrevocably.

Louis Napoleon seized complete power, crowning himself Napoleon III and established an anti-parliamentary constitution. Hugo openly called him a traitor to France. Expediently, he fled to Brussels, then the island of Jersey. His residence in Jersey was brief when he supported a local newspaper that had criticized Queen Victoria. He finally settled with his family in St. Peter Port on the island of Guernsey in the Channel Islands. He would remain there in exile from October 1855 until 1870.

Hugo fought a lifelong battle for the abolition of slavery and the death penalty that distinguished him internationally. His influence was credited with removing the death penalty from the constitution of Geneva, Portugal and Colombia.

During his exile, freed from the distractions of politics and visitors, he completed some of his best poetry and the classic *Les Miserables*.

He declined amnesty in 1859 because he concluded it would curtail his criticism of the government. He returned to France in 1870 when Napoleon III abdicated and the Third Republic was established. He was welcomed back as a returning hero. He was promptly elected to the National Assembly and the Senate and anticipated being offered the dictatorship of France. His expectation never materialized. The resulting 1871 Commune uprising split the country. He criticized both sides for the atrocities committed.

Despite his popularity as an artist, he lost his bid for re-election to the National Assembly in 1872. Four years later, he would be elected to a newly created Senate. His maverick personality could not bend towards compromise or conciliatory behavior. He achieved nothing substantial with his political career.

The following decade became a series of setbacks and declines in his health and for his intimates. He suffered a mild stroke in June 1878. His daughter Adele was interned in an insane asylum and his two sons died. His long-term mistress Juliette Drouet would precede him in death during 1883.

Hugo would die from pneumonia on May 22, 1885 at the age of 83. The nation mourned his passing as no previous literary icon. More than two million people joined his funeral procession from the Arc de Triomphe to the Pantheon, where he was buried. He shares a crypt with writers Alexandre Dumas and Emile Zola.

30 rue du Dragon

6 place des Vosges

37 rue de la Tour d'Auvergne

A Streaking Symbolist Meteor Influencing A Literary Future
Arthur Rambeau's Residence:
2 rue de Vieux Colombier, 75006 Paris

Poet Arthur Rambeau's writings were created exclusively between his late adolescence years until he reached the age of twenty. He then abruptly ceased. Despite the brevity of his career and lifespan, his work became an important influence for challenging existing social mores and articulating surreal and symbolic themes. Rambeau would become an important icon within the future Dadaist and Surrealism movements.

Rambeau's unhappy childhood was muddied by an indulgent and absent father and a strict mother who he described as *stingy* and *lacking a complete sense of humor*. Rambeau privately called her *Bouche D'Ombre* (Mouth of Darkness).

His father spent the majority of Arthur's childhood consigned to distant military outposts scarcely seeing his family. He missed his children's births and baptisms. His estrangement became complete following the birth of his youngest daughter.

Arthur chafed under his mother's discipline and obsessive scrutiny over his formal education. He excelled as a student, but summarized education as *merely a gateway to a salaried position*.

During the outbreak of the 1870 Franco-Prussian War, his restlessness and boredom provoked him to seek fresh adventure in Paris without funds or a railway ticket. He was arrested at the Gare de Nord train station for vagrancy and fare evasion. He was returned to his mother who received him with an emphatic slap in the face. By October at the age of fifteen, he left again permanently abandoning his formal education.

His outward rebellion then became provocative. He discarded his former neat appearance and manners, let his hair grow long and unkempt, drank excessively and became intemperate. Through a friend, he became acquainted in Paris with another rising poet, Paul Verlaine.

Beginning in 1871, the two men engaged in a turbulent, destructive and sexual relationship that briefly destroyed Verlaine's marriage. Their vagabond existence was accentuated by opium, hashish and absinthe. They would travel together to London in 1872 where both taught part time while squandering Verlaine's financial allowance from his mother. Rambeau continued his writings while spending many hours in the Reading Room of the British Museum. The pair was sarcastically labeled as *the geniuses of the tavern*.

Their relationship would ultimately spiral out of constraint with Verlaine returning to his wife in Paris. An attempt at reconciliation in Brussels resulted in Verlaine shooting Rambeau with his pistol following a drunken rage. Verlaine would be imprisoned for two years for the offense and convert to Catholicism while interned. He would encounter Rambeau on one final occasion during March 1875 in Stuttgart.

The Arthur Rambeau that he met had completely given up writing. His earlier celebrated works had become discarded as streaking meteors flaming out. What had distinguished his originality then both thematically and stylistically was his intermingling of profane imagery with sophisticated verse. Rambeau's works would often be coupled with Charles Baudelaire into the symbolist group of poets.

His earlier recklessness and tormented soul would compel him to shift the direction of his life. A professional occupation offered him a needed sense of financial security.

His more conventional routine was not accompanied by a publicly expressed remorse for abandoning his poetic voice.

Rambeau would travel extensively as a coffee merchant and retailer for his next fifteen years on three continents. Happiness proved elusive. His obscurity became absolute.

In March 1891, he returned to Marseille from Africa suffering from a presumed case of arthritis in his right knee. His crippling condition proved far worse. His right leg would be amputated on May 27. The post-operative diagnosis confirmed that he was suffering from bone cancer. Efforts to revive his health for a return to Africa proved futile. On November 10, 1891, he died at the age of 37.

2 rue de Vieux Colombier

The Patron Sinning Writer Depicting the South of France
Alphonse Daudet's Residences:
8 Place des Vosges, 75004 Paris
31 rue de Bellechaise, 75007 Paris

Alphonse Daudet was born in Nimes during May 1840, the son of a silk manufacturer. When he was nine, his father was obliged to sell his factory due to accumulating debts and relocate to Lyon. By 1857, his parents had lost all of their savings and Alphonse would join his eldest brother in Paris.

He began writing poetry and his first novel at fourteen. Despite his family's reversal of fortune, his compositions never ceased. He dedicated his only book of poems *Les Amoureuses* (The Lovers) to his mistress, model Marie Rieu. They shared a long and obsessive entanglement that he would write about later in his novel *Spaho*. He was active socially and sexually and employed the traits of many of the individuals he encountered into future literary works.

In 1860, he met Frederic Mistral, the recognized leader of a revival of Provencal language and literature. Mistral awakened his passionate and artistic sensibilities towards his formative life in the south of France. Daudet would channel those memories into short stories and novels recreating sentimental tales of provincial life. His most renowned included *Lettres de Mon Moulin* (Letters from my Windmill) and the character of *Tartarin de Tarascon* (Tartarin of Tarascon). The boastful and naive portrayal of Tartarin would often be used to ridicule perceived traits of exaggeration and buffoonery existing in the rural south.

His initial works achieved measured success, but sometimes incurred venomous criticism. In 1867, he married writer Julia Allard and the couple would have two sons and a daughter together. Daudet's health suffered from poverty, but his most debilitating impediment to writing became the venereal

214

disease that he'd acquired from earlier brothel activity.

During the Franco-Prussian War of 1870-71, he enlisted in the French army, but later fled Paris during the Commune uprising of 1871. Amidst middle age, he began to enjoy recognition and prosperity. His works would be described as clear-sighted storytelling intermingled with humor, irony and compassion.

His earlier excesses had not groomed him for longevity. His syphilis worsened into an agonizing ailment of the spinal cord. He wrote through the adversity via a book entitled *In The Land of Pain*. He was credited with being an encouraging patron of younger writers including Marcel Proust.

In 1895, he visited London and Venice until his pain and crippling paralysis became insupportable. He would die in Paris on December 16, 1897 at the age of 57 and is interned in Pere Lachaise Cemetery.

31 rue de Bellechaise

A Russian Literary Giant Follows His Muse
Ivan Turguenev Residences:
210 rue de Rivoli, 75001 Paris
30 rue de Douai, 75009 Paris

Ivan Turguenev had already published his famous short story collection *A Sportsman's Sketches* (1852) and *Fathers and Sons* (1862) when he decided to leave Russia. He took up residence in Baden-Baden in southern Germany and would publish one story entitled *Smoke* (1867).

He became deeply infatuated with famed opera singer Pauline Viardot after hearing her rendition of *The Barber of Seville* in Russia during 1843. She was permanently attached to the Saint Petersburg Opera between 1843 to 1846.

Her marriage to Louis Viardot, her manager, defined the boundaries of Turguenev's unrequited love. He would follow the Viardots to Baden-Baden and would eventually install himself into their household. He treated their four children as his own and adored Pauline until his death. She promoted his work extensively through her social connections.

The Franco-German War of 1870-71 forced the Viardot family to leave Baden-Baden. Turgenev followed. First they resided in London and then Paris. Turguenev became an established Russian cultural ambassador cultivating an impressive bevy of literary peers. His self-imposed exile from Russia generated no controversy. He earned honors in Paris, London and was still feted in Russia during his annual visits.

During the final decade of his life, his literary output reflected nostalgia for the past framed in elegant prose. His final novel *Virgin Soil* (1877) was an attempt to stimulate the seeds of revolution amongst the Russian peasantry. Aimed at establishing relevance to a younger generation, it became the least successful of his novels.

His health declined during his final years dues to an aggressive malignant tumor. Despite its removal, it had metastasized in his upper spinal cord. He remained in intense pain throughout the final months of his life. On September 3, 1883, he died at his home in Bougival, outside of Paris. His remains were shipped to St. Petersburg where he was buried in the Volkovo Cemetery.

210 rue de Rivoli

30 rue de Douai

How An Accusatory Editorial Helped Spare An Innocent Military Officer
Former Site of Cherche Midi Military Prison:
33 rue du Cherche-Midi, 75006 Paris
Alfred Dreyfus Residence:
6 avenue du President Wilson, 75008 Paris
L'Aurore Newspaper Offices:
142 boulevard du Montparnasse, 75014 Paris
Emile Zola Residence:
278 rue Saint-Jacques, 75005 Paris
Site of Zola's Accidental Death:
21bis rue de Bruxelles, 75009 Paris
Site of Defamation Lawsuit Against Writer Emile Zola (Palais de Justice):
10 boulevard du Palais, 75001 Paris

The *Dreyfus Affair* became France's most controversial legal theatrics of the late nineteenth century. Prejudice, injustice, abuse of authority and journalistic accountability became dominant themes staged amidst a series of trials, blunders and pointed accusations.

Many of the principal characters within the drama would have their reputations darkened, freedom compromised and lives shattered by a witch-hunt of debatable motivations.

In December 1894, thirty-five-year old Army Captain Alfred Dreyfus was accused of communicating French military secrets to the German Embassy in Paris. France's humiliating defeat by the Prussians in 1871 remained an open wound. Scapegoats were still sought out.

Artillery officer Dreyfus was convicted by a military tribunal for treason and sentenced to life imprisonment. The case lacked tangible evidence. Some observers felt Dreyfus' Jewish heritage singularly made him a credible suspect. He was incarcerated for nearly five years at the reviled Devil's

Island Prison in French Guiana.

The verdict initially generated public support until two years later when the head of French counter-espionage and Minister of War Georges Picquet examined the evidence more intimately. He became convinced of Dreyfus' innocence and arrived at a different conclusion toward the identity of the culprit. He concluded that the guilty party was a French Army major named Ferdinand Esterhazy.

Esterhazy had been a former member of French counterespionage during the 1870 war. He had direct access to the missing and presumed stolen files. His handwriting matched incriminating documents that were considered supporting evidence. He reportedly harbored a personality disorder and was deeply in debt. The *secret* documents sold to the German Embassy were voluminous in number, but passed on for a minimal amount.

The embarrassment of convicting the wrong man prompted high-ranking military officers to close ranks. They suppressed Picquart's findings and conducted a superficial closed two-day trial acquitting Esterhazy.

For an innocent man, the liberated Esterhazy behaved curiously. He would shave off his distinctive mustache and flee France. Following his investigation and evidence submission, Picquet was re-assigned to an obscure position in North Africa.

The Military tribunal who'd erred grievously during Dreyfus's first trial decided one colossal mistake deserved a follow-up. They brazenly decided to file additional charges against Dreyfus based on freshly acquired forged documents.

In 1889, Dreyfus was returned to France to stand trial for these additional charges. The political climate and attitude towards Dreyfus had altered significantly. Popular sentiment had shifted towards his acquittal and liberty.

Writer Emile Zola remained outraged over the sham verdict favoring Esterhazy. Zola had historically shared an affinity towards the oppressed and Dreyfus's persecution represented a blatant miscarriage of justice.

He wrote a famous open letter on the front page of the newspaper *L'Aurore* directed towards French President Felix Faure condemning the acquittal of Esterhazy and the proceedings against Dreyfus. His blistering commentary identified incompetent public and military officials and his personal commentary on the travesty. Zola's commentary was crowned by an epic headline *J'Accuse...!* reportedly composed by publisher and future French Prime Minister George Clemenceau.

Zola's letter ignited immediate response. The published attack galvanized reaction and criticism towards the handling of the Dreyfus Affair. His targets however were not amused.

Public and military officials condemned by Zola retorted to addressing his claims by filing a lawsuit suing him for defamation. Dreyfus became a cause celebre and perceived vulnerable victim of military ineptitude.

The military tribunal doggedly persisted with Dreyfus' second trial despite their credibility being universally dismissed. Their trial resulted in a second controversial conviction. Protests in major French cities and anti-French manifestations in twenty foreign capitals raged. The military judges were savagely criticized for their unfamiliarity towards the law and proper criminal proceedings.

The collective outrage and pressure preempted a planned third trial. Dreyfus was abruptly pardoned and released. In

1906, he would be exonerated of all charged criminal activities against him and reinstated as a major in the French Army. He would serve during World War I and retire with the rank of lieutenant colonel. He died in 1935.

Zola's article and suggestion that anti-Semitism motivated the Dreyfus decision triggered public backlash. His own libel trial would be contentious and fiery. He was convicted and sentenced to one year in prison along with being accessed a maximum fine of 3,000 francs.

He fled France for a year living as a celebrated exile in England. He returned when the public clamor had subsided. He might never serve a day in prison, but his existence would be altered as well. His act of public defiance may have cost him his life.

On September 29, 1902, he died mysteriously from asphyxiation traced to fumes unable to escape his chimney. His wife narrowly avoided the identical fate. His death would be ruled accidental, but persistent claims of murder were suggested although never substantiated. In 1953, a dying Parisian roofer claimed that he had murdered Zola by blocking the chimney passage of his house.

Ferdinand Esterhazy was discreetly discharged with a military pension. He was forced to resign at the rank of major. In September 1898, he relocated to England via Brussels. He settled in the town of Harpenden where he wrote venomous anti-Semitic articles for journals under the pen name *Jean de Voilement.*

As his name gradually receded from print, many observers concluded that he'd been a double agent. He lived until 1923 in obscurity. He is buried in Harpenden's St. Nicholas churchyard under his adopted pen name. His guilt was never substantiated in a court of law.

Former Site of Cherche Midi Military Prison

6 avenue du President Wilson

L'Aurore Newspaper Office

21bis rue de Bruxelles

Palais du Justice

The Fame and Crash of Irish Playwright Oscar Wilde

Oscar Wilde's Paris Residences:
Hotel Voltaire:
19 Quai Voltaire, 75007 Paris
Hotel Wagram:
208, rue de Rivoli, 75001 Paris
Hotel de l'Athennee:
15 rue Scribe, 75009 Paris
Hotel d'Alsace (Wilde's Death Site):
13 rue des Beaux Arts, 75006 Paris
Wilde's Funeral Mass (Eglise de Saint-Germain-des-Pres):
3 place Saint-Germain-des-Pres, 75006 Paris
Initial Performance of *Salome* (Theatre de l'Athenee):
7 rue Boudreau, 75009 Paris

At the age of twenty, Oscar Wilde first visited Paris with his mother Speranza during the summer of 1874. The experience would cement his affinity for the city that would become prominent during his literary rise and subsequent disgrace. During his initial visit, he stayed at the Hotel Voltaire renowned for such celebrated clients including Charles Baudelaire, Richard Wagner and Jean Sibelius. During this period he began publishing poems as a college student at Dublin's Trinity University.

His next visit would occur in late January 1883 staying initially at the Hotel Continental before returning to the Hotel Voltaire during April and May. One of his notable acquaintances during this visit was French literary writer, publisher and critic Edmond de Goncourt. Through several visits with Goncourt, he encountered actress Sarah Bernhardt and became enchanted by her performances and personality.

Goncourt described Wilde prophetically as *an individual of doubtful sex who talks like a third-rate actor and tells tall tales.*

He returned in triumph the following June as one of London's most popular playwrights on a honeymoon trip with his bride Constance Lloyd occupying three rooms at the Hotel Wagram. As his reputation continued to flourish, this visit was crowned as a *Grand Event* amongst the literary salons of Paris. During his stay, he worked on the play *Salome* that he composed in French. The play would premier with French dialogue on February 11, 1896 at the Theatre de l'Athenee by the Theatre de l'Oeuvre acting troupe. By that period, Wilde's life and fortunes had altered radically.

At the peak of his fame, Wilde presumed that his celebrity status elevated him above the dictates of society. He flaunted his wit, fame and indiscreetly his excesses. Since 1891, he'd begun a gay relationship with Lord Alfred Douglas, a young poet and aristocrat sixteen years younger. Douglas' father, the Marquess of Queensberry (curiously the originator of modern boxing rules) was outraged by their relationship. He left his calling card with the porter at the private Albemarle Club in London penning the words *For Oscar Wilde, posing sodomite.*

His action attracted public notice and created a potential public relations nightmare for Wilde's reputation. Homosexual acts between consenting adults were illegal in England and punished by incarceration. France had decriminalized homosexuality during the French Revolution in 1791. England maintained its illegality status until the 1960s.

Wilde ignored his friends' advice to temporarily relocate to France. Instead, he rashly sued the Marquess for defamation of character on April 3, 1895. Following three days of court proceedings, Wilde's lawyer withdrew the lawsuit. The trial exposed Wilde's sexual activities with Douglas and reportedly a dozen additional men. The repercussions against Wilde were immediate.

He was tried for homosexuality less than three weeks later pleading not guilty on 25 counts of gross indecency. The first trial ended in a hung jury, but the second staged three weeks later resulted in his conviction of *gross indecency* and a two-year sentence of hard labor.

One of the intriguing phrases used at the trial as evidence against Wilde was a line written by his lover Douglas to confirm their relationship. From Douglas' poem *Two Loves*, the phrase *the love that dare not speak its name* was infamously citied as the description of a homosexual relationship. Many have erroneously credited the line to Wilde.

On May 25, 1895, Wilde was incarcerated inside London's Pentonville Prison where he remained for several months. He would be transferred to London's Reading Gaol and released in 1897. During his internment, he had lost his health, reputation, and temporarily his means of financial sustenance. Upon his release, he returned to Paris once again living off the charity of friends and a significantly scaled down lifestyle. His spirit was fractured, but he did manage to write *The Ballad of Reading Gaol* based on his prison experiences. Over the next three years, he periodically traveled throughout Europe dodging creditors and being unceremoniously kicked out of lodging houses for failing to pay his bill.

His final residence became the Hotel d'Alsace where his declining health continued to gut his soul and spirit. He toyed with the idea of converting to Catholicism primarily to insure a priest would give him a proper funeral service. There is significant speculation that he was in a near canonic state when he lay on his deathbed and his entourage took the initiative for his *conversion*.

He would die at the age of 46 on November 30, 1900 from acute meningitis the same year as his tormentor the Marquess of Queensberry. His demise and creative rupture had become foreseeable upon his imprisonment. His funeral would be conducted at the church of Saint-Germain-des-Pres on December 3 in the presence of 56 individuals.

Father Cuthbert Dunne who conducted the ceremony would be expelled from France two years later following the passage of anti-clerical legislation. Wilde was initially buried in a pauper's grave at the Bagneux cemetery before his remains were transferred to Pere Lachaise Cemetery in July 1909.

A concluding insult to Wilde's legacy arrived with yet another unpaid hotel bill for his four-month stay at the Hotel de l'Alsace. The hotel owner Jean Dupoirier decided not to contest the bill for the room, necessities and luxuries that he provided for his tenant. His generosity of approximately $200 proved an excellent investment in future public relations. Wilde's posthumous royalties would ultimately become a billion dollar industry.

Hotel Wagram

Hotel Voltaire

Hotel l'Athennee

Hotel D'Alsace

Saint Germain des Pres

Theatre de l'Athenee

Lost Time Immortalized In Classic Literature
Marcel Proust's Residences:
9 boulevard Malesherbes, 75008 Paris
45, rue de Coucelles, 75008 Paris
8bis rue Laurent Pichat, 75116 Paris
44, rue Hamelin, 75016 Paris
Hotel Scribe: 1 rue Scribe, 75008 Paris
31 rue Bellechaise, 75007 Paris
102 boulevard Haussman, 75008 Paris

Marcel Proust saved for last his best and most enduring writings in the form of *A La Recherché du Temps Perdu* (In Search of Lost Time). The classic was a monumental compilation of his life experiences, encountered personalities and insightful glimpses of Paris and the upper bourgeoisie.

Proust was born two months following the signed treaty ending the Franco-Prussian War in 1871. The violence and suppression of the Paris Commune would occur during his infancy. Throughout his formative years, he would intimately witness the decline of the aristocracy and subsequent rise of the middle class.

At the age of nine, he began suffering from asthma that prompted extended holidays and doctor visitations. The majority of his doctors considered him a hypochondriac. His writings started early in school and later enabled his access into literary salons that he would portray in great detail.

Proust became the ultimate outsider voyeur in his writings. He was known to be gay, but remained in public denial. He would fight a duel in 1897 with a writer who publicly insinuating his sexual orientation. Both survived. He was linked with three relationships, but typically frequented male brothels. His maternal influence sustained him during his frequent dark periods. He lived at his parents' apartment until both were deceased.

Proust never worked. Once to appease his father, he accepted a volunteer position at *Bibiotheque Magazine* during the summer of 1896. He obtained a sick leave of absence that extended for years until it was finally acknowledged that he'd resigned.

At 38, he began his classic *Temps Perdu* consisting of seven volumes, over 3,200 pages and more than 2,000 characters. He would die before he was able to complete his revisions of the drafts and proofs of the final volumes. His last three volumes were edited by his brother Robert and published posthumously. Proust spent the final three years of his life confined primarily to his bedroom. He slept during the daytime and labored at night. He died of pneumonia and heart disease on November 18, 1922 at the age of 51. He was buried at the Pere Lachaise Cemetery.

Hotel Scribe

102 boulevard Haussman

A Woman of the Future Articulating Her Present Tense
Colette's Residences:
28 rue Jacob, 75006 Paris
9 rue de Beaujolais (Death Site), 75001 Paris

Sidonie-Gabrielle Colette was a creative force far ahead of her era. She was a mime, actress, journalist and writer whose insight and wit portrayed early twentieth century life from a bemused, cynical, but candid perspective. She wrote with honesty on forbidden subjects such as courtesans, libertines, outcasts and lesbian alliances that shocked her readership. Her observations and truths could not be discredited because she had lived this existence.

Colette frequently credited her writing initiative to her first husband Henry Gauthier-Villars, a well-known writer and publisher using the pen name *Willy*. He exploited her talent and prevented her access to the sizable earnings from her popularly authored *Claudine* series of books. Willy owned the exclusive copyright.

Willy introduced her into Parisian avant-garde intellectual and artistic circles. The members' exchanges, intrigues and lifestyles provided excellent inspirational material for her writings.

The couple separated in 1906, but didn't divorce until four years later. She struggled financially and performed in music halls throughout France. This stage of her life was portrayed in her autobiography *La Vagabonde* (1910). She often performed as *Claudine*, the primary heroine in her novels. During this period, she initiated a series of relationships with other women.

Her most scandalous liaison was with Natalie Clifford Barney whom she frequently shared the stage with. Barney went by the *Marquise de Belbeuf* or often simply Max. An onstage kiss between the pair during a pantomime entitled *Revu d'Egypte* at the Moulin Rouge nearly provoked a riot by the audience.

Colette married editor Henry de Jouvenel in 1912 and had a daughter also named Colette the following year. They nicknamed her *Bel-Gazou*. Their marriage lasted only until 1924 due to his infidelities and her own affair with her 16-year-old stepson, Bertrand de Jouvenel. Readers have noted the similarity between him and one of her most recognized literary figures *Cheri*. He would later become the lover of American journalist Martha Gellhorn, the third wife of Ernest Hemingway.

She would marry a final time in 1925 to Maurice Goudeket, who was sixteen years younger. They remained together until her death.

In 1920, she published one of her most popular works, *Cheri*, depicting a sexual entanglement between an aging woman and young man. Cheri, the male character would eventually leave his mistress for a woman his age. In the follow-up novel, he would commit suicide after evaluating tragically the mistake he made in discarding his older mistress.

During the German occupation of Paris in World War II, the Gestapo detained her Jewish husband for seven weeks. He was released due to the intervention of the French wife of the German ambassador. Colette remained in constant fear of his potential second arrest.

At the conclusion of the war, she wrote her most famous work, *Gigi*. The narrative is the story of a 16-year-old girl being groomed as a courtesan to entrap a wealthy lover. Instead she marries him. The novel was made into a 1949 French film and then adapted into a stage production casting then unknown actress Audrey Hepburn in the title role.

Colette selected her personally. In 1958, a Hollywood musical production movie won the Academy Award for Best Picture.

Colette spent her declining years crippled by arthritis and confined to her Palais Royale building apartment. She accepted visitations and numerous awards. Her writing style always stressed direct experience over invention and creative license. Many readers consider her to be the greatest French female writer of the twentieth century.

28 rue Jacob

26 rue Jacob

9 rue de Beaujolais

9 rue de Beaujolias

An Artistic Influence Who Outshone His Own Poetry
Guillaume Apollinaire's Residence:
202 boulevard Saint-Germain 75007
Chess Matches With Lenin and Trotsky La Closerie des
Lilas (Demolished):
171 boulevard du Montparnasse, 75006

Guillaume Apollinaire has been glorified as one of France's foremost poets from the early twentieth century. His work is scarcely read in Britain or the United States. The company of visual artists and writers that he kept pre-World War I enshrined him as an important component of the Parisian creative scene.

Apollinaire's work defied convention. He stressed the necessity that the act of creating must originate from imagination and intuition. He wrote his poems without punctuation attempting to be both modern in form and subject matter. He is credited with being one of the earliest Surrealist writers. He purportedly was the originator of the actual term in 1917 to describe the ballet *Parade* by composer Erik Satie.

He was an active journalist and art critic for numerous publications and coined the term *Cubism* in 1911 to describe the emerging art movement. He is further credited with introducing African art influences into his circle of Parisian contemporaries.

The longevity of Apollinaire's influence would be abruptly severed upon his enlistment during World War I. He served as an infantry officer and in 1916 suffered a serious shrapnel wound to his temple. He would never fully recover and perish during the 1918 Spanish flu pandemic on November 9 at the age of 38.

Apollinaire was considered the ultimate free spirit and one of the most popular members of the creative community. He reportedly played chess with Vladimir Lenin and Leon Trotsky at the café *La Closerie de Lilas*. His circle of friends included Gertrude Stein, Andre Breton, Jean Cocteau, Marc Chagall, Marcel Duchamp and Pablo Picasso. Picasso dedicated *The Head of Dora Maar* sculpture located in Laurent-Prache Square to him.

202 boulevard Saint-Germain

A Literary Influence, Fascist and Psychiatric Inmate
Ezra Pound's Residence:
70 bis, rue Notre-Dame-des-Champs, 75006 Paris

Ezra Pound became an important influence in the early modernist poetry movement. His own early formation stigmatized him as an outsider viewing society distantly. He is credited with his role in developing *Imagism*, a writing movement stressing sparse precision and economy of language.

His influence as foreign editor of several American literary magazines shaped and influenced notable peers including T. S. Eliot, Ernest Hemingway and James Joyce. His own distinguished works would include *Ripostes*, *Hugh Selwyn Mauberley* and *The Cantos* composed during 45 years of his life.

Pound moved to London in 1908 following travels there two years previously. He mixed within literary circles dressing extravagantly in varied color plumage. In March 1910, he visited a friend Walter Rummel in Paris and was introduced to American heiress and pianist Margaret Lanier Cravens. She offered to become his sole patron offering him $1,000 annually. Prior to her death two years later, she provided him with money regularly. He met the novelist Olivia Shakespeare at a social gathering and would later marry her daughter Dorothy in 1914 against her mother's wishes.

The beginning of World War I that same year altered the freedom that writers and poets had formerly enjoyed. Creative works were expected to be patriotic. Pound's own finances dropped precariously. His anti-war themes lessened his popularity. Close literary friends were killed in the conflict that he blamed on *financial capitalist interests*.

He relocated to Paris in 1921 and became part of the

impoverished Left Bank art and literary scene. He was older than many of his peers and wasn't a drinker. He became acquainted with the Dada and Surrealist movements.

Pound carved himself a unique niche. Paris was a cauldron of inspiration and creativity. He preferred the company of Natalie Barney's salon to the more popular Gertrude Stein's. The pair never got along, particularly after he sat down too heavily on one of her fragile chairs, causing it to collapse. Stein called him *a village explainer* and *not amusing*.

He cavorted throughout Paris with women other than his wife. He described her porcelain skin and ice-blue eyes as *a beautiful picture that never came to life*. His contemporaries considered him charismatic, robust with notable height and full color complimented by a mane of wavy red-blond hair. The couple lived on the small stipends from his reviews supplemented by her allowance and contributions from his family in Philadelphia.

He moved to Italy in 1928 and throughout the 1930s and 40s promoted Benito Mussolini's fascist philosophy and his own economic theory known as *social credit*. He admired Adolph Hitler during World War II and the Holocaust making hundreds of radio broadcasts on behalf of the Italian government. His contrarian views targeted the United States and Britain, President Roosevelt, international finance, Jews and munitions makers.

When American military forces entered Italy in 1945, he was arrested for treason. He spent months in a U.S. military camp in Pisa including three weeks in an outdoor steel cage.

Pound was shipped back to Washington D.C. where he pled insanity at his trial. Most of the doctors who examined him found him coherent and sane. Dr. Winfred Olverholster who was fascinated by the poet and his works protected him with his compromised testimony portraying him as *mentally disturbed.* The strategy succeeded.

Pound was admitted into St. Elizabeths Hospital where he would spend the next twelve years in the Chestnut Ward. The facility was plagued by drab surroundings and minimal light. His ward had a wide corridor with few rocking chairs, a television and cubicles for sleeping.

In 1948, Pound controversially won the inaugural Bollingen Prize for his *Pisan Cantos,* written during his imprisonment outside of Pisa. Awarding the highest national poetry award to a convicted traitor led Congress to disassociate the Library of Congress from the award. The Yale University Library would determine future award winners.

Examining psychiatrists did not conclude that Pound ever truly modified his core anti-Semitism or political doctrine. Several of his intimate artist friends including Robert Frost, Ernest Hemingway and T.S. Eliot advocated his release. Frost secured him complimentary legal representation.

At the age of 72, Pound was released in 1958 where he welcomed the awaiting press with a fascist salute. He returned back to Italy to write until his death in 1972.

A Movable Feast For A Lifestyle Gourmet
Ernest Hemingway's Residence:
74 rue Cardinal-Lemoine 75005 Paris
Writing Studios:
39 rue Descartes, 75005 Paris
9 rue Delambre, 75014 Paris

Ernest Hemingway described Paris as a *moveable feast*. He moved to the city with his first wife, Hadley in 1921 when he was twenty-two. The young couple lived in a diminutive apartment with no running water and a bathroom that consisted of primarily a bucket. He rented another space nearby where he concentrated on his writing.

Hemingway's fondest and most productive memory was his acquaintance with contemporary artists that fermented his development as a writer. The members comprising this legendary *Lost Generation* included Gertrude Stein, Ezra Pound, Picasso and James Joyce.

In 1923, the Hemingway couple left Paris for a year while Hadley had their first child in Toronto. They returned to Paris and he wrote with greater proficiency completing *The Sun Also Rises* and *Men Without Women*. His philandering ruined the marriage in 1927 when his wife discovered his affair with Pauline Pfeiffer, a fashion reporter.

They divorced. He would marry Pfeiffer a few months afterwards. They would depart for Key West the following year.

He summarized his Parisian experience best in his writing: *Wherever you go for the rest of your life, it (Paris) stays with you.*

74 rue Cardinal-Lemoine

A Pioneer in Independent Bookselling and Publishing
Original Shakespeare and Company Locations:
8 rue Dupuytren, 75006 Paris
12 rue l'Odeon, 75006 Paris
Sylvia Beach and Adrienne Monnier's Residence:
18 rue l'Odeon, 75006
Current Shakespeare and Company Bookstore:
37 rue de la Bucherie, 75005 Paris

Baltimore native Sylvia Beach was conducting research at the Bibliotheque Nationale in Paris when she read about a lending library and bookshop called *La Maison des Amis des Livres* (The House of the Friends of Books). Visiting the store in the Latin Quarter, she met vivacious proprietor Adrienne Monnier, one of the first women to operate an independent bookstore in Paris.

The two women became infatuated with each other. Monnier encouraged and offered invaluable advice to Beach to pursue her dream of opening an English language bookstore. Beach pooled all of her resources to begin *Shakespeare and Company* located initially on rue Dupuytren in the Latin Quarter. In May 1921 after outgrowing her location, she moved her store directly across the street from Monnier's replacing an antique dealer. The two women would became lovers and live together for 36 years until Monnier's suicide in 1955.

Shakespeare and Company attracted an immediate French and American clientele. The literary life of the Left Bank was vibrant. Both women hosted readings by notable contemporary authors. Beach offered books and frequently lodging hospitality to American writers in Paris. She befriended innovative authors such as Ernest Hemingway, Simone de Beauvoir, F. Scott Fitzgerald and James Joyce.

She met Joyce at a dinner party hosted by French poet Andre Spire. He had been trying unsuccessfully to publish his manuscript *Ulysses* into an English language version. Distribution had become blocked due to perceived obscenity in the text.

Beach offered to publish and distribute his work. Joyce gratefully accepted her offer and *Ulysses* was introduced to the literary world. Joyce would betray her generosity later signing with an alternative publisher. She suffered severe financial losses from his duplicity. The adventure however generated significant publicity for her shop.

During the Great Depression of the 1930s, her company faced daunting financial difficulties. Her longtime patrons, wealthy friends and artists that she'd encouraged created a sponsorship group called *Friends of Shakespeare and Company*. Subscription monies and high-profile authors readings sustained her during those bleak years.

What could not extend the lifespan of her store was the German occupation of Paris during World War II. Beach would be interned initially six months at Vittel in northeastern France. Art dealer William Tudor Wilkinson was able to secure her release in February 1942. Until the liberation of Paris, she reportedly sheltered allied airmen shot down in France. She hid her books in a vacant apartment upstairs above her bookstore. She would never re-open for business. She died in Paris on October 5, 1962.

American George Whitman would open a bookstore in the Left Bank during 1951 originally calling it *Le Mistral*. In 1964, following her death and capitalizing on the name recognition, he renamed his store *Shakespeare and Company* to honor Sylvia Beach. He died in 2011 at the age of 98, but the operation continues run by his daughter.

12 rue l'Odeon

**The Father of Surrealism and His Ungrateful Offspring
Andre Breton's Residences:
Hotel des Ecoles, 35 rue Delambre, 75001 Paris
42 rue Fontaine, 75009 Paris**

Andre Breton is the acknowledged founder of the Surrealist movement based on his theorist writings and unconventional tastes and aesthetics. He authored the *Surrealist Manifesto* in 1924 calling it *pure psychic automation*.

The movement was initiated from the remnants of the *Dada* Movement, popular during World War I. Many participants and observers have summarized surrealism as an exploration of the subconscious through dreams and unconventional forms of expression. The term is still employed today, generally towards difficult to label visual art and performance.

Breton was born and raised in Normandy and attended medical school. World War I interrupted his studies and he worked in a neurological ward throughout the conflict in Nantes. During his stint, he was introduced to Jacques Vache, whose anti-social attitude and disdain for established artistic traditions influenced his thinking. Vache committed suicide at twenty-four and his wartime letters to Breton would become one of his first publications.

Breton joined the French Communist Party in 1927, but was expelled in 1933 due to philosophical differences. His fascination with mental illness and atheism embarked him on an alternative path of discovery.

Salvador Dali would ironically become the public face of surrealism. Breton's opinion towards Dali would sour by the mid 1930s. He would create a famous anagram of Dali's name, *Avida Dollars* that translated into *greed for money*. Dali would be expelled from the movement in 1939, but

254

glibly responded: *I myself am surrealism.*

Breton accumulated allies and detractors with his writings and strict inclusionary rules for membership. He considered himself a French art and literature authority amassing a significant collection adorning his modern styled residence.

He joined the French medical corps at the outset of World War II. During the German occupation, the ruling Vichy government banned his books and writings. He migrated to New York City during the war continuing his writings and staging exhibitions exploiting his surrealistic reputation. The movement had evolved into a virtual monarchy under Breton's control. It steadily lost relevance to the post-war abstract expressionism movement.

Breton returned to France in 1946. He immediately began criticizing French colonialism and later the Algerian War. His own philosophy drifted towards pseudo-anarchy. His base of supporters had aged and eroded significantly. He died at the age of 70 in 1966. His contributions towards contemporary thought remain acknowledged, but his authoritarian stamp is often diminished.

42 rue Fontaine

A Literary Voice Of The Lost Generation
F. Scott Fitzgerald's Residence:
58 rue Vaugirard, 75006 Paris
F. Scott Fitzgerald's Writing Studio:
9 rue Delambre 75014 Paris

F. Scott Fitzgerald wrote *The Great Gatsby* during the summer of 1924 while renting a villa with his family in Saint Raphael on the French Riviera. He needed to escape from the social whirl of Great Neck, Long Island. He and wife Zelda were mainstays amidst the glamorous party set. Unfortunately the setting became a detriment to his writing productivity.

On the French Riviera, they were introduced to a wide circle of musicians and friends that included Cole Porter and Fernand Leger. Some of these acquaintances would inspire characters in later books.

Gatsby was published in 1925 and was initially a commercial failure compared to his previous works. Decades later it would become his most acclaimed and best-selling work.

Scott and Zelda decided to spend the summer in Paris. They made immediate acquaintance with many of the leading artistic and literary voices. Saturday evening salons at Gertrude Stein's apartment was a collection of the finest minds and talents of a collective Stein called *The Lost Generation*. This designation was bestowed on those *who'd lost their brothers, their youth and their idealism*. She considered Fitzgerald the finest writer of the age.

Fitzgerald would become close friends with Ernest Hemingway and actively promote and encourage his growing literary career and reputation. Hemingway disliked Zelda and considered her *insane*. Hemingway was convinced that Zelda was intent on destroying her husband.

In December 1926, the Fitzgerald's would return to the United States following another year of travel between Paris and the Riviera. Their marriage had begun to crack due to Zelda's jealousy, growing mental illness and the couple's alcoholism.

A stark decline of both over the next six years consumed their once illustrious future together. Fitzgerald's novelty and following were dimmed during the Great Depression era. He was considered *elitist* and *materialistic*. His book royalties plunged crippling him in debt to support the couple's lavish lifestyle.

The magic had vanished and his novel *Tender Is The Night* published in 1934 generated only mixed reviews and modest sales. Ironically it would later become one of his highest regarded works. He resorted to writing short stories for popular magazines and movie screenplays from other writer's compositions. He loathed the direction his career had plummeted.

His chronic alcoholism destroyed his health, hospitalizing him a reported eight times. He claimed to have achieved sobriety the final year of his life. He died in Los Angeles of coronary arteriosclerosis on December 21, 1940 at the age of 44. His unfinished fifth novel *The Last Tycoon* was published posthumously in 1941.

Zelda's future upon their return from France became even bleaker. Her behavior grew increasingly violent and erratic. She was diagnosed with schizophrenia in 1930 that was later modified to bipolar disorder. The rest of her life was spent being periodically institutionalized. She endured a decade of electroshock therapy and insulin shock treatment. She attempted writing and painting, but her growing notoriety and unpredictability resulted in rejection and indifference. The couple ultimately lived apart before his death.

In March 1948, she was sedated in a locked room on the fifth floor of Highland Hospital in Asheville, North Carolina. She perished in an arson fire that an investigation blamed on a disgruntled or mentally disturbed hospital employee.

There would be no second acts in American lives as F. Scott Fitzgerald wrote in *Gatsby*, particularly their own.

Being There But Remaining Blind To Surroundings
Gertrude Stein and Alice B. Toklas Residence
27 rue de Fleurus, 75006 Paris

Gertrude Stein cast an extended shadow on the literary and artistic community upon her arrival in Paris during 1903. She was born in Pittsburgh, but more renowned for her formation in Oakland, California. Her summation of Oakland was *there is no there there*. The insult became the ultimate dismissive description for a city.

Her apartment in Paris became the ultimate salon where the leading figures of modernism congregated during the 1920s. Amongst her best know acquaintances included Ernest Hemingway, Pablo Picasso, F. Scott Fitzgerald, Henri Matisse, Ezra Pound and Sinclair Lewis.

Her own literary work *The Autobiography of Alice B. Toklas* became a bestseller vaulting her into the limelight of mainstream attention. Toklas was her life partner and the memoir concentrated on their celebrated Paris years. She wrote additional works with more modest acclaim often from an expatriate or lesbian twist.

During the German occupation of Paris, there was widespread speculation that she sustained both her life and art collection through cooperation with the Vichy government. As a Jew she became a high risk to lose both. The regime would deport more than 75,000 Jews to Nazi concentration camps with only an estimated 3% surviving.

Following the war, she was one of the few voices expressing admiration for Vichy leader Marshall Petain. In wartime interviews, she compared Petain with George Washington while naively commenting once that *Hitler ought to have the (Nobel) peace prize*. She was a vocal critic of President Franklin Roosevelt and his *New Deal* policies.

She died on July 27, 1946 at the age of 72 following surgery for stomach cancer at the American Hospital outside of Paris.

Her life revolved around straddling unconventional boundaries. As a champion and collector of modern art, her influence became commendable. As a potential Nazi collaborator, her lasting legacy has become permanently divisive and tarnished.

27 rue de Fleurus

A Paris Portrait of The Artist As An Older Man
James Joyce's Residences:
Hotel Corneille: 5 rue Corneille, 75006 Paris
7 rue Edmond Valentin, 75007 Paris
71 Cardinal Lemoine, 75005 Paris
2 Square Robiac, 75007 Paris

By the time James Joyce resided in Paris, he was already middle aged and nearly blind. He had published *Dubliners*, *A Portrait of the Artist* and his manuscript for *Ulysses* was nearly completed.

He would live for twenty years in Paris, nearly as long as he had in Dublin. He lived frugally often spending extensive time reading in the National Library or engaging in literary discussions with his peers. The difference between life in Paris and Dublin was that he maintained modest social pursuits without the intention of documenting his frolics in print.

Paris offered him privacy, distance and an ideal working environment. During his residence, he underwent at least ten eye operations often inhibiting his ability to compose manuscripts and edit his proofs.

Shakespeare and Company owner Sylvia Beach financially enabled him to publish his classic *Ulysses* as a first edition. At the time, no other publishers dared risk their reputation on the controversial Joyce. Exclusively her shop sold her first 1,000-copy printing. Over the next 11 years, she sold approximately 28,000 copies of fourteen additional printings.

Joyce's stay in Paris coincided at the same period with many of the *Lost Generation* writers. Towards the end of his residence, he completed his gargantuan *Finnegans Wake* that still confounds readers today as much as when initially released.

71 Cardinal Lemoine

A Renaissance Man of Twentieth Century Arts
Jean Cocteau's Residences:
10 rue d'Anjou 75008 Paris
Hotel Biron: 77 rue de Varenne 75007 Paris
36 rue Montpensier, 75001 Paris

Jean Cocteau resisted labeling, but always considered himself a poet. Many considered him a *Renaissance Man* of twentieth century creativity distinguishing himself as a playwright, novelist, poet, designer, filmmaker, visual artist and critic.

His works contributed to shaping and influencing the surrealist, avant-garde and Dadaist movements. He collaborated with numerous renowned artists in diverse fields always maintaining his presence amidst the social pulse. He distinguished himself internationally as an avant-garde filmmaker via notable productions including *Beauty and the Beast* (1946) and *Orpheus* (1950).

His lifestyle was as equally unconventional as controversial. He lived openly gay without pretense or apology risking adverse commercial consequences and alienation. He professed no political views and once publicly praised the French republic for serving as a haven for the persecuted. He claimed to support pacifism and antiracism and professed disdain of anti-Semitism within France.

The German occupation during World War II clouded his moral courage and public pronouncements. He met regularly with French and German intellectuals at the George V Hotel in Paris. Their sessions and discussions minimized the horrors and atrocities surrounding their oasis. He brazenly accused France of disrespect towards Hitler whom a close friend had convinced him was a pacifist and patron of the arts.

Post war, he was arraigned on charges of collaboration. He

was cleared legally of wrongdoing, but probably because as with many high-profile suspects, he still possessed friends in influential places. He regrettably learned little from his exposure to fascism. He hailed Joseph Stalin as the *only great politician of the era*.

The grind of celebrity bored and distressed him with fans waiting outside or knocking on his door at his Palais Royal residence. He resolved the dilemma by purchasing a house in 1947 with his lover Jean Marais in Milly-la-Foret, located southeast of Paris, near Fontainebleau. He employed the property as his creative retreat and refuge from the urban chaos of Paris.

He would die of a heart attack there on October 11, 1963 at the age of 74. His friend, singer Edith Piaf died the day before. Many speculate that hearing the news may have literally stilled his heart. He is buried beneath the floor of the Chapelle Saint-Blaise des Simples in Milly-la-Foret.

36 rue Montpensier

An Action Figure and Author Heading A Cultural Crusade
Andre Malraux Residence:
Madison Hotel: 143 Boulevard Saint-Germain 75006 Paris
44 rue du Bac, 75007 Paris
Palais Royal (Ministry of Culture):
204 rue St. Honore 75001 Paris

Andre Malraux led an overflowing existence leading up to his most renowned political appointment. He became France's first cultural affairs minister during Charles de Gaulle's presidency between 1959-1969.

He was born in Paris and raised by his mother, aunt and grandmother who operated a grocery store in Bondy. His parents separated when he was five and his father, a stockbroker, committed suicide in 1930 with the onset of the stock market collapse and global Great Depression.

Malraux shared a fascination with adventure and archaeology. At twenty-two, he and his first wife traveled to Cambodia, then a French Protectorate. Their ambition was to explore uncharted areas to discover hidden temples and artifacts that could be sold later to art collectors and museums.

He wasn't alone. Numerous archaeologists were sanctioned by the French government to transport artifacts from the recently discovered 12th century Angkor Wat temple to France. Malraux was arrested and charged upon his return for removing a bas-relief from the Banteay Srei temple.

He contested the legitimacy of the charges, but was unsuccessful. The experience tainted his views on French Colonialism. He became highly critical of the colonial authorities. He assisted in starting a newspaper in 1925 to champion the cause of Vietnamese independence.

Malraux first began writing in the mid 1920s concentrating on Asiatic themes. In 1933, he authored *La Condition Humaine* (The Human Condition), a novel that earned him the literary Prix Goncourt that year. Additional works dealt with philosophical themes and the communist rebellion and movements within China and the Soviet Union.

In February 1934, he embarked with a colleague on a search to discover the lost capital of the Queen of Sheba referenced in the Old Testament. They flew for weeks over the deserts in Saudi Arabia and Yemen. They claimed to have discovered the ruins in the mountains of Yemen. Archeologists never substantiated these claims.

With the world in upheaval throughout the mid twentieth century, Malraux wholeheartedly plunged into causes. At the beginning of the Spanish Civil War in 1936, he joined the Republican forces. During the outbreak of World War II, he enlisted in the French Army. He was captured in 1940 during the Battle of France, but reportedly escaped and joined the French Resistance. The Gestapo arrested him in 1944 and executed his half-brother Claude, a special agent.

Immediately following the war, General Charles de Gaulle appointed Malraux as the Minister for Information. He continued his writings throughout his military adventures and political appointments. He earned the dubious distinction of being nominated for the Nobel Prize in Literature on 70 occasions, but never winning once.

When de Gaulle appointed him Minister of Cultural Affairs, he shaped the perception and role of the position. He launched a nationwide clean up campaign on the facades of historic buildings. This program would be emulated in numerous major international cities. He promoted contemporary French art, performance and creations worldwide.

Despite a focus on marketing culture, he remained outspoken on political issues. He was the target of a 1962 unsuccessful bombing of his apartment. Ironically the action was due to his perceived support for Algerian independence, a cause that he was lukewarm and relatively silent towards.

Malraux would die in November 1976 from a lung embolism. He was cremated and his ashes ultimately moved to the Pantheon in 1996.

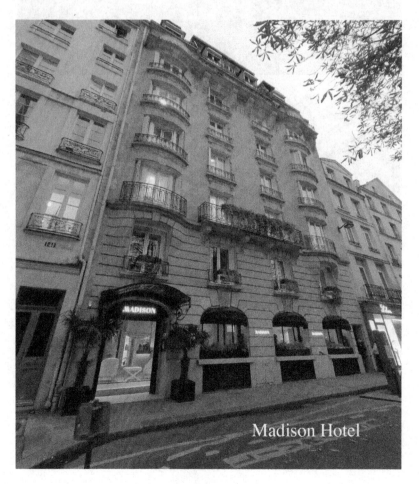

Madison Hotel

44 rue du Bac

Ministry of Culture

Paris As An Escape Destination From Racial Injustice
James Baldwin Residence:
8 rue de Vermeuil 75007 Paris

Writer James Baldwin arrived into Paris at the age of twenty-four in 1948. It was his first experience overseas and potentially an answer to a dream that he envisioned. He'd become disillusioned with his life in the United States with no foreseeable solution.

Baldwin was black, gay and poor. He carried only forty dollars in his pocket. His writings were virtually unpublished. His sole prospect in Paris consisted of the publication of his essay *Everybody's Protest Novel* in *Zero* magazine. By some means, he managed to navigate a lifestyle within the city. Baldwin would obsessively toil on his first novel *Go Tell It On The Mountain*. Paris offered him artistic freedom, camaraderie, color-blindness and models for his future fictional characters.

He settled primarily in the Saint-Germain district due to the numerous inexpensive lodgings and surrounding bars and nightclubs. The neighborhood was infused with artists and authors enabling him to disappear into work, rather than being an uncomfortable focus of attention.

He reportedly wrote for endless hours inside the Café de Flore and became intimates with the intellectual circle of Camus, de Beauvoir and Sartre. He was also known to frequent the Café Tournon and the Brasserie Lipp.

His succession of writings often evolved into moral essays targeting the eradication of bigotry and racial hatred. He unflinchingly exposed and combated these twin evils through his texts and lectures. Despite a supportive environment that he surrounded himself with, he remained as much a detached observer as later an inspiration to others.

His literary works provided him international recognition, controversy and wealth. The American Civil Rights movement offered him a kinship with other activists espousing shared ideals.

These relationships would be stolen from him. First, Medgar Evers was gunned down in 1963, Malcolm X in 1965 and finally Martin Luther King, Jr. in 1968. The succession of murder and violence became overwhelming and a radical step backwards in furthering racial tolerance and relations. Relocating to Turkey and then in 1971 to St. Paul de Vence in southern France provided him respite from his accompanying grief, depression and illness.

He would remain in the village enabling healing and cultivating local affection and acceptance. It was a calming society and environment that he had sought out his entire life. He would die there from stomach cancer on December 1, 1987. He was later buried in Hartsdale, New York. Posthumously, Baldwin's observations towards injustice remain as valid and timely as when he first unveiled them. Truth never ultimately fades from relevance.

8 rue de Vermeuil

The Second Sex and A Writer Who Transcended Labeling
Simone de Beauvoir's Residences:
11 rue Victor Schoelcher 75014 Paris
Hotel des Bains, 33 Rue Delambre, 75004 Paris
11 rue de la Bucherie, 75005 Paris
7 rue de l'Hotel Colbert, 75005 Paris

Simone de Beauvoir's written works offered women a unique perspective on activism and feminism. She wrote novels, essays, biographies, autobiographies and monographs on philosophy, social issues and politics. She has been called an *existentialist philosopher*, a label she was frequently uncomfortable with.

Her most renowned success *The Second Sex* was published in 1949. The work was her detailed analysis of women's oppression. Many consider it a foundation for contemporary feminism. Her memoirs were highly honored within literary circles expressing an unapologetic and candid appraisal of her life, her sexual identity and the challenges of maintaining a just society.

De Beauvoir first met philosopher and writer Jean-Paul Sartre during their college years. They began a romantic relationship that would evolve into a lifelong comradeship. Each significantly influenced the other's creative output and developing philosophies. She opted never to marry or have children. She preferred to write, advance her education, teach and engage in political causes.

Her relationship was sexually open with Sartre. Two notable men, Claude Lanzman and Nelson Algren shared long-term relationships with her. She lived with Lanzman between 1952 until 1959. Algren was the author of *The Man with the Golden Arm*, eventually made into a film starring Frank Sinatra about a heroin addict.

She died at the age of 78 on April 14, 1986 six years following her companion Sartre. She is buried at the Montparnasse Cemetery.

7 rue de l'Hotel Colbert

A First Time Novel and Success Elusive To A Triumphant Sequel
Francoise Sagan's Residence:
135 avenue de Suffren, 75007 Paris

Author Francoise Sagan sampled the intoxication of fame at eighteen with the publication of her novel *Bonjour Tristesse* (Hello Sadness). The story concerned the life of a young, spoiled and indulgent Cecile, her relationship with a boyfriend and her widowed father's philandering. Published in 1954, the book would earn international acclaim.

For the rest of her professional existence, Sagan would chase an elusive sequel of similar magnitude. Despite writing numerous plays, novels, song lyrics and an autobiography, she only modestly succeeded.

Her youthful success and accompanying royalties enabled her to pursue a lifestyle strewn with fast cars, drug addiction and flawed relationship with both sexes. Her destructive pace resulted in scandal and the depreciation of her work.

Her obituary self-composed succinctly capsuled her failed expectations: *Appeared in 1954 with a slender novel, Bonjour Tristesse, which created a scandal worldwide. Her death, after a life and body of work that were equally pleasant and botched, was a scandal only for herself.*

She died at the age of 69 in Calvados on September 24, 2004 following several years of declining health and a conviction for tax evasion.

Absurdism and Stolen Genius
Albert Camus Residences:
Madison Hotel: 143 Boulevard Saint-Germain, 75006 Paris
16 rue Ravignan-Hotel du Poirer, 75018 Paris
Place Emile Goudeau, 75018 Paris

During his brief forty-six years, Albert Camus remained an outsider within the literary universe. It would mirror the title of his most famous creation *L'Etranger* (The Stranger).

Many observers felt the content of the work mirrored his philosophy of *Absurdism*. He would be linked additionally with the existentialist movement, but rejected the association. He became integrated into a circle of intellectuals that included Jean-Paul Sartre, Simone de Beauvoir and Andre Breton.

He was born in 1913 in French Algeria to parents labeled *Pied-Noir* (Black Feet). The term applied to individuals of French and European descent born in Algeria during the period of French rule between 1830 until 1962. He was raised in a poor neighborhood and later studied philosophy at the University of Algiers.

He was living in Paris during the German invasion of 1940 amidst World War II. There was nowhere to escape, so he reportedly joined the French Resistance. He edited an outlawed newspaper called *Combat*.

His post-war writings would make him an international celebrity figure and lecturer. He declared himself a *moralist*, but did not fit comfortably into any specific cause. He opposed Joseph Stalin and the Soviet Union due to their totalitarianism. He stressed his preferences towards integration and multiculturalism. He remained neutral due to his pacifist beliefs during the Algerian Independence War prompting controversy and criticism from both sides.

He married twice, but had numerous extramarital affairs. He was awarded the 1957 Nobel Prize in Literature at the age of 44, the second youngest recipient ever.

Two years later at the height of his acclaim, he would be killed in a freak car accident near Sens. He was sitting in the passenger seat of a car driven by his publisher, Michel Gallimand. The vehicle swerved into a tree on an extended stretch of a national highway. Both men died in the wreckage. Gallimand's wife and daughter sitting in the back seat survived unharmed. Speculation followed that the KGB assassinated Camus due to his criticism of Soviet Union human rights abuses.

Surviving nearby the wreckage in mud was 144 pages of a handwriting manuscript called *Le Premier Homme* (The First Man). The uncompleted autobiographical novel was later transcribed by his daughter and published in 1994. Camus envisioned this work as his crowning masterpiece. Many book critics agreed citing its *physical intensity* and *uninhibited psychological* tone. They contrasted favorably this style with his normally restrained reserve from earlier novels and plays.

Madison Hotel

A Philosophical Contraction
Jean-Paul Sartre's Residences:
42 rue Bonaparte (Bombed Site), 75006 Paris
222 boulevard Raspail 75014 Paris

Jean-Paul Sartre was willing to become a martyr for his philosophical beliefs that he described as a special kind of anarchy. As an anti-colonialist during the Algerian War of Independence, he was the target of two bombing attempts. One detonated at the entrance of his apartment building.

He would become known as one of the key figures in the Existentialist movement and an intellectual defender of Marxism. He never joined the communist party.

Sartre was an extreme contradiction and a deeply flawed political propagandist.

He supported absolute freedom for individuals, but pandered to despots heading totalitarian regimes. He admired Fidel Castro, Gamal Adbel Nasser, Mao Zedong and Ernest Che Guevara. In a rare moment of objectivity, he compared Castro's persecution of homosexuals to the Nazi persecution of the Jews. He called Guevara the *most complete human being of our age*, despite the enormity of blood staining his hands. One journalist labeled him a *useful idiot* due to his generally uncritical positions.

In 1929 while attending the Ecole Normale, he first encountered Simone de Beauvoir who studied at the Sorbonne. The pair became inseparable and lifetime companions. They initiated a romantic relationship but were not monogamous. Following graduation, Sartre taught at various schools in Le Havre and then Paris.

During 1939, he was drafted into the French army where he served as a meteorologist. He was captured by German troops in 1940 and imprisoned for nine months in Nancy. He was released in April 1941 due to poor health and returned to Paris where he began a teaching position at the Lycee Pasteur. In October he was given a position that was previously held by a Jewish teacher at the Lycee Condorcet. Under Vichy government laws, Jewish teachers were forbidden to teach.

During this period, he participated in the founding of an underground organization *Socialisme et Liberte* (Socialism and Liberty) with several writers and students including de Beauvoir.

Sartre would evolve into a playwright, novelist, screenwriter, political activist, biographer and literary critic. His most regarded work *L'Etre et le Neant* (Being and Nothingness) was published in 1943. Many sources credit his work as having influenced sociology and critical theory. He and de Beauvoir would challenge the cultural and social assumptions attached with their middle class upbringings.

Their attempts at defining *authentic living* became popular literary works championed by its own elitist following. One of his most enduring quotes from his writings became *L'enfer, c'est les autres* (Hell is other people).

Consistent with his political beliefs, Sartre reserved the majority of his criticism for Americanism, French governmental policies, capitalism and democracy. The freedom that he was allowed in France was an irony to the fascist governments that he embraced.

He appeared oblivious to his ability to freely publish his work without censorship or travel liberally without restraint.

Sartre maintained a simplistic lifestyle with few possessions. His life was devoted towards his writings and causes, however questionable. When he was arrested during the May

1968 protests, President Charles de Gaulle expediently pardoned him and commented: *you don't arrest Voltaire.*

He won the 1964 Nobel Prize in Literature despite claiming that he attempted to refuse the award. He commented that he always declined official honors citing that a writer *should not allow himself to be turned into an institution.*

Whether willing participant or not, Sartre and Existentialism became institutions of thought and lifestyle. His café liaisons with de Beauvoir and their circle of intellectuals at Les Deux Magots became legendary. He suffered from poor health during his later years aggravated by his chain smoking, amphetamine use and high blood pressure.

As his physical condition deteriorated and he sensed that he was near death, he confided to a writer about his modified perception of God. He was previously regarded as an Atheist.

He stated in an interview: *I do not feel that I am the product of chance, a speck of dust in the universe, but someone who was expected, prepared, prefigures. In short, a being whom only a Creator could put here.* Simone de Beauvoir would reveal her contempt with his altered viewpoint by stating: *How should one explain this senile act of a turncoat?*

He died on April 15, 1980 at the age of 74 from pulmonary edema. He would be buried four days later at Montparnasse Cemetery. An estimated 50,000 mourners accompanied his entourage to the burial site. Simone de Beauvoir would die six years later. Despite their differences at the conclusion of his life, the couple would be buried together.

42 rue Bonaparte

TWISTED TOUR GUIDES.com

performance arts

Moliere Follows A Circuitous Exile To Sustain His Voice and Creative Expression
Moliere's Birthplace (Demolished):
96 rue Saint-Honore, 75001 Paris
Moliere Residence and Death Site:
2 rue de Richelieu, 75001 Paris
Moliere Fountain:
28 rue Moliere, 75001 Paris
Final Performance (Theatre du Palais-Royal):
40 rue de Richelieu, 75001 Paris
Comedie-Francaise:
2 rue de Richelieu, 75001 Paris

Jean-Baptiste Poquelin lived a varied, contentious and distinctive lifetime that mirrored his most renowned theatrical productions. Even in death, Poquelin, better known as Moliere remained in character, collapsing on stage and then dying afterwards while performing *Le Malade Imaginaire* (The Imaginary Invalid).

Poquelin was raised as a royal insider as his father had purchased a prestigious valet title within the court of Louis XIII. He would assume the identical post in 1641 affording him access to innumerable lucrative contacts. He studied to become a provincial attorney in Orleans, but abruptly abandoned this path at 21 to pursue a lifelong career on the stage.

His intermingling with the nobility and legal studies would service his future writings providing him critical and intimate insight.

His first performance collective involved the founding of the theatre troupe *Illustre Theatre* with actress Madeleine Bejart. She added her siblings to the entourage. The troupe failed financially and he ended up in debtor's prison. During this period he changed his name to Moliere to spare his father the shame of association. Actors during this era of were considered immoral individuals and not allowed to be buried within sacred ground.

Moliere traveled a performance circuit outside of Paris for twelve years following his imprisonment. This period sharpened his writing craft, acting dexterity and penchant for mockery. His writing style and performances endeared him to audiences, but often fractured friendships and relationships with the subjects and subject matter that he portrayed.

By 1658, Moliere's theatrical fame prompted his return to Paris and the critical capital audiences. His first performance was before Louis XIV at the Louvre that was available to rent as a venue. Moliere's satirical farces and musical comedies made uncomfortable viewing for many of the royal and aristocratic viewing audience as they were bluntly lampooned by his characterizations.

He was often spared the venom from his legion of enemies and critics due to his patronage by Philippe I, the Duke of Orleans and the king's brother.
At the height of Moliere's renowned, he navigated a taught line between social tolerance and censorship for his works. The higher his professional rise ascended, the riskier his status wavered.

The effects of Moliere's youthful imprisonment affected his health for the balance of his adult life. He suffered from chronic pulmonary tuberculosis that culminated in his death on February 17, 1693. He collapsed on stage during an extreme fit of coughing and hemorrhaging. The play was a condemnation of medical practices and quackery employed during that era. Moliere insisted on completing the performance. He was taken home semi-conscious where he continued to bleed profusely.

His prior antagonism with the clergy prompted two priests to refuse to administer him last rites. A third arrived too late and he expired at the age of 51. Actors were still not permitted proper funerals, but Moliere's widow Armande appealed to the King to permit a service at night. The King consented and his body was buried in a portion of the cemetery reserved for unbaptized infants. In 1817, his body would be exhumed and transferred to Pere Lachaise Cemetery.

He would be credited with writing 85 plays and numerous collaborative projects with his peers. Despite his frequent conflicts with authorities, rivals and conventional thinkers, his public success would never diminished. The variety, magnitude and depth of his plays have been widely translated internationally. His observations regarding human nature remain relevant presented in contemporary productions.

The Comedie-Francaise would be founded in August 1680 by the decree of Louis XIV seven years following Moliere's death. The organization is the oldest theatre company in the world. The theatre has also been known as the *Theatre de la Republique*, but more commonly as *La Maison de Moliere*. He is considered the supreme standard for French acting and his influential shadow has never been extinguished.

Comedie Francaise Theatre

2 rue de Richelieu

Moliere Fountain

Theatre du Palais-Royal

A Lifetime Of Contradictions Noteworthy By Classic Creations
Pierre Beaumarchais Residence (Hotel Amelot de Bisseuil):
47 rue du Temple, 75004 Paris

Pierre-Augustin Caron de Beaumarchais is best known for his three Figaro plays entitled *The Barber of Seville*, *The Marriage of Figaro* and *The Guilty Mother*. His sixty-seven years compacted numerous overlapping vocations including diplomat, spy, inventor, financier and musician.

He was born within the lower class, but earned a great fortune in his lifetime without expending his own money or holding an official title.

Beaumarchais was the name of a small estate owned by his wife. He was freely admitted into the highest society of King Louis XV, but amongst the earliest promoters of the revolution that dethroned Louis XVI. He lobbied the French government vigorously on behalf of the American revolutionary cause. He personally oversaw the transfer of covert aid from the French and Spanish governments to the rebel colonies.

He was described unflatteringly as *vain, conceited, petulant and immoral*. He lost his fortune upon returning from Holland in the midst of the revolution. He became an enthusiastic Bonapartist. He died suddenly on the morning of May 18, 1799 from a stroke although rampant speculation suggested suicide.

The Pleasures Of Paris Terminate A Composer's Productivity
Gioachino Rossini's Residence:
2 rue de la Chaussee d'Antin 75009 Paris

Gioachino Rossini opted to enjoy the pleasures and platitudes derived from a prolific start in opera composition within Italy. He was responsible for thirty-four completed operas and seemingly destined to compose significantly more. At thirty-one, in his prime and at the peak of popularity, he and his wife arrived in Paris during November 1823. He was greeted as a celebrity and fawned over. A fresh generation of opera enthusiasts embraced him.

Initially, several of his classics were performed. Paris was the center of the opera universe. Once established, he enthusiastically composed *Il Viaggio a Reims* (The Journey to Reims) to honor the coronation of King Charles X. He had ambitions of modifying his popular style by injecting greater intensity and focusing more importance with the role of the chorus. Over the next five years he would compose three new works, one that had been modified from an earlier composition. His working gait slowed from a gallop to a leisurely stroll.

Rossini reveled in the offered pleasures during his residence in Paris, overindulging and adding significant girth. His wife discovered the joys of shopping while nagging him incessantly over being left unoccupied.

In August 1829, Rossini premiered the *Guillaume Tell* (William Tell) opera that was received in Paris with great acclaim. A critic credited the composition of the middle act to God. The work pursued popular themes of nationalism and liberty. It was planned to be the first of five new operas performed at the Paris Opera House. Following the 1830

Revolution, the new government put Rossini's contract on hold.

Rossini responded to their symbolic gesture by announcing his retirement from theatre composition. Some sources suggested that he'd become increasingly lazy, while others citied jealousy with popular German composer Giacomo Meyerbeer and/or increasing hostility towards his pace and completed works.

Whatever motivated his decision, he never rescinded it. At thirty-seven, he felt that he had reached his summit. He composed minimally afterwards, published nothing and concentrated on religious themes. He preferred to savor his wealth and spoils for the next 38 years. He entertained and hosted sumptuous dinners for the greats of the musical and literary world. He would remarry in 1846 following the death of this first wife the year before.

He returned to Italy briefly to reside, but as his own health deteriorated, he returned to Paris in April 1855. The move reinvigorated his *joie de vivre*. He shifted living quarters between his apartment near the opera house and a villa that he had constructed in Passy on the periphery of Paris. He and his new wife established a famous salon at both locations for Saturday evenings. For ten years, they continued the gatherings until two months before his death from colon cancer on November 13, 1864. He was originally buried in Pere Lachaise Cemetery, but twenty-three years later his remains would be moved and be permanently interned in a Florence, Italy cemetery.

2 rue de la Chaussée d'Antin

A Delicate Bloom Flourishes and Prematurely Withers
Frederick Chopin's Residences:
5 rue Tronchet, 75008 Paris
5 rue de la Chaussee d'Antin, 75009 Paris
38 rue de la Chaussee d'Antin, 75009 Paris
9 rue St. Lazare, 75009 Paris
12 Place Vendome (Death Site), 75001 Paris

Polish pianist Frederick Chopin arrived in Paris on October 5, 1831 after bypassing Italy, his originally intended destination. Violent political unrest had created a dangerous situation within the country.

As a child prodigy, Chopin had completed his musical education and established a reputation within his country. Upon his arrival in France, he would never return to Poland.

He quickly integrated himself into the Parisian cultural society and became acquainted with the city's great talents and artistic celebrities. By the end of 1832, Chopin had integrated himself amongst the musical elite. His published musical compositions earned him a substantial income. The majority of his live performances were done within the intimate atmosphere of artistic salons. He reportedly would give only 30 public performances, which he never enjoyed.

One of the most influential relationships he cultivated during his life in France was with writer Aurore Dupin (George Sand). Although initially repulsed by her non-conventional appearance, he grew dependent upon her strength, generosity and artistic support. He composed some of his most memorable works during their troubled relationship. They severed their relationship towards the end of his life and he became financially supported by another admirer Jane Stirling. She arranged for him to visit Scotland in 1848.

Chopin suffered from poor health throughout the majority of

his adult life. He died in Paris during 1849 at the age of 39. The cause was presumed to be pericarditis aggravated by chronic bouts of tuberculosis.

9 rue St. Lazare

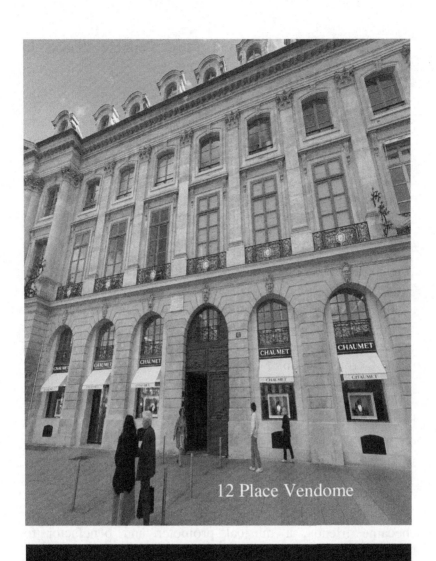

12 Place Vendome

TWISTED TOUR ⟨UIDES.com

The Reputed Greatest and Most Popular Pianist In Europe
Franz Liszt's Residences:
13 rue du Mail, 75002 Paris

Franz Liszt arrived in Paris during 1823 with his parents already an acclaimed musical prodigy in Central Europe. In Vienna, Ludwig van Beethoven has christened his ascent with a kiss on the forehead. His initial piano concerts would be enthusiastically received within Paris' cultural community.

During the 1830s and 1840s, Liszt toured Europe and developed a strong female following due to his handsome appearance. His concerts broadened beyond upper class audiences and elevated him into a stardom and popularity not achieved by his predecessors. The Hungarian born Liszt was classified as one of the most important representatives of the New German School.

His diverse compositions would influence numerous forward aspiring artists. His stylistic symphonic poem, thematic transformations and experimental musical form would be credited with stimulating innovations in harmony. Many observers still consider him the finest piano player in history.

His popularity did not alienate him from his colleagues. He became friends, a musical promoter and benefactor to contemporary peers including Frederic Chopin, Richard Wagner, Gioachino Rossini, Hector Berlioz and Robert Schumann. He extended his friendship to literary figures including Alfred de Musset, Alexandre Dumas, George Sand and Victor Hugo.

He shared an extended relationship with the Countess Marie d'Agoult, six years his senior. She left her husband in 1835 to join Liszt in Geneva. He taught at the newly founded Geneva Conservatory where he wrote a manual of piano technique and contributed essays for the Paris based *Review*. For the next four years, they traveled throughout Italy and Switzerland inspiring the composer to create some of his finest and most memorable works.

The couple had three children together. One who would become the future wife of French Prime Minister Emile Ollivier and another the wife of composer Richard Wagner. Agoult and he never married and following their rupture, she would return to Paris and establish a famed salon under the pen name, Daniel Stern.

The 1860s became a turbulent and sad period in Liszt's life. He lost his one son and daughter to their early deaths. He spent the majority of his time living in Rome, Weimar and Budapest. As his health declined during the 1880s, he suffered a grave injury when he fell down a flight of stairs as a Weimar hotel on July 2, 1881. He continued to be dogged by numerous ailments including heart disease, asthma, insomnia and dropsy.

He gradually descended into desolation, despair and a preoccupation with death. He would die in Bayreuth, Germany on July 31, 1886 at the age of 74 from pneumonia.

A Maestro Fleeing Debts and Seeking Operatic Inspiration
Richard Wagner's Residences:
14 rue Jacob 75006 Paris
Hotel de Quai Voltaire, 19 Quai Voltaire, 75007 Paris
3 rue D'Aumale, 75009 Paris

Composer Richard Wagner determined to seek his fortune in Paris during September 1839. The city was considered the capital of the operatic world. Nothing would be easy both entering the country or throughout his first three-year residence.

His accumulating debts had cost him his passport in Riga, Latvia. He and his wife Minna were smuggled across the border into Prussian Konigsberg. They booked passage on a ship that should have required eight days to Paris. Instead, the boat docked in London as foul weather, his wife's foreboding and stormy seas would extend the trip to three and a half weeks.

Arriving in Paris, the operatic world was dominated by the music of German composer Giacomo Meyerbeer, one of Wagner's detested rivals. Part of Wagner's hatred stemmed from his growing anti-Semitism. This disgust extended to already successful composer Felix Mendelssohn who had lost or mislaid Wagner's Symphony in C major from 1832 sent to him in hopes of a performance.

During his time in Paris, Wagner completed his opera *Rienzi* and managed to arrange a future performance at the Dresden Court Theatre. He began work on *The Flying Dutchman*, a plot based on the writings of Heinrich Heine. He would depart Paris for Dresden where he would reside for the next six years. The move became an epiphany for the artist. He claimed that upon viewing the Rhine River with *hot tears in my eyes*, he swore *eternal fidelity to my German fatherland*.

Rienzi was a great success in Dresden. Wagner mixed within premier artistic circles. His socialist political views abruptly ended his welcome. A May 1849 political uprising resulted in his fleeing Dresden. Following a stopover in Paris, he then established residence in exile in Zurich for nine years.

Wagner's second and final residence in Paris starting in 1859 was motivated by his overseeing preparation and production of *Tannhauser*. The performances staged during 1861 became a catastrophe. Protests launched by the conservative Jockey Club targeted his reversal of the ballet featured in the first act rather than the traditional second act. The opera was withdrawn following the third performance and he left shortly afterwards. He would settle in Biebrich along the Rhine River. Although critically panned, he cultivated an appreciative admirer in poet Charles Baudelaire who wrote an appreciative and favorable review of *Tannhauser*.

19 Quai Voltaire

14 rue Jacob

3 rue d'Aumale

A Maestro Better Known For Conducting Than Composing

Hector Berlioz's Residence:
31 rue de Londres (Demolished), 75009 Paris
96 rue Richelieu, 75002 Paris
4 rue de Calais (Death Site), 75009 Paris
Berlioz's Sculptural Monument:
Square Berlioz. 75009 Paris

Louis-Hector Berlioz became one of France's greatest Romantic era conductors during the mid 19th century. He was oldest son of a small town doctor from the Isere region. Although expected to follow his father's career direction into medicine, he rebelled. Following a brief attendance at a Parisian medical college, he informed his family that he would pursue music as a profession.

Throughout his professional career, his independent, headstrong and reputed tyrannical behavior created conflict within the traditional Paris music establishment. In 1830, he won the prestigious *Prix de Rome*, the highest honor in French music.

He only achieved marginal success as a composer with three completed operas and four larger-scale works he credited as symphonies. He increasingly shifted his energies towards conducting and became sought out internationally. He received his highest acclaim in Germany, Britain and Russia, both as a conductor and composer.

He augmented his earnings with his music journalistic writings. Many were preserved in his book *Treatise on Instrumentation* published in 1844. This work was considered highly influential during the latter 19th and 20th centuries. His own composition admirers gradually diminished. His most performed work remains the *Symphonie Fantasique*.

Berlioz returned to Paris in 1867 following a performance tour of St. Petersburg and Moscow. He hoped that the concerts might revive his failing spirits following the news of his son's death that year in Havana, Cuba from yellow fever.

The performances were widely praised, but failed to improve his health. A recuperative visit to Nice was shortened abruptly due to his fall on shoreline rocks after a probable stroke. He returned to Paris to convalesce, but continued his decline expiring on March 8, 1869 at the age of 65.

31 rue de Londres

4 rue de Calais

A Benevolent Composer of the Dance Parisian
Jacques Offenbach Residence:
8, boulevard des Capucines, 75002 Paris

Jacques Offenbach was born in Cologne, then part of Prussia in 1819. At six, his father taught him to play the violin and at nine, he took up the cello and began composing songs and dances. During his teenage years, his father sent he and his older brother to Paris to study. Despite their age and nationality, both brothers were admitted following an audition before Luigi Cherubini, the director of the Paris Conservatoire.

Jacques was bored by academic study and left the school after only a single year. He earned temporary employment performing before securing a permanent position with the Opera-Comique the following year as a cellist.

His reputation as a virtuoso and genius at composition steadily grew. He undertook tours of France and Germany and was engaged to perform with the most famous musicians and audiences of the era.

He would convert to Catholicism from his Jewish origins to marry Herminie d'Alcain. Their marriage endured lifelong and was perceived as happy despite periodic extramarital dalliances on his part.

He gradually shifted away from performing and concentrated on composition. He composed nearly 100 operettas between the 1850s into the 1870 leaving one famous score *The Tales of Hoffman* unfinished. He became a profound influence on future composers including Johann Strauss Jr. and Arthur Sullivan. His works were and have remained continually revived over the past two centuries.

Offenbach was renowned for his abundance of long dark hair, which he wore hanging down his back. He earned a reputation for hospitality and generosity towards performers and craftsmen suffering from ill fortune and poverty.

During the final decade of his life, his music briefly fell out of favor in Paris. He had become associated with the Second Empire of Napoleon III who would abdicate. He was granted French citizenship and the Legion d'Honneur. During the Franco-Prussian War in 1870, his imperial German connections and Prussian birth tarnished his reputation. His music remained popular in Vienna and London. By the time of his death in 1880, a revival had already begun of his works. He died suddenly from gout on a day that he had attended a reading of the *Cabaret du Lilas* for the Varieties. He was 61-years-old.

8 boulevard des Capucines

The Devine Goddess of International Theatre
Sarah Bernhardt's Birth Site:
5 rue de L'Ecole-de-Medicine, 75006 Paris
Sarah Bernhardt's Residences:
16 rue Auber (Demolished), 75009 Paris
56 boulevard Pereire, 75017 Paris

Sarah Bernhardt entered the world within the Latin Quarter. She was the illegitimate daughter of Dutch courtesan Judith Bernard and the presumed son of a wealthy Le Havre merchant. Her father's name was never officially recorded. Her mother traveled frequently due to her profession and spent minimal time with her daughter during her formation. She placed her in the care with a nurse in Brittany and then a cottage in a Paris suburb.

As her mother rose to the upper echelon of Paris courtesans, Sarah began acting in theatrical performances at her boarding school. Her mother consorted with politicians, bankers, generals and writers. Several of her patrons were well placed government officials.

Bernhardt gravitated towards performance both on the stage and throughout her life. She was accepted to the Paris Conservatory despite an unconventional audition. In her memoirs, she indicated that her schooling taught her diction, grand and sublime gestures and simplicity. Her two years with the Comedie-Francaise were disappointing, so she bolted to the popular Gymnase Theatre that proved an even a worst disaster.

She traveled to Brussels with letters of introduction from famous writer and friend Alexander Dumas, She was admitted to the highest levels of society where she met aristocrat Henri, the hereditary Prince of Ligne at a masked ball. The couple consummated a brief affair that resulted in a son named Maurice. Henri's uncle wanted no family affiliation with the unknown actress and the future Prince denied any responsibility for the child. Once Bernhardt became famous he would regret his decision. His son Maurice by then had no interest in assuming his surname.

Aware that her career had stalled and her future appeared even bleaker supporting herself with a son, Bernhardt resumed acting. She supported them both by playing minor roles and understudies at the Porte Saint-Martin theatre, a popular melodrama venue. In 1866, she auditioned before the director of the Odeon Theatre. She was accepted and initially cast in highly stylized frivolous comedies.

Gradually her roles and technique improved. Her breakthrough performance arrived in 1868 with a revival of *Kean* written by her consistent supporter Dumas. Her performance raised both her professional esteem and salary. Triumph was followed by further success and a six-year tenure with the Odeon.

Throughout her career, Bernhardt became renowned for blurring the distinction between performance and reality. She acted the roles of Hamlet, Phedre and Cleopatra as though they'd been written exclusively for her. She would be called the *Golden Voice* by writer Victor Hugo and *La Divine* by her international audiences.

She became one of the first touring superstars of the theatre first conquering London and United States stages. She would extend her exposure worldwide with performances in South and Central America, the Middle East, Scandinavia, Russia, Australia and New Zealand. There were few destinations that she missed during her lifetime. Her performances were consistently sold out. Her earnings were arguably the highest of any global performer of her era.

She required immeasurable income due to her traveling performance expenses, gambling debts and extravagances that kept her perpetually in debt. She was incapable of saving money or spending prudently. In one instance when she had nearly paid off her obligations, she impulsively purchased a lion cub.

She would become one of the first actresses to star in silent motion pictures beginning in December 1895. She made other artists famous including Alphonse Mucha, who designed her distinctively ornate promotional posters. He would ultimately become one of the most sought after commercial artists during the Art Nouveau era.

La Divine would embrace several lifetimes within her own solitary span. Even an amputation of her right leg to the hip in 1915 due to gangrene couldn't slow her career. The injury had resulted from a stage fall years before in Brazil. She refused an artificial leg, crutches or a wheelchair. She would perform seated, or supported by a prop with her leg hidden. She often recited poetry or her acting lines that did not require much movement.

She worked up until her death. She was in the process of rehearsing a new 1922 production by playwright Sacha Guitry called *Un Sujet de Roman*. On the evening of the dress rehearsal, she collapsed and remained in a coma for an hour.

She recuperated for several months. As her condition improved, she began preparations for a film and play paying extravagantly. She had become so frail that she could no longer travel. A film set was constructed inside her apartment with background scenery, lights and camera.

On March 21, 1923, she collapsed once again during pre-production. This time she expired three days later in the arms of her son. Her death at 78 was caused by kidney failure. At her request, her funeral was conducted at Saint-Francois-de-Sales the next day with an estimated 30,000 people in attendance. An enormous crowd followed her procession to Pere Lachaise Cemetery where she was buried.

There have been many celebrated actresses throughout the history of theatre. It is unlikely one has or ever will become as influential or as well traveled as Sarah Bernhardt. From the humblest of origins, her talent and appeal elevated her into a singular stratum of deity.

5 rue de l'Ecole-de-Medicine

The Grand Finale Crowning A Career of Consistent Disappointment
George Bizet's Residence:
22 rue Douai, 75009 Paris

For the entirety of his adult life, George Bizet relentlessly pursued fame and recognition as a composer. He enjoyed a brilliant student career at the Conservatory of Paris winning numerous prizes including the most prestigious *Prix de Rome* in 1857. His works following his return from Rome to Paris were generally ignored or out of sync with the prevalent times.

He attempted numerous theatrical projects during the 1860s. The majority were abandoned. As his career steadily leveled, he earned his livelihood by arranging and transcribing the music of others. During the Franco-Prussian War of 1870-71, he served in the National Guard. He returned to Paris with his presumed appointment as chorus-master of the Opera confirmed. Hector Salomon would assume the position.

The reason was never officially divulged. Speculation persisted that Bizet protested the director's closing of Ernest Reyer's opera *Erostrate* following only two performances.

In May 1872, his one-act opera *Djamileh* opened and closed after only 11 performances at the Opera-Comique. During that summer, his incidental music to Alphonse Daudet's play *L'Arlesienne* was dismissed by many critics as *too complex* for popular tastes. He began work on composing *Don Rodrigue*, an adaptation of the El Cid story. The opera house burned to the ground during the late evening of October 28. The production was shelved.

Discouragement, ill fortune and timing had plagued Bizet's professional career since its promising beginning. Towards the late 1860s, he began suffering from a recurrent throat complaint. His heavy smoking worsened these severe bouts of what he perceived was throat angina.

Between June 1872 and 1874, he launched into an operatic project based on author Prosper Merimee's short novel *Carmen*. Adolphe de Leuven, the co-director of the Opera-Comique vehemently opposed the production due to the themes of betrayal and murder. He perceived the plot would offend audiences. His resignation in early 1874 cleared the path for the production planned to originally begin rehearsals in October.

Bizet was pleased with the overall outcome of *Carmen*. He noted: *I have written a work that is all clarity and vivacity, full of colour and melody.*

Bizet had lined up his ideal Carmen in the form of famed mezzo-soprano Celestine Galli-Marie. Rumor floated that the pair engaged in a brief affair as Bizet was living apart from his wife. During that period, he would father a daughter with his housekeeper.

Rehearsals unleashed unforeseen complications. The orchestra had difficulty with the score announcing some portions *unplayable*. The chorus declared that much of the music was impossible to sing. They bitterly complained over having to act their parts on stage. Customarily they stood in a chorus line. The management of the Opera-Comique wanted to tone down the perceived improper actions in the script. Bizet and his core singers refused to compromise.

The opening night was delayed until March 3, 1875. Ironically, that morning Bizet was appointed as a Chevalier of the Legion of Honour. His wife would be unable to attend due to an abscess in her right eye. The first performance extended to four and a half hours and the final act did not start until after midnight.

Most of the press reviews were negative. Composer Charles Gounod maintained after the performance that Bizet had plagiarized his work. Public reaction was documented as *lukewarm*.

Bizet convinced himself that *Carmen* would become yet another commercial fiasco. Despite his Legion of Honour designation, he considered himself a failure.

Depressed, he fell ill in May and at the end of the month traveled to his holiday home at Bougival, ten miles outside of Paris. On May 31, he went for a swim in the Seine River and reportedly began feeling better. The next day, he endured pain and high fever followed by an apparent heart attack. During

the early hours of June 3, coincidentally his wedding anniversary, he suffered a second and fatal heart attack. He was 36 years old.

Bizet's premature passing left his legacy in chaos. Many of his manuscripts became lost. Other composers stole some of his music scores creating their own modifications. Few of his existing works were immediately performed in the years following his death.

During the beginning of the twentieth century, Bizet and particularly *Carmen* would begin to find a receptive audience. Some music critics suggested that with a longer lifespan, he would have revolutionized French opera. With genius, there is rarely a gauge to measure unrealized potential.

22 rue Douai

The Symphonic Musical Maestro of Finland
Jean Sibelius' Residence:
Hotel de Quai Voltaire, 19 Quai Voltaire, 75007 Paris

Finnish musician Jean Sibelius is widely regarded as his country's greatest composer. His music became an important part of establishing a national identity following its independence struggle from Russia. His set of seven symphonies along with his other renowned works remains performed internationally. Most are inspired by nature and Nordic mythology themes.

Paris became an influential venue for him during his February 1900 European orchestral tour promoting a revised version of his First Symphony. Critics were highly favorable of his work bringing the composer his first taste of international acclaim. In 1906, he resided in Paris during the early part of the year. The stay proved uneventful and he relocated to Ainola (Jarvenpaa) in southern Finland. His major work during that residence became *Pohjola's Daughter*.

Three years later he would return to Paris followed by Berlin after a near-death scare. He had a tumor surgically removed from his throat. After the operation, he vowed to abstain from smoking and drinking permanently. The promise would remain unfulfilled. His last recorded major stay in Paris was in 1911 when he arrived to view a performance of Richard Strauss's *Salome*.

He spent the next decade touring internationally to widespread approval and composing some of his most memorable works. He continued his overindulgence with food and drink. The combination stimulated his output. By 1926, Sibelius increase in alcohol consumption stymied his musical production and social activities. He had developed a severe tremor and self-medicated by drinking, which reduced the symptoms. For the last three decades of his life, he would compose only minor regarded works.

His most blatant character blemish came in 1935 with his acceptance of the Geothe Medal from the German Nazi regime. A certificate signed by Adolf Hitler accompanied the award honoring his 70th birthday. Alarmed by the threat of communism and a deep-rooted hatred of Russia, Sibelius advocated that Finnish soldiers march alongside German forces during the invasion of the Soviet Union on June 22, 1941. His bargain with the devil conveniently neglected references to the German atrocities with the genocide of the Jewish population.

On the evening of September 20, 1957, Sibelius died of a brain hemorrhage at the age of 91 at his property in Ainola. He had long before retreated to the countryside, rarely visiting Helsinki. His absence from the limelight and music industry commentary became mythological and was called the *silence of Jarvenpaa*. He was honored with a state funeral and buried in the garden of Ainola.

19 Quai Voltaire

A Blithe Spirit Capriciously Flittering Through Tragedies
Isadora Duncan's Residence/Studios:
Hotel Biron, 77 rue de Varenne, 75007 Paris
9 rue Delambre, 75014 Paris
Performance Venue: Theatre de la Gaite
3-5 rue Papin, 75003 Paris

Dancer Isadora Duncan was already an international star when she rented space at the Hotel Biron in Paris. The early eighteenth century town house was used between 1820 and 1904 for the teachings and worship by the Society of the Sacred Heart of Jesus. In July 1904, the society was dissolved, the sisters evicted, and the property placed in the hands of a receiver.

The following year, the estate was put up for sale and while awaiting a buyer, tenants were allowed to occupy the property. Isadora Duncan rented space between 1909 and 1913 along with other notable artists including Jean Cocteau and Henri Matisse. Auguste Rodin would ultimately occupy the ground floor that would later become the Musee Rodin.

Duncan toured Europe extensively performing and lecturing while cultivating a reputation as a passionate and unconventional spirit. Her romantic liaisons became chaotic when she engaged in an affair during December 1904 with actor and designer Edward Gordon Craig in Berlin. The couple had a daughter in September 1906. Her Grunewald dance school closed in 1908 and she returned to Paris.

During one of her performances at the Parisian Gaite-Lyrique Theatre, she encountered Eugene Singer backstage. Singer was a wealthy heir to the Singer sewing machine empire. As his own marriage was in the process of crumbling, he became her lover and financial benefactor. The couple shared incompatible personalities. Both were accustomed to having their caprices accommodated. He was not an artist and could not share Duncan's creative vision. She would have a son by him on May 1, 1910.

Their shared bliss would turn to grief three years later while they met for lunch in Paris. A chauffeur was driving her two children home with their governess. Their vehicle stalled on a slope. The driver exited to crank the engine. The car began to roll downhill before he could get back inside. The vehicle accelerated before crossing Boulevard Bourdon and plunging over a grassy knoll into the Seine River. Frantic efforts to save the passengers were futile. All three drowned.

Duncan's grief became insupportable. She sought out a young Italian lover shortly afterwards to impregnate her. They succeeded but the infant died in August 1914. In November, she would sail to New York City as World War I commenced. She returned financially destitute after traveling throughout Europe and South America. Singer bailed her out financially.

Singer's inability to understand or appreciate her unconventional dance doomed their relationship. He offered to buy her Madison Square Garden. She refused and their relationship terminated. He divorced his wife and married a senior nurse at a military hospital. During the week of her rupture with Singer, the Russian Revolution ignited. She relocated to Moscow for two years sympathetic to the revolutionary cause. Her stay resulted in an abbreviated marriage to Russian poet Sergei Esenin. His alcoholism and violent behavior darkened the union. He would be hospitalized and die in a mental institution.

Duncan returned to Paris and began composing her memoirs. Singer continued to financially support her. Her own life would end bizarrely on September 14, 1927 in Nice. The scarf that she was wearing got caught in the wheels of a moving car strangling her. Her ashes would be buried in Pere Lachaise cemetery.

Symbol of the Roaring Twenties and Civil Rights Activist
Josephine Baker's Performance Venues:
Theatre des Champs-Elysee, 15 Avenue Montaigne, 75008
Folies Bergere, 32 rue Richer, 75009 Paris
Casino de Paris, 16 rue de Clicy, 75009
Bobino Music Hall, 20 rue de la Gaite, 75014 Paris
Le Carrousel, 40 rue Pierre Fontaine, 75009 Paris
Josephine Baker's Funeral:
L'Eglise de la Madeleine
Place de la Madeleine, 75008 Paris

Josephine Baker refused to accept the restrictive conditions of southern American Jim Crow laws and segregation. She renowned her American citizenship in 1937 following her brief marriage to French industrialist Jean Lion. She would become a French national and sing in her popularly recorded song that her two loves were *my country and Paris*. At the peak of her fame, she refused to perform before segregated audiences in the United States.

She was born and raised in St. Louis, but dropped out of school. She drifted between waitressing, street corner dancing, homelessness and finally marriage at thirteen. The marriage lasted less than a year and at fifteen she remarried. She left that husband when her vaudeville troupe was booked into New York City. She began to experience modest success while dancing in the chorus that enabled her to sail for Paris in September 1925 at the age of 19.

She became an instant sensation opening on October 2nd at the *Theatre des Champs Elysee*. Her erotic dancing style nearly nude and singing onstage captivated audiences. She followed up that success with a brief tour of European cities. She abruptly severed that engagement and returned to Paris in 1926 to star at the *Folies Bergere*. Her act included her pet cheetah that she'd named *Chiquita*. The cheetah, adorned with a diamond collar, frequently fled the stage during her performances terrorizing the musicians and audience.

The timing of Baker's public emergence was opportune. African influenced visual art was in vogue. Her carefree attitude and outgoing personality ideally symbolized the *Jazz Age* and the *Roaring Twenties*. She vaulted into international stardom and endorsed various licensed beauty products including gels and cosmetics that enabled her distinctive appearance. She assimilated effortlessly into French culture and would appear in numerous films that had success only within Europe. Her comic stage presence was enhanced by her loose-limbed athleticism and feigned clumsiness.

During World War II, she left Paris and relocated to her home that she named the *Chateau des Milandes* in the Dordogne. She clandestinely housed individuals anxious to help the *Free French* effort led by General Charles de Gaulle and reportedly supplied them with visas. Her continued performing enabling her a pretext to travel freely around Europe and also visit neutral countries. She assisted with the French counterintelligence and resistance movements with her access to embassies and social gatherings of German, Italian and Japanese high-ranking officials. Post war, she was honored by the highest French military commendations for her espionage activities.

During 1950s, Baker enthusiastically supported the American Civil Rights Movement. Her outspoken views against racism and segregation frequently cost her bookings and income. Her uncompromising perspective, public statements and racy past sometimes made her controversial even to proponents of the cause. She was frequently labeled in the media as a *communist*. The resulting fallout was that she was denied an American work visa for nearly a decade. She was the sole female speaker during Martin Luther King Jr.'s *March on Washington* in 1963.

Baker lived consistently with her multiracial philosophy by adopting eleven children of different ethnicities and religions. They entertained paying visitors to her chateau. She had numerous relationships and would marry four times. She had one stillborn child of her own in 1941.

Her self-described *Rainbow Tribe* traveled with her throughout France during her performances. The toll of financially supporting such an enormous family compelled her to perform until the end of her life. She lost her chateau in 1968 due to her accumulating and unpaid debts.

Her final performance was conducted at the Bobino Music Hall in Paris. The performance entitled *Josephine a Bobino 1975* was a retrospective of her show business career. Her single April 8th show drew a sold-out attendance and generated rave reviews. Four days later, she suffered a cerebral hemorrhage while lying in bed reading her reviews. She slipped away peacefully at a local hospital at the age of 68. She was honored with full French military honors and a 21-gun salute at the L'Eglise de la Madeleine, attracting a reported 20,000 mourners. She was buried at the Cemetery of Monaco.

40 rue Pierre Fontaine

Eglise de la Madeleine

TWISTED TOUR ЯUIDES.COM

A Fragile Singing Sparrow Navigating The Brutalities of Life
Edith Piaf's Residences:
72 rue de Belleville (Birthplace), 75020 Paris
Grand Hotel de Clermont, 18 rue Veron, 75018 Paris
Hotel Au Clair de Lune (No Longer in Existence), rue Andre-Antoine, 75018 Paris
L'Etoile de Kleber, 3rd Floor: 4 rue Paul Valery, 75016 Paris
5 rue Crespin du Gast, 75011 Paris

Edith Piaf is typically the first name mentioned when the subject of renowned French female singers is raised. She developed an international following during her career. Her life was a succession of tragedies culminating in the ultimate deterioration of her health.

She was born Edith Giovanna Gassion in the Bellevue neighborhood of Paris on December 19, 1915. World War I British nurse Edith Cavell was the inspiration for her first name. Cavell was executed two months before Edith's birth for assisting French soldiers escaping from German imprisonment.

Her father was a street performer of acrobatics and mother a singer and circus artist. Her grandmother on her father's side was a Madame of a brothel in Normandy. Her parents divorced when she was fourteen.

When her father enlisted in the French military in 1916, Piaf was taken to her grandmother's brothel where the prostitutes looked after her. In 1929 at the age of fourteen, she accompanied her father during his street performances and began singing in the red-light Pigalle district. She was able to afford a room at the Grand Hotel de Clermont. She roomed with her half-sister Simone *Momone* Berteaut who also sang and participated in their father's acrobatic performances.

Three years later, she met Louis Dupont who moved into their small hotel room. Dupont did not get along well with Momone and didn't want Piaf performing or roaming the streets. She became pregnant and briefly worked in a factory. Their daughter would be named Marcelle.

Piaf would leave Dupont following an intense quarrel taking Momone and Marcelle with her. They lodged at another hotel and returned to street performing. Marcelle was frequently left unattended although Piaf paid for limited childcare. She would die of meningitis at the age of two.

Local nightclub owner Louis Leplee would discover Piaf in 1935. He groomed her stage presence, told her to wear a black dress and gave her the pet name *La Mome Piaf* (The Little Sparrow). Their brief association would profoundly influence Piaf for the rest of her career. On April 6, 1936, mobsters with alleged ties to Piaf murdered Leplee. She was accused as an accessory but acquitted.

She distanced herself from the negative attention by changing her stage name to Edith Piaf and barring undesirable acquaintances. She commissioned Marguerite Monnot to write songs for performances that reflected her previous life on the streets.

Piaf sang with a passionate fervor that reflected her experiences. Her reinvention became complete and she branched out into theatre. The German occupation of Paris did little to slow her career momentum. It elevated her exposure. She continued performing in Paris in various nightclubs and brothels, many reserved for German officers and collaborating French Vichy officials. In 1942, she participated in a concert tour to Berlin and prisoner-of-war camps, sponsored by the German Reich.

Her actions were deemed *traitorous* and her conduct *collaboration*. She was obliged to testify during a wave of trials that followed the liberation of France and fall of the Vichy regime. Her personal secretary Andree Bigard, a reported member of the Resistance claimed that she was instrumental in helping a number of prisoners in Germany escape. The fury passed and she would be cleared of charges, but not freed from condemnation.

Her career and record sales skyrocketed internationally following the war. Her legendary performances between January 1955 and October 1962 at the Paris Olympia music hall cemented her French legacy. Her eight appearances on *The Ed Sullivan Show* and two concerts at Carnegie Hall introduced her to American audiences.

Years of alcohol and medication abuse gradually deteriorated her health. She suffered from rheumatoid arthritis, insomnia, stomach ulcers and a deteriorating liver. A series of car accidents further increased her drug dependency.

By the end of her life, her weight plummeted to 66 pounds and she spent 1963 drifting in and out of consciousness for several months. She ultimately died on October 10, 1963 from liver failure at the age of 47 inside her villa in Grasse. Her old friend Jean Cocteau would follow her in death the next day. He reportedly suffered a fatal heart attack upon hearing the report of her demise.

Greatness Extending Beyond A Long Paternal Shadow
Jean Renoir's Residences:
7 avenue Frochot 75009 Paris
Jean Renoir's Studio (Musee de Montmartre):
12 rue Cortot, 75018 Paris

Of all the traditional filmmakers critiqued by members of the French *Nouvelle Vague* (New Wave) movement, Jean Renoir escaped their scathing criticism. He was regarded as a revered influence and innovator. His two most popular films *La Grand Illusion* (1937) and *The Rules of the Game* (1939) are considered by critics amongst the greatest movies of his era and potentially all time.

Renoir had the expectation burden of being the son of internationally famous painter Pierre-Auguste Renoir. Despite the extended shadow of his father's fame, he would become an actor, screenwriter and director in over forty films stretching from the silent era to the end of the 1960s.

He was born in the Montmartre district of Paris and raised by his nanny and mother's cousin. She exposed him to guignol puppet shows. In his memoirs, he credited her with *seeing the face behind the mask and the fraud behind the flourishes. She taught me to detest the cliché.*

As a child, Renoir moved to the south of France with his family. He and his two brothers were the subjects for many of his father's paintings.

He joined the French cavalry during World War I and was shot in the leg leaving him with a permanent limp. He later served as a reconnaissance pilot. His injury prompted him to develop an interest in films while he recuperated. Postwar, his father suggested that he experiment with making ceramics. He decided to abandon visual art and concentrate on making films.

The relationship between father and son was often fraught with conflicting egos. His father's last nude model before his death was Catherine Hessling. Renoir would marry Hessling and cast her in most of his first nine silent films. They remained married until 1943.

Renoir had economic difficulties financing his early films. He gradually sold many of his father's inherited paintings to raise capital. During the 1930s, he experienced his initial success with sound movies.

One of his greatest triumphs *The Rules of the Game* initially was a commercial failure. He had co-financed the production. The timing of the film's release coincided with the outbreak of World War II. The existing French government banned the film. Part of their motivation stemmed from Renoir's known communist sympathies and pacifism. The ban was briefly lifted in 1940, but upon the occupation of France by Germany in June, the prohibition was reinstated.

An Allied bombing raid destroyed the original negative of the film. During the 1950s, French film enthusiasts with Renoir's cooperation reconstructed a near print of the film.

Renoir fled France for the United States upon the German invasion in 1940. He continued to make films, but had difficulty finding projects that suited him.

Over the next three decades, he completed numerous films, few of which were successful. He experimented with techniques adapted from live television and incorporated industry innovations in filming and editing. Eventually the film industry discarded him following his final production *Le Petit Theatre de Jean Renoir* (The Little Theatre of Jean Renoir) in 1970. Unable to secure financing for his projects, he spent his declining years entertaining friends at his

Beverly Hills home. As his health steadily declined, he began concentrating on writing novels and his memoirs. In 1975, he received a lifetime Academy Award for his contributions to the movie industry.

Four years later, he died from a heart attack at the age of 84. His body was shipped back to France for burial at Essoyes in the Aube region. He would become lionized upon his death as an innovator and icon within the film industry. Fellow director and friend Orson Welles wrote an article in the *Los Angeles Times* citing him as *the greatest of all directors.*

7 avenue Frochot

A Filmmaker's Glimpse Into A Sterile Future
Jacques Tati's Residence:
30 rue Ponthieve, 75008 Paris

Jacques Tati established a lasting legacy in French cinema despite only completing six feature length films. He distinguished himself as a filmmaker, screenwriter and actor. He created a character, *Monsieur Hulot*, perpetually confused by his surroundings. Wearing his trademark raincoat, umbrella and pipe, Hulot remained an icon of resistance towards modernity.

Tati's professional career began in the 1930s Parisian music halls performing as a mime. The writer Colette who'd begun her own career similarly lauded him in print.

During that decade, Tati began experimenting with short films oriented around mimed sports performances. In World War II, he enlisted in the French army fighting in the Battle of Sedan during May 1940. Upon the Armistice signing in June, his division was demobilized. He returned to Paris where he survived as a cabaret performer.

Tati's perspective on modern evolution offered a dark and comic outlook towards future dependence on technology. In his films, he graphically showcased a predictable schism resulting from technology promised convenience and the complications resulting from terminating social interaction. His first notable film *Mon Oncle* (My Uncle) won him the 1958 Academy Award for *Best Foreign Film*.

His most prophetic and celebrated movie would require nearly a decade before its release in 1967. *Playtime* resurrected his popular Hulot character, a group of disoriented American tourists and an assortment of consumer obsessed shoppers and sellers. The collection of personalities is isolated in a development complex featuring high-rise futuristic glass and steel buildings. The roadways resemble a carnival ride without any particular concluding destination. This futuristic suburban metropolis is positioned on the outskirts of Paris that is periodically referenced by images of national monuments.

The interaction between the personalities is minimal and irrelevant. The volume of the American conversations is elevated with subtle jabs at French and American cultural peculiarities sprinkled liberally. The sterile and superficial environment is parodied by its disposability and impermanence. An elegant restaurant opening night is staged lavishly to an overbooked patronage. The formalities steadily erode into calamity during the latter stages of the film. The disaster concludes with the patrons assembling inside an early morning coffee café. The tourists ride off into oblivion inside their bus towards their exiting airport.

The frightening imagery and portrayal of accelerated obsolescence is uncomfortably believable. The film production bankrupted Tati. Despite initially being a commercial failure, his movie peers, films critics and future viewers serenaded him lavishly with acclaim. His insightful glimpse was acknowledged as a bold perspective in filmmaking without precedent. The disjointed and confusing future that he abhorred would become our present tense.

His failed finances stalled future film projects. His last completed film *Parade* was produced for Swedish television in 1973. The movie filmed a circus performance that featured Tati's mine act and other performers.

Tati had planned additional films that would ultimately be released posthumously. None captured or surpassed the foresight of *Playtime*. Accompanying health problems plagued his declining years. He died from a pulmonary embolism on November 5, 1982 at the age of 75.

30 rue Ponthieve

TWISTED TOUR GUIDES.com

Beauty, Animal Rights and Controversial Public Statements
Brigitte Bardot's Residences:
5 Place Violet (Birthplace), 75015 Paris
35 avenue la Bourdonnais, Fifth Floor (Demolished), 75007 Paris
79 rue Chardon Lagache, 75016 Paris
71 avenue Paul Doumer, 75016 Paris
1 rue de la Pompe, 75016 Paris
22 avenue Foch, 75016 Paris

For twenty years, Brigitte Bardot became a sustained luminary within the French film constellation. She was born in Paris and raised in an apartment located near the Eiffel Tower. The building was razed and is now a public swimming pool. Bardot had few childhood friends due to her mother's intervention and the German wartime occupation mandating strict civilian surveillance.

Her family was wealthy as her father was an engineer and proprietor of several industrial factories in Paris. Her parents imposed strict behavioral standards upon her. She attended school three days a week and took ballet lessons in between at a local studio. In 1949, she was accepted to the *Conservatoire de Paris* where she attended ballet classes for three years. During the same period, she was hired as a fashion model appearing on the cover of *Elle* at the age of fifteen.

Her first film prospect *Les Lauriers sont Coupes* came after the cover exposure. Following her audition, Roger Vadim, employed by the production team informed her that she did not get the role. The pair would fall in love despite the opposition by her parents who demanded that she continue her education in England.

Reportedly, the headstrong Brigitte reacted by sticking her

head into an oven with an open fire. Her parents stopped her questionable suicide attempt and consented to the relationship. She would be obliged to marry Vadim at eighteen based on her their ultimatum.

The relationship would sour following five years. Bardot's exposure in the cinematic world began accelerating through small roles. Following her divorce, she appeared in four consecutive hit films that displayed her acting range and versatility from dramatic to comedic. In the 1956 Italian movie *Mio figlio Nerone*, Bardot was asked by the director to appear as a blond. She dyed her natural brunette hair. She was so pleased by the effect that it became her permanent public, modeling and film color.

Her rebellion against her parents extended into the cinema and society's expectations for young women. She became famous for portraying accessible sexually emancipated characters. Her perceived hedonistic lifestyle and portrayals lifted her into comparisons with American actress and sex symbol Marilyn Monroe during the 1950s and 1960s.

Her life became a movable circus with the public fascination towards her insatiable. She married Jacques Charrier and then Gunter Sachs between the years 1959 and 1969. She was lauded by French intellectuals particularly Simone de Beauvoir as *the most liberated woman of post-war France*.

Her character differed markedly from Marilyn Monroe. In 1973, following two decades as a major cultural icon, she severed her ties with the entertainment industry. She was credited with 47 films, 60 songs and several musical productions. She admirably retired to become an animal rights activist and create the *Fondation Brigitte Bardot*.

Her inner need to express herself never diminished for better or worse. She continued her outspokenness and public speeches on animal defense. In 1992, she married Bernard d'Ormale, a former adviser to far-right political gadfly Jean-Mari Le Pen. Her public statements drifted from exclusively promoting animal rights towards a controversial critique of French immigration policies and the Muslim community. That shift and her statements have resulted in multiple fines for *inciting racial hatred*.

Evaluating the legacy of a celebrated personality is fraught with contradictions. The public persona is often a paradox to an individual's private values and beliefs. Bardot has tested the polemics of physical and civil tolerance throughout her life. She has inspired many with her unflinching candor. Several of her later incendiary statements have undermined that positive impact.

35 avenue la Bourdonnais

An Undisputed Crusader of French Cinema's New Wave Francois Truffaut's Residence: 33 rue de Navarin 75009 Paris

The French *Nouvelle Vague* (New Wave) film movement emerged during the late 1950s. The movement was characterized by a rejection of traditional filmmaking conventions. These traditions were replaced by experimentation. Filmmakers explored innovating approaches to portable filming equipment, editing, visual styling and narratives that mirrored the social issues of the era.

The magazine *Cahiers du Cinema* galvanized the New Wave faction spotlighting like-minded filmmakers including Jean-Luc Godard, Eric Rohmer, Claude Chabrol, Alain Resnais, Agnes Varda and Jacques Demy. Their budgets were limited and each worked expediently. Their most prominent proponent became Francois Truffaut who denounced banal, safe and unimaginative films of literary classics in a 1954 manifesto essay.

Truffaut shaped his worldview and perspective through cinema. His shortened life would still result in twenty-five completed films and cement his legacy as a French film industry icon.

His earliest work mirrored his turbulent upbringing. His father was never publicly revealed. He took the surname of his stepfather who accepted him as an adopted son. He was shuffled between nannies and his grandmother during his formative years. He habitually stayed with friends avoiding his parents as frequently as possible. He became a truant and expelled from various schools. At fourteen, he decided to become self-taught. He snuck regularly into movie houses lacking the money for admission fees.

He joined the French Army in 1950 at the age of 18 and spent the subsequent two years attempting to escape his enlistment. He was arrested for attempting to desert and incarcerated briefly in a military prison. His salvation arrived in the personality of friend and art critic Andre Bazin. He used his political contacts to get Truffaut released and then established him as a writer for *Cahiers du Cinema*.

Truffaut leapt into his new position with passion and fury. He became noteworthy for his scathing and brutal movie reviews earning the moniker of *The Gravedigger of French Cinema*. He would ultimately become editor and write more than 500 articles during his four years affiliated with the publication.

Anxious to put theory into visual practice, he made his first film *The 400 Blows* in 1959. The movie traced the troubled adolescent upbringing of lead character Antoine Doinel. The film was highly autobiographical and received critical and commercial acclaim. He won the Best Director award at the 1959 Cannes Film Festival. The honor was particularly ironic because he was the sole French critic not invited to the previous year's event.

Truffaut embraced a philosophy of film productivity. Over his twenty-four year filmmaking career, he completed an astonishing twenty-five productions. His attention to detail, superb actors and diverse subject matter made several of his films appealing classics for international audiences. He appeared in roles for over half. His outspoken commentary and fiery expressive writing became legendary, periodically estranging him from contemporaries.

His publicly stated goal was to complete thirty films before a planned retirement to concentrate on writing books. There was no evidence that he shared a premonition towards an early demise. In July 1983, he was diagnosed with a brain tumor that would steadily incapacitate him. His sprinting gait would slow to a crawl. He had numerous film projects in preparation that would remain uncompleted. He died on October 21, 1984 at the age of 52 and is buried in Montmartre Cemetery.

Many industry observers continue to lionize Truffaut for his enduring contributions to cinema. It is unlikely that a future filmmaker will ever replicate his level of productivity in such a condensed career span.

33 rue de Navarin

An Actress Who Helped Define The Film Industry Nouvelle Vague
Jeanne Moreau's Residence:
39bis Square du Roule, Fifth Floor 75008 Paris
Burial: Cemetery of Montmartre
20 avenue Rachel, 75018 Paris

Jeanne Moreau began her acting career with the Comedie-Francaise eventually becoming one of their leading actresses. She played small roles in films beginning in 1949 and earned prominence with her starring roles in *Elevator to the Gallows*, *La Notte* and *Jules et Jim*. She became prolific during the 1960s and appeared regularly in films by notable avant-garde directors from the French *Nouvelle Vague* (New Wave) film movement.

Moreau had creative passions in multiple outlets. She combined film with theatre acting, but also was a notable vocalist, once performing at Carnegie Hall in 1964 with Frank Sinatra. She also worked in the movies as a writer, director and producer.

She would be honored extensively for her industry performances and roles in over 100 productions. Her final movie *Le Talent de Mes Amis* was released in 2015.

Moreau would be married twice and have a son. She was linked romantically to film directors Tony Richardson, Louis Malle, Francois Truffaut and fashion designer Pierre Cardin.

She lived an extended life of 89 years, but indicated that shortly before her death she felt *abandoned*. Her cleaning maid discovered her body inside her Paris home on July 31, 2017. She was buried at Montmartre Cemetery.

The Lasting Gainsbourg Mystique
Serge Gainsbourg's Residence:
5 bis rue de Vereuil 75007 Paris

Lucien *Serge* Gainsbourg was unique amongst his musical contemporaries and successors. He became known for his innovative and often provocative musical releases that defied finite classification. His partially sung and half spoken songs set him on a musical direction that integrated jazz, rock, funk, reggae and electronica. Much of his work appeared experimental as though intended to perforate previous genres. He achieved near mythical status within the French music industry and a cult following as a public figure.

The two women most associated with Gainsbourg were Brigitte Bardot and Jane Birkin. In 1967, he engaged in a brief affair with Bardot and contributed four songs for her album *Brigitte Bardot 67*. One track that was not included was *Je t'aime...moi non plus* (I Love You...Me Neither).

Bardot had reportedly asked Gainsbourg to write her the most beautiful love song he'd ever written. He succeeded with one of the most sensual composition perhaps ever recorded.

The steamy and erotic duet was recorded inside two intimate glass booths at a Paris recording studio. The lyrics were written as a dialogue between two lovers amidst sexual intercourse. The whispering voices are interspersed with heavy breathing sequences culminating in an orgasm by Bardot at the conclusion.

The authentic sound of the recording convinced listeners that the intercourse was real. Both parties denied it. Gainsbourg maintained that the song *was about the desperation and impossibility of physical love.*

Gossip surrounding the recording session stimulated interest within the music press. Bardot's then third husband, German businessman Gunter Sachs became enraged by the news and demanded that the single be withdrawn. Bardot pleaded with Gainsbourg not to release it and he complied. Sachs would divorce Bardot in 1969 and later commit suicide in 2011 as his father had done in 1958.

Gainsbourg reportedly unsuccessfully asked numerous actresses and singers to replace Bardot in the duet. The year following, he began a relationship with English actress Jane Birkin after meeting her on the set of the movie *Slogan*. After filming, he asked her to record the song with him. They completed their version together in a London studio that was released in February 1969. The single had a plain cover with a caution strip forbidding listening for anyone under 21.

The sensationalized publicity made the record an enormous success throughout Europe despite being banned by many radio stations. The Vatican reportedly excommunicated the record executive who released the title in Italy. The couple's simulated lovemaking was considered too risqué for even American radio audiences. Various pop groups and singers have covered the song numerous times since. Bardot later regretted not including her version in her 1967 album. In 1986, she petitioned Gainsbourg for permission and her version was released.

During the 1980s, Gainsbourg's health began a steep decline. His disheveled appearance, slurred speech and performances became an embarrassment. He continued his songwriting despite sinking into the depths of alcoholism.

He desperately underwent liver surgery in April 1989, but could not curb his excesses. He reportedly smoked five packs of unfiltered cigarettes daily. He died of a heart attack at his home on March 2, 1991, a month before his 63rd birthday. French President Francois Mitterrand comparing him to Baudelaire and Apollinaire while eulogizing him. He was buried in the Jewish section of Montparnasse Cemetery.

His Parisian house that he resided in from 1969 until 1991 has become a shrine befitting and symbolizing his cultural defiance. The exterior wall is saturated with graffiti punctuated by photographs of significant figures in his life and assorted attached memorabilia.

5 bis rue de Vereuil

A Cinema Gangster and An Unsolved Contract Killing
Stevan Markovic Fateful Taxi Pickup Site:
22 avenue de Messine, 75008 Paris
Alain Delon Residence:
42 avenue du President-Kennedy, 75016 Paris

Alain Delon enjoyed a popular film career between the 1960s and throughout the 1990s. He was considered one of France and Europe's leading male acting draws working with a celebrated selection of directors. His films and roles had a minimal impact within the American market, despite his international acclaim.

Delon shared a fascination with criminals and gangsters. He claimed that his Corsican background offered him unique insights and acquaintances in the underworld. He often portrayed them in his movies and proudly boasted of several being his closest confidants.

In 1962, Delon arrived in Belgrade (then Yugoslavia) to star in a feature movie about Marco Polo. The film would be aborted and never complete production. Delon hired Milos Milosevic as his bodyguard. The pair traveled to Venice for filming and then Paris. Milosevic would remain in his employ until 1964, when he departed to relocate to Hollywood.

His tenure with Delon lasted only two years. He married showgirl Cynthia Bouron who was linked with several extramarital affairs with prominent personalities. Milosevic would be found dead at the home of actor Mickey Rooney in 1966 along with Rooney's estranged wife Barbara Ann Thompson. Both had been shot to death with Rooney's revolver. Cynthia Bouron would be discovered seven years later stuffed in the trunk of a car parked outside a grocery store in Studio City, California. She'd been tied up and beaten to death.

Before Milosevic left for the United States, he suggested to Delon that he should hire his cousin Stevan Markovic as his replacement. Delon reportedly secured Markovic's release from prison and employed him. He was a close associate of Serbian crime figure Nikola Milinkovic.

Markovic established his own dangerous enterprise while employed by Delon. He was a heavy gambler, deeply in debt and renowned for arranging sex parties targeted towards the affluent of Paris. He concealed secret cameras throughout his party locations, particularly in the bedrooms.

He allegedly accumulated compromising videos and photographs of his guests. Some of the photos he offered to various publications for a fee. He attempted blackmailing some of the more influential public figures. The most prominently rumored included Claude Pompidou, the wife of then Prime Minister and future presidential candidate George Pompidou.

Delon's role in the scam was never disclosed although speculation was rampant that he was acutely aware of Markovic's activities.

On September 22, 1968, Markovic left his Messin Avenue apartment and entered a black Peugeot 404 taxi. Witnesses identified a man awaiting his entree in the back seat inside the cab. His name was Uros Milicevic and purportedly a friend.

Markovic would never be seen alive again. He was discovered inside a public garbage dump in the village of Elancourt, outside of Paris. His legs and arms were bound and his body wrapped inside a sheet. He'd been viciously beaten and then shot execution-style.

The relationship between Delon and Markovic had reportedly deteriorated significantly. Rumors circulated that Markovic was having an affair with Delon's wife Nathalie Barthelemy. Delon had apparently offered him a large severance buyout that he refused. He had grander intentions with his damaging photography and videos. He wrote to his brother cautioning him that if he met his death, it was *100% the fault of Alain Delon and his godfather Francois Marcantoni*. The latter was a notorious Corsican mobster with an extensive criminal history.

Markovic was deeply over his head with his blackmail threats and rapidly cultivating lethal enemies. By the request of the police, Delon would return to Paris following his murder. He was in the midst of filming *La Piscine* (The Swimming Pool) in Saint-Tropez. He denied initially knowing Markovic. Investigators had sufficient documentation confirming their professional relationship, his liaison with Marcantoni and even the infamous sex parties.

Marcantoni would spend 11 months in custody for the murder, but was released in December 1969 due to a lack of evidence. He died during August 2010 in Paris at the age of 90. George Pompidou would win the 1969 presidential election, but die in office at the age of 62 during April 1974. His wife Claude would survive the gossip and continue her role as a philanthropist and patron of contemporary art. She would die in July 2007 at the age of 94.

Delon would divorce Nathalie Barthelemy in 1969. He continued to appear regularly in gangster films, many self-financed. He continued collaborating with popular European actors Lino Ventura, Jean Gabin, Jean-Paul Belmondo and Yves Montand. As he aged and his appearance worsened, he concentrated on character acting roles and talk show appearances.

He relocated to Switzerland permanently for tax avoidance purposes. He diversified his commercial interests and endorsed products. He suffered a severe stroke in June 2019 prompting a subsequent deathwatch. He died on August 18, 2024 at the age of 88 in Douchy-Montcorbon, France.

Stevan Markovic's violent death remains a distant and forgotten anecdote in his life. The murder remains unsolved and there exists no sustained interest in apprehending and/or punishing his killer.

Stevan Markovic Apartment

Taxi Pick Up Location

TWISTED TOUR GUIDES.com

A Songwriter Eventually Discovers and Then Loses His Public Voice
George Moustaki's Residence:
26 rue St. Louis en L'ile. 75004 Paris

Unconventional songwriter George Moustaki received his first big break when his lover Edith Piaf recorded his hit song *Milord*. He began his own performance career after spending a decade composing songs for some of France's most popular voices including Yves Montand, Barbara, and Serge Reggiani.

His music scarcely penetrated the American music scene, but his 1969 album *Le Meteque* propelled his own French career. He was born in Alexandria, Egypt to Greek parents and settled in Paris during 1951. He was considered *an artist with conviction who conveyed humanist values*. His vagabond lifestyle and bohemian association with artists and intellectuals became the inspiration for many of his ballads and love songs.

His career ended abruptly in 2009 during a packed concert performance in Barcelona. He informed the audience that he was no longer capable of singing. His irreversible bronchial illness prompted him to relocate from Paris to the French Riviera for health reasons. He died in May 2013 at the age of 79.

26 rue St. Louis en L'île

The Decadent Decline of Doors' Lead Singer Jim Morrison
Jim Morrison Paris Lodgings:
George V Hotel, 31 Avenue George V, 75008 Paris
Hotel d'Alsace, 13 rue des Beaux Arts, 75006 Paris
17 rue Beautreillis, 3rd Floor, 75004 Paris
Gravesite: Pere Lachaise Cemetery:
Division 6, rue du Repose, 75020 Paris

Door's lead singer Jim Morrison was a disaster when he arrived in Paris during March 1971 with his girlfriend Pam Courson. She had been his long-term companion since 1965, but their relationship was never exclusive. She was a heroin addict and the perfect enabler for his final act of self-destruction.

Morrison at twenty-seven was no longer the lean, leather clad *lizard king* that fans remembered. His excessive beer drinking had bloated his face and figure. An unkempt beard and mustache obscured his exotic and iconic look.

He was burned out and creatively fizzled. His final performances were dismal and often erratic. He was awaiting a verdict following his 40-day trial after being charged with exposing himself on stage in Miami.

He'd arrived in Paris to clean and sober up, Instead, his stay would seal his coffin permanently. The couple initially lodged at the George V Hotel before relocating to the Hotel d'Alsace where writer Oscar Wilde had perished in 1900.

They eventually settled into a third floor rented apartment near the Marais and Bastille districts. He attempted to write and spent time wandering the local cultural tourist attractions.

His final evening included dinner at a Chinese restaurant, the film *Pursued* followed by a return to their apartment.

According to Courson, his labored breathing awakened her. He told her that he was going to take a bath. Reportedly he suffered a fatal heart attack and died in the tub. She discovered his body at dawn..

The story later became murkier with claims by other acquaintances that he died of a heroin overdose in a toilet stall. It was rumored that his body was wrapped in plastic and packed in ice inside the tub for three days before an undertaker would remove it. No autopsy would be performed and his death certificate simply stated *heart failure*.

Pam Courson would die three years later from a heroin overdose in Los Angeles at twenty-seven. The narrative behind his death would remain mysterious and open to speculation. He would be buried in the Pere Lachaise Cemetery and ultimately become one of the most frequently visited and desecrated gravesites.

17 rue Beautreillis

A Songstress Who Reveled and Died Amidst Melodrama
Dalida's Residence:
11bis rue d'Orchampt, 75018 Paris

Iolanda Cristina Gigliotti, better known as *Dalida* would become a French-Italian singing sensation performing in eleven languages and selling millions of records internationally.

She was born in Cairo, Egypt on January 17, 1933 to Italian parents and studied music in school while also playing violin in taverns. The family lived a modest existence focused on music. In 1940, her father and other Italian men from their neighborhood were imprisoned inside the Fayed camp near the city due to World War II. When he was released four years later, he became embittered and violent.

During her teenage years, she acted periodically, participated in a Cairo beauty pageant and began modeling. She adopted the stage name *Dalila* that was commonly used in Egypt. On Christmas Day, 1954, she left Cairo for Paris attempting to broaden her career prospects.

Struggle coupled with extensive training by a vocal instructor characterized her early years. In 1956, she participated in and won a singing contest called *Les Numeros 1 de Demain* (The Number One's of Tomorrow). Following her victory, she would receive her initial recording contract. She modified her name to *Dalida* upon the advice of author and screenwriter Alfred Marchand.

Her career would steadily blossom with a series of successful hits and concert appearances between the late 1950s through 1987. She battled reoccurring eye problems originally from her youth and severe bouts of depression.

Repeated failed relationships and personal emotional issues darkened her private life. Her husband from 1956 to 1961 Lucien Morisse died in 1970 by shooting himself in the head. One of her close friends, singer Mike Brant (1975) and lover Richard Chanfray (1983) would also kill themselves.

On the evening of May 2, 1987, Dalida would follow their lead by overdosing on barbiturates. The melodrama, passion and tragedy portrayed in many of her songs played out definitively in her life.

visual artists

Genius Prized, Lost and Then Rediscovered
Jacques-Louis David's Residence:
10 rue de Seine, 75006 Paris

Jacques-Louis David followed the prevailing winds of political change until cross currents singed him for pursuing too closely. David became responsible for some of the most celebrated and notorious paintings of the French Revolution and Napoleonic era. His historical depictions became renowned for their austerity, severity and captured moments. He is considered the preeminent French artist of his era.

He attended the French Royal Academy and earned the prestigious *Prix de Rome* in 1774. He was denied the award for three consecutive years before his selection. He staged a fast following his second denied application. While in Rome, David closely studied High Renaissance painters creating a profound effect on his own future works.

His return to France fell short of the triumph that he'd anticipated. The government, due to fears that it might incite violence initially censored one of his works *The Lictors Bring To Brutus the Bodies of His Sons*. The authorities were forced to rescind their decision due to public protest. The painting would be hung in a public exhibition protected by art students.

David was an early supporter of the Revolution, member of the Jacobin Club and friend of Maximilien Robespierre. As a participant in the National Convention, he voted for the execution of King Louis XVI.

He captured some of the monumental events of the revolution through symbolic works gleaned from the ancient past. His first masterpiece would become *The Death of Marat*. He painted the work in 1793 following the stabbing death of friend and leader Jean-Paul Marat in his bathtub by Charlotte

Corday. Despite his venomous writings advocating a *Reign of Terror*, Marat would ultimately be viewed as an important martyr to the movement.

David organized the ill-fated *Festival of the Supreme Being* at the Champ de Mars that elevated Robespierre and the Revolution to its apex of prominence. The fall of the ideology would descend shortly afterwards. David narrowly escaped the guillotine when Robespierre was arrested and executed. He had missed the session when the arrest occurred due to stomach pains. He would be imprisoned for his association with the Revolutionary Council. The majority of his internment was restricted to the Luxembourg Palace where he continued his paintings in relative comfort.

During his incarceration, he conceived of a series of paintings entitled *The Rape of the Sabine Women*. He considered the transitional style of these works *Greek*, evolving from his earlier Roman influences. Napoleon Bonaparte became aware of their existence and would later employ David for his own personal glorification.

David's wife Marguerite Charlotte Pecoul had divorced him previously in 1793. She managed to secure his release in 1796. They remarried following his profession of love towards her. His status would become restored and he retreated to his studio, announcing a permanent retirement from politics.

He may have lowered his public profile, but his propaganda value became useful for Bonaparte. Upon seizing power via coup d'etat in 1799, he commissioned David to paint *Napoleon Crossing the Saint-Bernard*. The work commemorated Bonaparte's daring travels over the Alps to defeat the Austrian army at the *Battle of Marengo*. Bonaparte had crossed the mountains on a mule, but requested David to substitute a *fiery steed* as his mode of transportation.

David would be honored as a Chevalier of the Legion of Honor in 1803 and twelve years later promoted to Commandant. He became the appointed court painter of Bonaparte's regime in 1804. Between 1805 and 1807, he painted the celebrated and controversial *The Coronation of Napoleon*. Pope Pius VII sat in his studio for the painting. Bonaparte reportedly stared at the completed canvas for an hour. He saluted David's genius and the Pope blessed the artist.

David's esteem plummeted following Bonaparte's two abdications. His prior association with the Revolution, execution of Louis XVI and Bonaparte's regime made his status vulnerable. During the Bourbon restitution, King Louis XVIII offered him a position as court painter. He refused the post preferring exile in Brussels.

He continued painting and living a modest existence with his wife. In December 1823, he declared that his canvas *Mars Being Disarmed By Venus and the Three Graces* would become his final work. On December 29, 1825, he was struck by a carriage while leaving a theatre. He died from his injuries. He would be buried in Brussels as his exile prohibited a return to France.

Shortly following his death, an auction of his once celebrated portraits was conducted in Paris. The sales prices were disappointing. *The Death of Marat* was previewed in a separate viewing room due to its controversial content.

David's legacy would require a perspective of time and separation from then ongoing political events to fully recognize and appreciate his genius.

28 Place Saint-George

A Dramatic Action Painter Renowned For His Liberty
Eugene Delacroix's Residences:
13 Quai Voltaire, 75007 Paris
54 rue Notre Dame de Lorette, 75009 Paris
Musee Delacroix, 6 rue de Furstemberg, 75006 Paris

Eugene Delacroix was described by poet Charles Baudelaire as being *passionately in love with passion, but coldly determined to express passion as clearly as possible*. His sense of depicting the dramatic in frozen action scenes elevated him from the outset of his career to leadership of the French Romantic movement.

He sought the exotic during his travels to North Africa. His style borrowed liberally from masters such as Peter Paul Rubens and painters of the Venetian Renaissance. He shared a dynamic kinship with poet Lord Byron portraying classical scenes from Greece and Rome legends emphasizing color and movement.

His most famous painting *Liberty Leading the People* reflects a symbolic and curious scene of a female character (Liberty) leading a charge of partisans during the 1830 Revolution. The battle and upheaval would unseat King Charles X, replacing him with King Louis-Philippe. Liberty remains determined, poised and lifting the fluttering French flag. She is partially disrobed amidst the carnage and catastrophe littering the battlefield.

The painting would be purchased by the French government but considered too inflammatory for display. Upon the abdication of Louis Philippe and election of Louis Napoleon, the painting would be exhibited in the Louvre. Delacroix would be considered one of the last Old Masters of Painting and an inspiration for artists expressing the Symbolist movement.

Many sources indicate that Delacroix worked himself into an early and preventable grave. His constitution was considered fragile and his housekeeper Jenny Le Guillou is credited with prolonging his life by guarding his privacy and providing constant care. His work was fatiguing and exhausting. During the winter of 1863, he developed a serious throat infection that continued to worsen.

He waited until June to visit his doctor. Two weeks later, he appeared to be recovering and left for his country home. His condition returned and he suffered a relapse. In mid July he returned to Paris for a second doctor visit. This time, his doctor confided that there was nothing he could do for him. He had been reduced to eating only fruit.

Delacroix realized the severity of his predicament and wrote up his will. He left a gift for each of his friends, suitable compensation for his trusted housekeeper and a demand that everything in his studio and art inventory be sold. He inserted a clause forbidding any representation of his features by drawing, death mask or photography. Curiously he was one of the first artists to have himself photographed. He died at the age of 65 on August 13, 1863. He was buried in Pere Lachaise Cemetery.

13 Quai Voltaire

54 rue Notre Dame

6 rue de Furstemberg

The Insightful and Illustrative Eyes of Nineteenth Century France
Honore Daumier's Residences:
221 rue St. Denis, 75002 Paris
9 quai d'Anjou, 75004 Paris

Honore Daumier's razor sharpened caricatures and cartoons of political figures satirizing their behavior earned him a lasting legacy. In 1832, his publication *Gargantua* earned him a jail sentence for several months. The reason for his arrest was an offensive and discourteous depiction of reigning King Louis Philippe. His timing proved poor, but his aim proved true. It would require decades before the Paris public would appreciate his full palette of artistic insight.

Daumier's fearlessness paved the thoroughfare for future generations of political cartoonists. His concurrently created paintings and sculptures were largely overlooked. Poet and art critic Charles Baudelaire as well as Daumier's painting peers recognized his genius in multiple mediums.

Daumier was an equal opportunity lampoonist. He attacked the bourgeoisie, church, lawyers, judges, politicians and the monarchy. His clear-sighted visuals illustrated uncomfortable depictions of excess, inhumanity and vulgarity. Unlike vernacular or text, his brilliant imagery could only be responded to by weaker verbal and printed denouncements. There was no capable illustrator able to counter his wit.

He was a prolific artist throughout his lifetime and credited with over 500 paintings, 100 sculptures, 1,000 drawings, 1,000 wood engravings and 4,000 lithographs. His printed works represented an accurate commentary on the social and political life within France between 1830 and 1870. Despite his success and recognition, he lived humbly and eventually outside Paris due to debt and failing eyesight. An old friend Jean-Baptiste Corot deeded him a small house in Valnondois that he'd been renting to live out his remaining years.

In 1878, a circle of friends and admirers arranged for a large exhibition of his paintings at the Durand-Ruel Gallery in Paris. The public and critics finally recognized that Daumier's talents exceeded simply illustration. The show helped broaden his appeal as a visual artist and widen his acclaim. He died on February 11, 1879 unable to financially capitalize on this newfound appreciation. The recognition did elevate his legacy into the subsequent century and beyond.

9 Quai d'Anjou

The Maestro Of The Book Illustration Trade
Gustave Dore's Residence/Studios:
7 rue St. Dominique, 75007 Paris
1 rue Bayard, 75008 Paris

Paul-Gustave Dore elevated book illustration into an artistic form that frequently made his imagery more in demand than the texts he accompanied. At his peak of productivity, he employed more than 40 woodcutters in the creation of over 90 illustrated books.

His depictions often resembled bizarre fantasies cast in expansive dreamlike scenes. His attention to precise detail separated his designs from peers. His most famous works included the *Oeuvres de Rabelais* (1854), *Balzac's Works* (1855), *Dante's Inferno* (1861) and a large folio *Bible* (1866)

He earned a staggering income during his lifetime and his production was prolific. He slept very little and devoted his energies and daylight hours almost exclusively towards his craft. He had a reputation for rapid completion of his designs. He owned other studios in Paris, but his headquarters were centered at his rue St. Dominique studio/residence. He lived in London for several years where his talents were likewise appreciated and well compensated.

His large paintings of historical figures and religious scenes never emulated the success that he generated as a book illustrator. He experimented with sculpting, but fared even worse.

Despite his wealth, fame and talent, Dore did not fare well in the longevity department. He was known for his merriment, violin and fiddle playing, practical jokes and sumptuous Sunday evening dinners and receptions. The frenetic pace of his work schedule resulted in an apoplectic seizure and death in 1883 at the age of 51.

7 rue St. Dominique

TWISTED TOUR ᏁUIDES.com

An Artist Lax On Enforcing Provenance
Jean Baptiste-Camille Corot's Residences:
125 rue du Bac (Birthplace/Demolished), 75007 Paris
10 rue des Beaux Arts, 75006 Paris
13 Quai Voltaire, 75007 Paris
56 rue du Faubourg-Poissonniere (Death Site), 75010 Paris

Jean Baptist Corot became a pivotal figure in French landscape painting during the mid nineteenth century. His stream of productivity crossed both the Neo-Classical traditional style and innovations by Impressionism.

He was born in Paris in July 1796 and raised in a middle class family. His father was a wig maker and mother a milliner. Her shop became a famous shopping destination for Paris socialites. His family earned a sound and stable income. Corot never suffered for lack of income but despised his first apprenticeship as a draper and business in general. He continued the profession until the age of twenty-six when he determined that art would become his sole profession.

Corot's paintings eluded controversy, but also acclaim with critics. He remained well respected by his peers. His early travels to Italy influenced many of his landscapes enhanced by the lighting, architecture and ruins. Throughout his painting career, he rarely strayed from his artistic vision. He stuck to an objective of blending harmonious tones and avoiding shocking excess in his colors. The cumulative effort often appeared muted.

By the time of his death in February 1875, a strong market for his work flourished. The interest stimulated both collector acquisitions and a thriving underground market for Corot fakes.

Corot became one of the most forged artists between 1870-1941 due to his straightforward immitigable style. He did little to discourage the practice reportedly allowing his students to copy his work and loaning his paintings to professional copiers and rental agencies. It is estimated that the thousands of still circulating fakes easily outnumbers his acknowledged originals.

10 rue des Beaux Arts

13 Quai Voltaire

A Painter Fleeing Fame and Recognition
Gustave Moreau Residence:
14 rue de la Rochefoucauld 75009 Paris

Gustave Moreau became his own worst public relations enemy. At the peak of his acclaim, the sting of adverse press criticism deeply affected him. His painting *Prometheus* received a medal at the Paris Art Salon of 1869, but the critics turned on him following his success. He would not submit another painting to the Salon until 1876 and permanently withdrew after 1880.

The highpoint of his career was seemingly when he was decorated *Officier de la Legion d'Honneur* in 1883. From that achievement, events slid downhill. He became reluctant to sell his work, seldom exhibited, rejected a professor's position and turned down several prestigious offers including decorating buildings at the Sorbonne.

He took over his friend Elie Delaunay's studio at the Ecole de Beaux Arts in 1891 upon his death. He devoted himself to teaching. Henri Matisse and George Rouault became two of his celebrated pupils. Moreau was a prolific artist credited with producing over 15,000 paintings, watercolors and drawings. He painted allegories and traditional biblical and mythological subjects. His works were described as *giving new freshness to dreary old subjects*.

The top floor of the townhouse his parents purchased in 1852 was converted into his working and living studio. He remained as a solitary bachelor for the rest his life. He died of cancer in 1898 and bequeathed the townhouse complete with 1,200 paintings and 10,000 drawings to the State to become converted into a museum. The Musee Gustave Moreau was opened in 1903 and operates today. It is likely the greatest concentration site of output by a single artist in history.

371

14 rue de la Rochefoucauld

A Vision of French Polynesia That Launched An Artistic Legacy
Paul Gauguin's Residences:
16 Rue Antoine Bourdelle (Impasse du Maine) 75015 Paris
Hotel des Ecoles, 35 rue Delambre, 75001 Paris
35 rue Milton, 75009 Paris
6 rue Vercingetorix, 75014 Paris
8 rue Carcel, 75015 Paris

Painter Paul Gauguin would likely have remained an obscure talent had the Paris stock market not crashed in 1882. He had established a comfortable livelihood as a stockbroker throughout an eleven-year career. He painted recreationally with modest success and exposure.

In 1873, he had married a Danish woman, Mette-Sophie Gad and they had five children together. The abrupt loss of income prompted Gauguin to move his family to Copenhagen, He attempted to become a sales representative for French manufactured tarpaulins. He spoke no Danish and there was no demand for his product line. His wife became their primary source of income offering French lessons to diplomat trainees.

The marriage and family bond disintegrated after his wife and her family requested his departure. He had denounced their middle class values and lifestyle.

He returned to Paris in 1885 with his six-year old son Clovis and worked as a translator and French teacher. He was determined to earn a livelihood from his paintings. He was obliged to accept a series of menial jobs to escape poverty. His art production and inspiration stalled due to his predicament. He ranted ceaselessly regarding the decline of traditional European originality.

His first major step towards breaking his creative ceiling came via a June 1887 visit to the Caribbean island of Martinique. His color palette began to brighten and broaden. His looser detailed figuratives altered radically the perception of his subject matter. His island stay widened his vision and subject matter. He completed eleven paintings during his June to November stay. This influential sojourn changed his entire approach to depiction.

Art dealer Theo van Gogh, Vincent's brother, purchased three of his paintings and arranged to have them showcased in his gallery. This exposure introduced his newest creations to wealthy patrons. Vincent van Gogh simultaneously cultivated an adoration and friendship with Gauguin. Theo would suggest that the pair paint together at Vincent's yellow house in Arles located in southern France.

Their relationship evaporated quickly within such close quarters. Gauguin decided to leave after nine weeks. One of the legendary accounts of their lodging occurred on December 23, 1888. Vincent threatened Gauguin with a sharpened razor. Later that evening, he would sever off his own left ear. He wrapped the tissue in a newspaper and handed it to a prostitute at a brothel both men had recently frequented.

Despite Gauguin's complex personality and financial difficulties, his career finally began to attract notice towards the conclusion of the decade. He visited his wife and children one final instance in Copenhagen. He promised fresh prosperity based on an upcoming planned voyage to French Polynesia. She had tired of and ignored similar promises in the past. His vision that she dismissed involved a complete escape from European civilization that he claimed represented *everything that is artificial and conventional.*

He set sail for Tahiti on April 1, 1891. The experience would ultimately elevate his professional novelty and distinction. It would benefit his lifestyle only marginally during the remainder of his lifetime. For the next decade, he would live intermittently between French Polynesia and Paris. His marriage became irretrievable shattered over financial disputes.

He lived comfortably within artist colonies initially near and sometimes inside the capital Papeete. As his sales steadily increased, he constructed a spacious reed and thatch house outside of the city. He installed a large studio, quarreled with officials and began an active involvement in local politics.

His canvas portrayed an idyllic existence of simplicity. Parisians had no more concept of life in Polynesia than Jupiter. His reality was more complicated. He was hospitalized several times for a variety of ailments including debilitating sores that restricted his movement. He claimed the sores were byproducts of eczema. Many biographers have attributed them to syphilis. He would father multiple children during his residence.

His health continued to deteriorate. By July 1902, Gauguin was resorting to laudanum and morphine dosages to address his chronic pain. His eyesight was beginning to fail him. Art critics noted the shift in his painting style.

He contemplated returning to Europe to get treatment for his ailments. He was discouraged within certain marketing circles due to his increasing fame and geographical distance from his critics. His work set him apart from mainstream artists and he was warned that this legacy might become tarnished with his reappearance.

At the beginning of 1903, Gauguin initiated a campaign intended to expose the incompetence of the island's police force. Several angry written exchanges resulted in a libel charge being lodged against him. He was very weak and resumed injecting himself daily with morphine. He died suddenly on the morning of May 8, 1903.

The advice to remain in Tahiti proved prophetic. Following the announcement of his death, the Parisian avant-garde embraced him. A vogue for his work began almost immediately. Numerous emerging artists including Picasso and Matisse credited his inspiration with their more liberal application of colors. Several posthumous exhibitions of his works established his prominence as a modern master. His creations would be absorbed into the Primitivism movement characterized by exaggerated body proportions, totems, geometric designs and stark contrasts.

A Solitary Intolerant Struggle to Depict Realism
Edgar Degas' Residences:
13 rue Victor Masse (1859-1873), 75009 Paris
77 rue Blanche (1873-1876), 75009 Paris
4 rue Frochot (1876-1877), 75009 Paris
50 rue Lepic (1877-1978), 75009 Paris
19 rue Pierre Fontaine (1879-1882), 75009 Paris
21 rue Jean-Baptiste Pigalle, 75009 Paris
23 rue Ballu (1890-1897), 75009 Paris
37 rue Victor Masse (1897-1912), 75009 Paris

6 boulevard de Clichy, 5th Floor (1912-1917) 75009 Paris

Edgar Degas' fascination with the female form and dancers set him apart from most of his Impressionist peers. He rejected the term and preferred to call himself a *realist*. He substantiated his disdain by criticizing *plein air* artists and rarely painting outdoors.

His draftsmanship set him apart by his accurate depicting of stilled dance transitional movements. He was able to capture even commonplace settings with a discerning eye for detail.

As Toulouse-Lautrec had access to cabarets and brothels for subject matter, Degas had intimate admittance to dance studios, the domain of adolescent girls. Most of his finished design imagery was created in his studio from memory, photographs or live models. He never wearied of depicting women, frequently in uncomfortable or awkward positions. The meanings behind his completed works was often ambiguously interpreted.

His use of photography was not simply for drawing references. He developed a genuine passion for the art often filming portraits of his friends by lamplight. Degas experimented with sculpture throughout his forty-year career. The only public showing of a solitary piece was in 1881 when he exhibited *The Little Dancer of Fourteen Years*. Critics praised the realism, but denounced the appearance as *ugly*. Following his death, over 150 wax sculptures were discovered, many in disrepair. Seventy-four were concluded to be suitable for casting in bronze.

Degas subscribed to a credo that *the artist must live alone, and his private life must remain unknown.* His work generated equal doses of contempt as admiration. In 1877, he developed a friendship with American artist Mary Cassatt after inviting her to exhibit in the third Impressionist exhibition. They shared similar tastes in art and literature and both came from affluent backgrounds. They remained independent and never married. She posed for several of his paintings, but detested his 1884 *Mary Cassatt Seated, Holding Cards* work that she felt represented her *as a repugnant person.*

As Degas aged, his solitary and uncompromising character stripped away pre-existing friendships and relationships. His anti-Semitism surfaced during the controversial Dreyfus Affair in the 1890s resulting in a complete rupture with all Jewish acquaintances, artists and models. His beliefs never softened until his death. His frequent clashes with Mary Cassatt on the issue estranged their friendship during his declining years.

Throughout his professional career, Degas confined his residences to within the Montmartre district. By 1890, his eyesight began a steady deterioration. He ultimately ceased working by 1912. During the final years of his life, nearly blind, he restlessly wandered the streets of Paris. He died on September 27, 1917 at the age of 83.

6 boulevard de Clichy

False Accusations of Life Casting And A Genius of Modern Sculpting
Musee Rodin (Former Hotel Biron):
77 rue de Varenne, 75007 Paris

Sculptor Francois Auguste Rodin converted his modest classical training with modeled clay into life. He became renowned for shaping complex and turbulent human figures into naturalistic sculptures. The definition and contouring accentuated his subject matter's physicality. His style became so pronounced and distinctive that he could only be admired, jealously criticized or poorly replicated.

Inspired by a liberating 1875 voyage to Italy, his naturalist style would elevated him into France's preeminent sculptor of the era. His public commissions would crown him a distinctive niche in posterity, but not without controversy. He refused to modify or compromise his personal vision for changes in fashion. Shortly following his death, his work temporarily fell out of favor. Acknowledged genius cannot be forever suppressed. His public regard would later undergo a renaissance and enshrine him among the immortals.

His best known works include: *The Thinker*, *Monument to Balzac*, *The Kiss*, *The Burghers of Calais* and *The Gates of Hell*. With his eventual commercial acceptance, his resulting career productivity would become staggering.

His path to acceptance and recognition was littered with embedded stones. He was essentially self-taught only attending formal school until seventeen. His studies concentrated on drawing and painting. He met adversity early. He was rejected three times for admission to the Ecole des Beaux-Arts. His work clashed with the admission judge's prevailing *Neoclassical* tastes.

For twenty years, he labored as a craftsman and ornament designer fabricating architectural objects and embellishments. He briefly stopped creating art due to his grief and perceived guilt following his sister's death. He joined a Catholic order with the intention of becoming a cleric. The head of the congregation recognized his art talents and unsuitability for the clergy.

He drifted to Belgium at the invitation of a colleague for six years where he further honed his skills and experience. He labored on the ornamentation for the Brussels Stock Exchange building. He first experimented with life size figurative sculpture creating *The Age of Bronze*. The sculpture was considered so lifelike that he was accused of casting a living model.

His future works would vary in proportion to prove this lingering presumption was erroneous. Returning to Paris, he earned his livelihood collaborating with more established sculptors on public commissions. His own applications in competitions were consistently rejected.

He would find part-time employment at the Sevres national porcelain factory. He would steadily enhance his reputation and creative credibility with his designs for vases and table ornaments. His work earned him introductions into the prestigious Paris Art Salon. These contacts proved substantive.

In 1880, he was awarded a commission to create a planned portal for a museum of decorative arts. Over the next four years, he constructed the elaborate *The Gates of Hell*, a monumental scene taken from Dante Alighieri's *Divine Comedy*.

The commission was accompanied by access to a free studio that enabled him a newfound level of artistic freedom. The museum would never be constructed. Several of the component sculptures including *The Thinker* and *The Kiss* would become recognized works apart from *The Gates of Hell*. He ceased designing for the porcelain factory as his income increased through private commissions.

The signature Rodin styling continued to evolve and earn recognition and public commissions. His submissions were no longer ignored. As his reputation soared, his private life underwent greater scrutiny until it detonated into a public scandal.

In 1883, he agreed to supervise a course for sculptor Alfred Boucher who was offered a sabbatical in Rome. During Boucher's absence, Rodin encountered his talented pupil, 18-year-old Camille Claudel. The pair developed a stormy relationship while influencing each other artistically. Claudel would work on several of Rodin's commissions and sculpt a noteworthy bust of him that earned public acclaim.

Claudel evolved into his lover and muse. She chafed impatiently at sharing only a secondary role in his life.

In 1864, Rodin had begun to live with a young seamstress named Rose Beuret. They would stay together throughout the remainder of their lives. He refused to sever his ties with her in preference to Claudel. Beuret had stuck with him through his leanest years and countless infidelities with models. Rodin felt a deep obligation towards her.

Claudel and Rodin would separate bitterly and conclusively in 1898. She would suffer a nervous breakdown afterwards and be confined to a mental institution by her family permanently in 1913.

By 1890, Rodin's subject themes became radicalized in the pursuit of fragmentation. He was breaking the barriers of traditional holistic and heroic sculpture and infusing contemporary themes. He experimented with combining figures of different sizing scales and isolating singular sections of anatomy. He was deconstructing the human figure and critics were frequently confounded by his innovations.

His growing fame opened international opportunities including the 1893 Chicago World's Fair and fresh celebrity followers and admirers. By the new century, his reputation was entrenched. A special pavilion of his artwork was established at the 1900 Paris World's Fair. His fleet of working assistants and protégé artists expanded to accommodate the inundation of orders for busts and portrait commissions by prominent individuals.

His principal studio was established in Meudon on the outskirts of Paris. He purchased the isolated and unkempt country estate in 1897. Following major renovations, he was able to host royalty, celebrities, leading artists and intellectuals.

In 1908, he decided to indulge in a Paris presence. He rented several rooms on the ground floor of the 18th century Hotel Biron townhouse to sell and store his sculptures. Some of the rooms were employed as working studios. He continued new commissions and entertained friends amongst the overgrown gardens. He left Beuret to oversee the Meudon property.

Fifty-three years into their relationship, Rodin decided to marry Beuret on January 29, 1917. She died two weeks later. He was suffering was chronic influenza that remained throughout the year. Part of his suffering was aggravated by he lack of heating inside his Meudon property.

His request to lodge at the Hotel Biron as an alternative was declined. Ironically, he had bequeathed the property, his archives and the contents of the studio in 1916 to the French government. His earlier generosity likely contributed to his demise. By November 1917, his lungs were fully congested severely weakening him. On November 17th, he died at his Meudon villa at the age of 77. A casted replica of *The Thinker* was placed next to his tomb on the grounds.

The Hotel Biron would officially become the Musee Rodin in 1919. The property has since been greatly enhanced, remodeled and landscaped. Several of Rodin's largest and most revered works are displayed on the grounds within a complimenting natural environment.

Musee Rodin

An Artist Who Devoured Herself and Her Finest Works
Claudel Family Residence: 135 Boulevard du Montparnasse, 75006 Paris
Camille Claudel Art Training (Academie Colarossi):
10 rue de la Grande-Chaumiere, 75006 Paris
Camille Claudel Art Studio: 111 rue Notre-Dame des Champs, 75006 Paris
Camille Claudel Residences:
Hotel de Jassaud, 19 Quai de Bourbon 75004 Paris
31 boulevard de Port-Royal, 75013 Paris

Camille Claudel will forever be linked with sculptor Auguste Rodin. Their association commenced in 1883 when she began working in his studio. She evolved into his muse, model, confidant and lover. They never lived together. He refused to terminate his 20-year relationship with Rose Beuret straining their relations.

Claudel ended her romantic affiliation with Rodin following an abortion nearly a decade later. They reportedly continued to see each other on a regular basis until 1898. She depended upon Rodin's financial support. His funding would cease abruptly the following year. After viewing her sculpture *The Mature Age* for the initial time, Rodin prompted their rupture. He was rumored to have put pressure on the Ministry of Fine Arts to cancel funding for her commission on the piece.

There has been significant historical debate over how much Rodin influenced Claudel...and vice versa. She was clearly talented, innovative and one of the only female artists that became distinguished from that era.

By 1905, she exhibited signs of mental illness. She disappeared for long stretches, destroyed many of her sculptures and was diagnosed with schizophrenia. She accused Rodin of stealing her ideas, ostracizing her from proper recognition and even plotting to kill her.

Her father tried to assist and support her financially. She lived secluded in her workshop. His death on March 2, 1913 altered her life dramatically. Wearied of her erratic behavior and unpredictable lapses, her younger brother Paul initiated drastic action towards her life.

He would become a noteworthy poet, dramatist and diplomat. Eight days following their father's death that she had not been notified about, he committed her into the Montfavet psychiatric hospital.

She would remain institutionalized for the next thirty years until her death. Her doctors attempted to convince her family that internment was unnecessary. Family members infrequently visited her. She died on October 19, 1943 during the German occupation. No family member attended her funeral and she was buried in a communal grave at the asylum.

The blurred distinction between genius and madness conceptualized the life of Camille Claudel. Approximately ninety of her surviving statues, sketches and drawings remain. Some may be viewed at Rodin-related exhibition venues. During the 1980s, several biographies and films sparked a resurgence of interest towards her life and work.

19 Quai de Bourbon

The Supporting Force Behind Starry Nights
Theo Van Gogh Residence:
54 rue Lepic, 75018 Paris

Goupil and Company Art Gallery (Closed Permanently):
19 Boulevard Montmartre 75009 Paris

The story of Vincent Van Gogh's life and suicide has been well documented in the annals of art history. Lesser known is the role of his younger brother Theo who became his champion and benefactor long before the world would become familiar with the Van Gogh name.

The brothers were born in Groot-Zundert in the Netherlands with a four-year age difference. Theo joined the Dutch office of the Parisian art dealers Goupil and Company in 1873 at the age of sixteen, their youngest employee. He was transferred next to their London and The Hague locations before settling in 1884 at the Paris main office. He then began Vincent's financial support in the form of art materials and cash enabling him to concentrate exclusively on painting.

The intimate lifeline between the brothers enabled Vincent to continue creating throughout his darkest bouts of depression and financial misery. Their written correspondence were characterized by Theo's praise and encouragement. Vincent would send over 650 letters to Theo. It is probable that Theo sent an equivalent number. Vincent did not keep any of Theo's communications.

Theo had an immaculate eye in gauging talent, trends and introducing contemporary Dutch and French art to the public. He personally promoted Claude Monet and Edgar Degas to his employers to exhibit and purchase their works.

During March 1886, he invited Vincent to live with him at his apartment in Paris He introduced his socially inept brother to the leading local artists. Two years later, he encouraged Paul Gauguin into an experimental living arrangement with his brother by financially covering the travel and living expenses.

The collaboration ended badly with Vincent assaulting Gauguin with a large razor and then later severing off his own right ear. Vincent's action cast him as the role of a madman within art circles. Their living experiment did result in a proliferation of paintings between both artists.

Around 1889, Theo met his future wife Johanna in Paris. She initially deferred his engagement proposal. She was already in a relationship headed towards marriage. When that union failed, she accepted his proposal. They were wed on April 17, 1889. Her later role in Vincent's future and artistic recognition would be greatly understated.

The death of Vincent by a self-inflicted gunshot wound on July 30, 1890 devastated Theo. He was unable to come to terms with the loss. His health had never been robust, but worsened rapidly following his brother's death.

Six months following Vincent's passing, he would follow at the age of 33 on January 25, 1891. The cause was determined as a disease of the brain caused by syphilis. Contributing factors cited included heredity, overwork and sadness. He left his widow with a one-year-old infant and nearly Vincent's entire art inventory.

Although Vincent had not been successful commercially while living, his death prompted a deeper appreciation of his work and technique. Theo's widow was able to draw on the connections that her husband had previously made to promote Vincent's body of work. Within a single year following his death, major memorial exhibitions were held in Brussels,

Paris, The Hague and Antwerp.

Suddenly his genius was recognized, missed and mourned. The story of his struggles and obscurity in the southern French village of Arles became a compelling narrative. Greater exposure translated into sales and artistic influence. His vivid color palette was credited with inspiring the subsequent Fauvist movement led by Henri Matisse. Other major artists would additionally acknowledge his influence.

In the United States, prevalent knowledge regarding Vincent Van Gogh's work and life story would not become widespread until a 1934 novel *Lust for Life* was published by writer Irving Stone. The edition was based on Vincent's letters to Theo. A film by the same name would be released in 1956, further enhancing his regard.

Van Gogh's vision would ultimately translate into some of the world's most valuable paintings. In 1914, Theo's wife Johanna had his body exhumed from the original burial location in Utrecht, Holland. It was relocated to a burial site adjacent to his brother in Auvers-sur-Oise. The act symbolically represented the intimacy the brothers shared with each other.

The Van Gogh name would resurface sixty year later in Holland. Theo's great-grandson sharing the same name was a controversial film director who created a short film critical of the treatment of women in Islamic culture. He would be gunned down on the streets of Amsterdam by an Islamic extremist.

54 rue Lepic

19 boulevard Montmartre

A Ridiculed Appearance Masks Empathetic Portrayals
Henri Toulouse-Lautrec Residences and Studios:
19bis Rue Pierre Fontaine. 3rd Floor, 75009 Paris (1884-87)
19 rue Pierre Fontaine, 75009 Paris (1887-1891)
21 rue Pierre Fontaine, Second Floor 75009 Paris (1891-1893)
21 rue Caulaincourt, Third Floor, 75018 Paris (1893-95)
30 rue Pierre Fontaine, Mezzanine, 75009 Paris (1895-1897)
5 avenue Frochot, Second Floor, 75009 Paris (1897-98)
9 rue de Doual, First Floor, 75009 Paris (1898-1901)
Moulin Rouge Cabaret: 82 boulevard de Clichy, 75018 Paris

Henri Toulouse-Lautrec was born into nobility at the Hotel du Bosc in Albi on November 24, 1864. His younger brother was born three years later, but died the following year. His parents would separate soon afterwards and a nanny would raise him. At eight, he began living with his mother in Paris, but returned to Albi due to his mother's concern for his health.

During his early teenage years he fractured both of his legs and the breaks did not heal property. The cause was attributed to a genetic disorder that afterwards ceased growth entirely in his legs. He developed an adult-sized torso with stunted legs and stood an even five foot tall.

He began to draw at a young age and both parents recognized his talents. At eighteen, he returned to Paris to study painting under artists Leon Bonnat and later Fernand Cormon. He accumulated art school friendships that he would maintain his entire life.

He settled into the Montmartre district known for libertine lifestyles and the haunts of creative artists, writer and philosophers. He would station himself permanently there for the next two decades developing his signature style. He became a fixture at brothels and nightclubs. His most famous works became commissioned posters for the Moulin Rouge cabaret opened in 1889.

Life within Montmartre was liberating for Lautrec's soul, but damaging to his health. He endured a lifetime of ridicule for his short stature and physical appearance. He compensated by drinking, first only beer and wine. Eventually his consumption gravitated into absinthe, a toxically lethal alcohol. He walked with a hollow cane filled with the liquor to keep him perpetually intoxicated.

His work became noteworthy for depicting individuals in their working environments, particularly in saloons and brothels. It was a universe untouched by contemporary peers who lacked his intimate access. Attributes from his primary characters were often highly detailed with undefined backgrounds and silhouettes employed to further sharpen focus. Many of his characters, distained by society, were described as *sympathetic*.

By the age of 34, his alcoholism had ruined his health. He was committed to a sanatorium for three months. He returned to his studio afterwards and then traveled throughout France. His physical and mental health continued to decline compounded by more drinking and syphilis that he reportedly contracted from one of his primary models and sleeping partners, Rosa La Rouge.

He would die on September 9, 1901 at his mother's estate of Chateau Malrome in Saint-Andre-du-Bois. He was buried a few kilometers away.

19bis rue Pierre Fontaine

19 rue Pierre Fontaine

21 rue Pierre Fontaine

30 rue Pierre Fontaine

5 avenue Frochot

9 rue de Doual

The Consummate Impressionist Painter
Claude Monet Residences:
45 rue Lafitte (Birthplace), 75009 Paris
35 Boulevard des Capucines 75002 Paris
6 rue Furstemberg, 75006 Paris

Claude Monet established his fame as a painter through his impressionist works of the French countryside. His landscapes and water-lily pond paintings remain his signature style.

He was born on the fifth floor of a Parisian apartment house, but raised in LeHavre in Normandy. His father wanted him to remain in the family grocery business and his mother, a singer herself, died when he sixteen. Monet rejected his father's desire and moved in with his widowed and wealthy aunt.

He studied at the Academie Suisse where one of his classmates was painter Auguste Renoir. He concentrated on landscapes, seascapes and portraits, but his work attracted minimal attention.

The best advice he ever received was from his peer Eugene Boudin who encouraged him to paint outdoors in *plein air*. Monet's objective became to document the French countryside by painting a scene multiple times capturing the changing of light and passing of the seasons.

Monet would be credited as one of the founders of Impressionism. His contemporaries included Renoir, Pissarro, Sisley, Cezanne and Degas. The path to acceptance and success proved arduous, but Monet rarely strayed from his vision and experimented deeper with his style. Acclaim would accompany during his lifetime and posthumously.

In 1883, Monet lived in Giverny in northern France. He purchased a house and property. He began a massive landscaping project that featured his legendary water-lily pond. For the next twenty years, his obsession towards painting his water lilies would consume him artistically.

He outlived two wives and died famous on December 5, 1926 at the age of 86. His popularity continued to soar during the second half of the 20th century. It has never receded nor dimmed.

45 rue Lafitte

35 boulevard des Capucines

An Artistic Prophet Nearly Ignored in His Homeland
Alphonse Mucha's Residences:
13 rue de la Grande Chaumiere, 75008 Paris
6 rue Val-de-Grace, 75005 Paris

The professional fate and ultimate destinies of Czech Republic artist Alphonse Mucha and actress Sarah Bernhardt coincided in alchemy. Mucha had moved to Paris initially in 1887 studying at the Academies Julian and Colarossi. He simultaneously produced magazine and advertising illustrations.

During the Christmas season of 1894, Mucha visited a neighborhood print shop. He learned of a pressing demand for a new poster required to promote a play starring Bernhardt at the Theatre de la Renaissance. The unknown Mucha agreed to design a lithograph poster within a tight deadline of two weeks.

The completed work when displayed publicly generated tremendous recognition. Bernhardt became so satisfied by the public response that she entered into a six-year contract with Mucha to design her future advertising posters. In addition to posters, he designed Bernhardt's theatrical programs, costumes and jewelry. She wisely set aside a number of posters to market exclusively to collectors, an early example of product licensing.

Their collaboration elevated Mucha's reputation within the Paris art world. He began producing on commission a significant inventory of paintings, book illustrations and advertisements. His distinctive style and lettering became associated with the *Art Nouveau* movement.

Mucha believed that art existed specifically to communicate a spiritual message. He rejected the notion of creating for commercial purposes stating his objectives as more idealistic and lofty.

He pragmatically understood aesthetics and public interest. He featured beautiful and healthy young women. They were ornamented in neoclassical robes surrounded by flowers that often gave the appearance of decorative halos behind their head.

His collaboration with Bernhardt brought international fame, greater income and an upgraded lifestyle. The 1900 Paris Universal Exposition became a showcase for *Art Nouveau*. He earned the title of *Knight of the Order of Franz Joseph* from the Austrian government.

With his career firmly established, he would marry and move to the United States. He taught illustration and design and became a visiting professor at the Art Institute of Chicago. He rejected the majority of commercial proposals. He replicated his Bernhardt style promotional posters for actresses Caroline Louise Dudley and Maude Adams. His stay and commissioned portraits completed in America were considered only marginally successful.

He would relocate to Prague and ultimately complete his grand painting vision. He labored over his *Slav Epic* series consisting of twenty 20x26 feet paintings detailing the historical legacy of his homeland. He experimented with other themes and artistic projects including ceiling murals, stain glass windows and even the artwork for a 1920 Czechoslovakian 100 korun currency bill.

Throughout the 1930s, political turmoil in his country relegated his artwork into near obscurity. A 1936 retrospective was staged at the Jeu de Paume museum in Paris reviving interest within the European art community.

Czechoslovakia became in grave peril of losing their

independence during the rise of Adolph Hitler and Germany. Mucha began work on a fresh triptych series depicting the Age of Reason, Age of Wisdom and Age of Love between 1936 to 1938. The works would never be completed. On March 15, 1939 the German army paraded through Prague and annexed Czechoslovakia into the German Reich.

Mucha was a visible public target due to his widely professed Slav nationalism. He was arrested and interrogated for several days before being released. He contracted pneumonia on July 14th and died at the age of 78, a few weeks preceding the outbreak of World War II.

As prophets are often historically underappreciated in their homeland, Mucha's legacy mirrored that injustice. His perceived greatest triumph the *Slav Epic* series would be displayed in Prague only twice during his lifetime. After 1928, the canvases were rolled up and placed into storage for twenty-five years.

He shared little regard for his *Art Nouveau* work that crowned him with his greatest recognition. He proudly described himself as a historical painter, even when he was perceived differently.

With time, his works have regained the reputation that they merited. The National Gallery in Prague currently displays his *Slav Epic* series. *Art Nouveau* remains contemporarily popular and fashionable.

The Towering and Enduring Art Legacy of Pablo Picasso
Musee National Picasso
5 rue de Thorigny, 75003 Paris
The Head of Dora Maar Sculpture:
Square Laurent-Prache 75006 Paris
Pablo Picasso Residences:
11 boulevard de Clichy, 75009 Paris
Bateau-Lavoir: 13 Rue Ravignan 75018 Paris
49 rue Gabrielle, 2nd Floor, 75018 Paris
242 boulevard Raspail 75014 Paris
5-7 rue des Grands-Augustins, 75006 Paris

Pablo Picasso had a grandiose vision of greatness installed in him during infancy by his mother. He was born in 1881 as Pablo Ruiz with enough middle names to complete a bulbous paragraph. His earliest works he signed Pablo Ruiz, but began using his mother's maiden name of Picasso around 1901.

Picasso would define an empire. As an artist, he completed approximately 50,000 works. The asset value of his fortune today would be incalculable. He holds the dubious distinction of having more of his paintings stolen than any artist in history. His paintings rarely are auctioned, but exceed fresh pricing expectations on each occasion. During his lifetime, he augmented his paintings with sculpting, printmaking, ceramics and theatre design.

Pablo Picasso cannot be categorized into a single stylistic category. He led the charge of innovation and his peers and contemporaries could only follow. His first Parisian works, anointed the *Blue Period*, were inspired by the suicide of his intimate friend, painter Carlos Casegemas. These works were produced between 1901 and 1904 during a somber period of poverty and critic rejection.

He shifted into more vibrant works following with his *Rose*

Period depicting circus performers, harlequins and clowns. As his peers experimented with cubism, primitivism, rectangular or conic shapes, Picasso defined each artistic movement with his distinctive output.

Picasso lived exclusively for his artwork, often alienating acquaintances and those closest to him. He abandoned creative movements, impulses and people once he no longer sensed their stimulation. He became difficult to comprehend, but never lingered long enough to wallow in reflection or sentimentality.

Paris offered him the ideal urban environment to create and innovate for nearly fifty years. His finest works were completed inside his various studios. *Les Demoiselles d'Avignon* was painted at the Bateau-Lavoir residence.

His longest lasting residence was between 1936 until 1955 located within the Saint Germain district. The building was the former 17th century Hotel de Savoie featuring wrought iron gates, an enormous skylight, impressive hall and spiral staircase. The property was where he reportedly painted *Guernica* in 1937 and spent the German occupation years.

Picasso's life was riddled with contradictions and a revolving door of failed female relationships. Some he immortalized in creations, most he systematically manipulated and then humiliated. His most famous and accessible depictions is arguably the sculptural *Head of Dora Maar* located adjacent to the Church of Saint Germain-des-Pres, the site of Oscar Wilde's funeral service. The sculpture is hideous intentionally and was dedicated to his friend poet Guillaume Apollinaire who died during the 1918 Spanish flu pandemic.

During his declining years, Picasso moved to the south of France, an environment that mirrored the climate of his native

Andalusia. In comfortable surroundings, he continued producing art although critics panned much of the quality. He cared little for critique and rarely explained the meaning behind his works. In his eyes, these were creations by Picasso and that was significant explanation.

By the 1960s his health declined and his productivity slackened. He died from pulmonary edema and heart failure on April 8, 1973 during a dinner party that his final wife, Jacqueline and he were hosting with friends. She prevented his children Claude and Paloma from attending his funeral. Devastated by his death, she committed suicide via a self-induced gunshot thirteen years later at the age of 59.

The largest collection of his art (approximately 5,000 pieces) is displayed at the Musee Picasso in the Marais district. An additional 4,000 works are located in the Museu Picasso in Barcelona. His prodigious outlet is unlikely to ever become duplicated. Each new child art prodigy is often but unfairly christened *Petit Picasso*. It is an unmerited moniker that is unattainable.

The Head of Dora Maar Sculpture

11 boulevard de Clichy

5-7 rue des Grandes-Augustins

An Innovative Artist Until His Final Breath
Henri Matisse Residence/Studios:
Hotel Biron, 77 rue de Varenne 75007 Paris
19 Quai St. Michel, 75005 Paris

Henri Matisse showed little inclination towards art until he was 20 years old. He attended secondary school in Saint-Quentin following a year of legal studies in Paris. He remained as a law clerk there. While recovering from appendicitis, he began sitting in on a drawing class and painted leisurely. His earliest works were color reproductions and soon he was filling his grandparent's house walls with his art.

Some artists are born innately talented. Others forge themselves into masters by sheer will, tenacity and productivity. Matisse fit into the latter category. He abandoned law and gravitated to Paris to become a professional artist.

His first decade produced marginal results. He studied initially at the privately operated Academie Julian. He then transferred to the Ecole des Arts Decoratifs for evening classes. At that school, he studied under Symbolist painter Gustave Moreau and submitted four works in 1896 at the prestigious Salon de la Society Nationale des Beaux-Arts. The government purchased one painting, *Woman Reading*.

His triumph emboldened his personality and heightened his artistic confidence. Over the next decade, he became a familiar face within Parisian art circles exhibiting in various group exhibitions. His first one-man exhibition in June 1904 at Ambroise Vollard's Gallery was a failure. He was experimenting with pointillism and others avant-garde styles, but his vision was stymied and not his own.

During the summer of 1905, he traveled to Collioure, a French fishing village on the Mediterranean near the Spanish border. He liberated himself from his urban design shackles and began experimenting with vivid colors. He contrasted traditional polar extremities against each other. His completed works represented a violent confrontation and clash of traditional painting maxims. He emerged as one of the leading figures of a painting movement labeled *Les Fauves* (The Wild Beasts) by Paris art critic Louis Vauxcelles.

The designation was not intended to be complimentary. It separated Matisse's work from the artistic pack. His financial situation ironically improved markedly as his work became fashionably sought and collected. By 1908, he was exhibiting in New York City, Moscow and Berlin. While living in Paris, he became a regular attendee at Gertrude Stein's salons and encountered influential contemporaries such as Pablo Picasso.

The two men would become intense rivals, but also inspirations to each other based on a bond of genuine respect. Picasso reportedly considered Matisse his sole rival for innovation and shaping 20th century painting.

Fauvism became simply a short-term gateway for Matisse. Many of the labeled adherents retracted back into Expressionism or other traditionalist painting modes. Some explored newer directions such as Cubism. He found no kinship with these movements. Matisse chased color, chromatic equilibrium and linear economy. His was an obsessive pursuit that he hunted industriously.

As he reached middle age, his fresh prosperity enabled him to relocate towards the welcome climate of the Cote d'Azur in southern France. He branched out into theatrical backdrops, sculpture, murals, etching, drypoint and printmaking. He traveled leisurely and often.

His health abandoned him during the 1940s and he spent the declining years of his life, solitary and bedridden. He saved one of his most compelling works towards the end. Following three years of planning and execution, he designed the Chapelle du Rosaire in Vence, a French Riviera hillside town where Matisse had owned a villa from 1943 to 1948. His contribution was inspired by gratitude towards the local Dominican nuns. One had nursed him to recovery during a nearly fatal illness in 1941. The chapel was completed in 1951.

As his life ebbed away during the early 1950s, he began work on a series of large-scale colored-paper cutouts. The cutout illustrations would once again launch him into the forefront of contemporary design. His final work became a drawing for a stained-glass window installation at the Union Church of Pocantico Hills, north of New York City. He died on November 3, 1954 from a heart attack at the age of 84. His body had ultimately abandoned him, but not his intellect, industry or creativity.

Hotel Biron

A Creator of Vividly Whimsical Mysticism
Marc Chagall's Residences:
110 avenue General Lederc 75014 Paris
La Ruche-The Beehive, 2 Passage de Dantzig, 75015 Paris
4 Villa Eugene-Manuel, 75016 Paris
18 Rue Antoine Bourdelle (Impasse du Maine), 75015 Paris

Marc Chagall was born Moishe Shagal in Liozna, Belarus, then part of the Russian Empire. His artistic formation began with studies in Saint Petersburg before immigrating to Paris at the age of twenty-three during 1910.

He enrolled at the Academie de La Palette, an avant-garde painting school and spent his free hours visiting galleries, salons and museums, particularly the Louvre. His early days were oppressively lonely, as he did not speak French. He eventually cultivated friendships with numerous creative peers.

The popular and dominant Cubist painting style influenced his early works. Chagall approached his dreamscape canvases with vivid color. His work aimed towards expressing poetic imagery amidst overlapping themes. He declined to publicly state literal interpretations of his paintings. He frequently returned to themes of memories from his homeland.

He would return to Russia in 1914 to marry Bella Rosenfeld and staged a successful exhibition before arriving of his work in Berlin. Upon reaching Belarus, World War I erupted closing the borders indefinitely. He began exhibiting his works in Moscow and St. Petersburg the following year. The communist takeover in October 1917 stilled his production briefly.

Due to his preexisting artistic reputation, he was offered a position as Commissar of Arts in Vitebsk. Chagall distanced himself from politics. His aim was to establish a collective of independently minded artists. His objective met with resistance from key faculty members who preferred structural compositions. He resigned and moved to Moscow to accept a job as stage designer for the newly established State Jewish Chamber Theatre. He created notable large murals enabling his integration of large-scale symbolism into his work.

Conditions in Russia worsened during the Bolshevik reign. Reduced to living in primitive conditions, he applied for an exit visa to France that was surprisingly approved.

He would return to Paris and continue following his poetical visions and mysticism through his paintings. He added biblical themes. His travels through Europe broadened his landscape imagery. During World War II, he fled France for the United States bonding with numerous exiled European artists. The German government branded his artwork as *degenerate* stating it represented an assault on Western civilization.

He lost his wife Bella during September 1944 with a viral infection that was not treated due to the wartime shortage of medicine. Initially many of his peers did not appreciate or even like his work. Broader exposure and exhibitions organized by his representative Pierre Matisse (son of Henri) softened their criticism. His work remains an acquired taste.

The Museum of Modern Art in New York City would exhibit forty years of his output in 1946 cementing his stature amongst prominent twentieth century artists. He returned to France in 1948 relocating permanently in Saint-Paul-de-Vence located in the south. Henri Matisse lived nearby, but the pair remained only acquaintances respecting the other's work.

Chagall would remarry in 1952. He accumulated numerous high-profile commissions including the ceiling for the Paris Opera and stained glass installations in various churches across Europe. He ventured into other mediums including tapestries, ceramics and sculpture. Each creation magnified his obsession with color and mystical imagery. He would continue working up until his death in July 1985 at the age of 97.

The Patriarch of Modern Sculpture and His Open Studio
Constantin Brancusi's Studio/Residences:
8 Impasse Ronsin, 75019 Paris
11 Impasse Ronsin, 75015 Paris
La Ruche (The Beehive): 2 passage de Dantzig, 75015 Paris
Atelier Brancusi: Place George Pompidou, 75004 Paris

Constantin Brancusi is a familiar name to visitors attending the Centre Pompidou Contemporary Art Museum. In 1997, an exact reconstruction of his art studio was created on the piazza opposite the museum to house his collection of work. Nearly 2,000 creations are featured including over 1,600 glass photographic plates and original prints.

Born and raised in Romania, he arrived into Paris studying at the Ecole des Beaux Arts between 1905 until 1907.

His style would evolve into clean geometrical lines that formed symbolic allusions of representational art. He was a difficult artist to classify and resented labeling. His inspirations were often primitive and exotic work from non-European cultures originating from Africa and the Mediterranean.

His fresh approach to sculpture elevated him as a pioneer of *modernism*. He worked briefly inside the workshop of Auguste Rodin, but parted after only two months. He concluded that the extended shadow of Rodin could permit no sustained growth or development.

He worked with plaster, wood, marble and bronze, but his abstractions established a distinctive and simplistic style seldom replicated. His work was periodically controversial due to his obsession with genitalia.

He developed a wide base of international collectors and his circle of intimates included Parisian artists and intellectuals. Despite his avant-garde surroundings and cultural refinement, he never lost contact with his Romanian roots. During the 1910s and 20s, he was regarded as a bohemian and pleasure seeker. He had one child with New Zealand pianist Vera Moore who he never acknowledged.

As his health began to deteriorate with age, a Romanian refugee couple cared for him. He became a French citizen in 1952 in order to designate his caregivers as his heirs. He bequeathed his studio and contents to the Musee National d'Art Moderne. One of the conditions was that his workshop was required to be rebuilt in the exact condition he left it on the day of his death. Architect Renzo Piano designed the airy atelier in accordance with the artist's wishes.

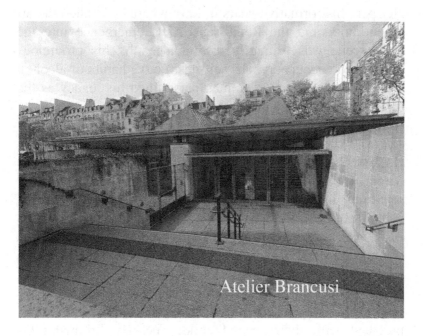

Atelier Brancusi

A Tragic Bohemian Artist Recognized Posthumously
Amedeo Modigliani's Residences:
3 rue Campagne-Premiere, 75014 Paris
La Ruche-The Beehive: 2 Passage de Dantzig, 75015 Paris
Bateau-Lavoir: 13 Rue Ravignan, 75018 Paris

Amedeo Modigliani became as equally known for the company he kept as his distinctive portrait, figurative and nude paintings. In 1906, he arrived in Paris and quickly gravitated into the company of fellow artists Pablo Picasso, Constantine Brancusi, Diego Rivera, Juan Gris, Max Jacob and Jean Cocteau. Modigliani cultivated a style defined by elongated faces and necks, often in cubism styling. His figurative works were not well received during his lifetime. They skyrocketed in value and appreciation posthumously.

He spent his formative years in Italy where he studied the art of antiquity and the Renaissance. His emergence into the Paris scene was primarily distinguished by his prodigious output and debauchery. His self-destructive habits of alcohol, drugs and promiscuous women personified his legacy as the tragic and bohemian artist.

The role suited him and stimulated his artistic productivity. He would not live long enough to savor the fruits of his output. Continually on the fringe of poverty and frequently squatting in communes for penniless artists, Modigliani contracted incurable tuberculosis that plagued him during his final years. Towards the end, he frequently experienced alcohol-induced blackouts. He was found in bed by a neighbor suffering from delirium clutching his girlfriend, Jeanne Hebuterne. He expired on January 24, 1920 at the age of 35. His 21-year-old muse Hebuterne was eight months pregnant with their second child. The day following his death, she leapt to her death from the fifth-floor window of her parent's home. His funeral was well attended by the Parisian artistic community and he is buried in Pere Lachaise.

The Mystique Of An Art Influencer and Unproductive Icon
Marcel Duchamp's Residences:
71 rue Caulaincourt, 75018 Paris
29 rue Campagne-Premiere, 75014 Paris

Marcel Duchamp became a cosmic jester amidst serious art historians during the early twentieth century. His sense of humor manifested itself publicly when he submitted a *Readymade* sculpture entitled *Fountain* which was a porcelain urinal laying sideways and hand signed *R. Mutt* at the base.

His submission during the Spring 1917 exhibition sponsored by the Society of Independent Artists in New York provoked shock, outrage and commentary. The irreverence behind the work questioned the essential adoration of art and ultimately what constitutes art.

The debate has raged since. Duchamp never felt an inclination or obligation to explain the motivations behind his work. His collective art has been associated with Cubism, Dadaism and conceptualism. His actual productivity as a painter and sculptor was marginal. Art historians have elevated him as one of the primary influential personalities of modern art. Duchamp would likely shrug his shoulders or smirk to himself at the designation.

More likely, he would return to his chessboard. He developed an obsession towards strategizing and playing chess. It may have been the sole occupation he took seriously even publishing books on complex chess theory. His talent level would never achieve elite playing status, but his artistic reputation made him one of the most celebrated followers of the game.

Duchamp was essentially a dabbler and sampler in grand artistic movements. He participated briefly as a Cubist creating two notable paintings, *Nude Descending a Staircase* and *The Bride Stripped Bare By Her Bachelors*.

He participated sporadically with the Dada group during World War I. Their activities included public gatherings, demonstrations and passionate coverage of unconventional art, politics and culture. The movement was credited with influencing subsequent styles such as surrealism. Duchamp ended his affiliation following World War I. He collaborated periodically with the surrealists, but never joined.

By mid-century, Duchamp rarely created artwork, keeping himself behind the scenes. Young artists including Robert Rauschenberg and Jasper Johns credited his influence with their production evolution. Duchamp became a fashionable icon to namedrop.

He continued to consult with artists, art dealers and collectors. Periodically he became involved with film projects. His final recorded art piece was released in 1966 entitled *Etant Donnes*. The work in typical Duchamp understatement required twenty years to create. The image is a disturbing view of a female nude cadaver, legs spread, visible through a peephole in a wooden door. The landscape background features a glowing lantern offering no plausible explanation for its appearance. The work is permanently installed in the Philadelphia Museum of Art.

The mystique behind Marcel Duchamp ended abruptly and peacefully in the early morning of October 2, 1968 at his home in Neuilly-sur-Seine. He had dined with friends the evening before, going to bed at 1:05 a.m. He collapsed in his studio and died of heart failure at the age of 81. The epitaph on his gravestone in Rouen aptly represents his whimsical life perspective reading: *Besides, it's always the others who die.*

A Groundbreaking Mixed Media Maestro
Man Ray's Residences:
31 rue Campagne-Premiere 75014 Paris
2bis rue Ferou, 75006 Paris

Emmanuel Radnitzkyl arrived in Paris during 1922 from New York City. He rechristened himself as *Man-Ray* as he shifted from painting to photography.

That same year, he composed his initial *rayographs*. He placed objects, materials and portions of his or his model's body onto a sheet of photosensitized paper and exposed them to light. These created negative images. Man Ray took an already existing technology and fashioned it into art. The irrational combinations and random arrangements of objects emphasized an abstraction of images. His collage compositions would become the forerunner of digital and Photoshop layered artwork.

Man Ray's work paralleled the evolution of the Dada movement into the more publicly accessible Surrealism. His pioneering photography evolved with a succession of muses and models between the two world wars. His first and most significant collaboration was with Kiki de Montparnasse (Alice Prin) who remained his companion during the 1920s.

When they met, she was already a celebrated character within Paris bohemian circles. Together she became the subject of some of his most celebrated photographic images and experimental films.

In 1929, the couple ended their relationship and he gravitated towards Surrealist photographer Lee Miller. She became his new photographic assistant replacing Kiki de Montparnasse. Together they collaborated on the photographic technique of solarization. Their relationship would only last until 1932.

Man Ray began a fresh series of iconic works capitalizing on the emerging vogue for African art.

His next partner two years later became Adrienne Fidelin, a Guadeloupean dancer and model who appeared in many of his photographs. By the beginning of World War II, Man Ray's international fame as a portrait photographer enabled him wisely to flee Paris during the German occupation. Fidelin opted to remain behind to care for her family.

During the war, he settled in Los Angeles until 1951, returning to his painting roots. He met and married dancer Juliet Browning. The couple would return to Paris in 1951 where he continued his work on new paintings, photographs, collages and art objects. His groundbreaking photography and experimental media prototypes became recognized and honored throughout the visual arts industry. He died in 1974 at the age of 86 from a lung infection.

A Celebrity Muse Whose Illumination Cruelly Dimmed
Kiki de Montparnasse's Residence:
31 rue Campagne-Premiere 75014 Paris

Kiki de Montparnasse is habitually linked to the artist Man Ray (Emmanuel Radnitzky). She herself was an accomplished artist. Their torrid seven-year love affair and working collaboration produced the most memorable artwork for both. She was the model for his photograph *Le Violon d'Ingres* that portrayed de Montparnasse's naked back marked in the dark room with the shapely f-holes of a violin. The effect was to compare the curves of a woman's form to the instrument.

She became Man Ray's primary avant-garde photographic muse, but also for numerous other artists, recreating her persona as fleetingly as changing costumes. She was a part-time actress, cabaret performer, painter and conceptual artist.

She was born Alice Ernestine Prin in a small Burgundy village and gravitated to Paris at the age of 12. She attended school only one year before working a series of dead-ended menial jobs. In 1917, she modeled nude for a sculptor and was disowned by her mother. She headed to the Montparnasse district homeless and befriended artist Chaim Soutine. He introduced her into a wider network of artists. The following year, she began an affair with Polish artist Maurice Mendjisky who painted her six times and branded the name *Kiki* on her, which would make her famous.

Kiki was local slang that varied widely in meaning, but often referred to an act of sexual intercourse.

In 1922, she changed partners becoming Man Ray's creative obsession and assistant. She managed his schedule, kept house and aided with translations due to his limited French skills.

She cultivated a personal following hanging out amongst the artistic community and becoming their pet celebrity. She dabbled in film, painting and even writing her memoirs at 28 with an introduction by Ernest Hemingway.

Her longevity within the spotlight peaked in 1929 following her rupture with Man Ray. She began dating cartoonist Henri Broca, even paying to publish his magazine *Paris-Montparnasse*.

Novelty can be as cruel as rewarding. She drifted steadily into obscurity. She gained weight adversely affecting her modeling career, drank and developed a dehabilitating cocaine habit leading to two arrests. She died destitute and sickly at the age of 51.

Childlike Abstractive Compositions By A Mature Artist
Joan Miro's Residence:
42 rue Blomet, 75015 Paris

Joan Miro Ferra was born in Barcelona in April 1893 and raised in the Barri Gotic neighborhood. His father was a middle class watchmaker and Miro initially followed a similar path towards commerce. At fourteen, he attended business school in Barcelona and classes in art studies at another local school. Following three years, he took a banal position as a clerk.

The world of conformity never appealed to him and shortly afterwards, he suffered a nervous breakdown. He resumed his art studies and began attending Francesc Gali's Escola d'Art academy between 1912 and 1915. In 1918, local art dealer Francis Picabia gave him his first solo show in his Barcelona gallery.

In 1920, Miro made his first trip to Paris where he encountered Spaniard Pablo Picasso. He befriended several local artists and became a fixture in Dada activities. He began dividing his time between Paris and Montroig, Spain.

Miro found Paris liberating and his exposure widened with his participation in Surrealist sponsored events. His work became showcased with a solo show at the Galerie la Licornia in 1921 and was included in the Salon d'Automne of 1923.

Over the subsequent fifteen years, he experimented with collages, pasted papers, lithography, etchings, ceramics and sculptures. His escapist themed works were often abstractive detached objects or figures composed in childlike simplicity. His early works were lumped with the cubist and fauve movements, despite their unique composition. Many defied literal explanation or even the appearance of trained draftsmanship.

In 1936, Miro left Spain due to the civil war. He returned upon its conclusion in 1941. During the post-war years, he began accumulating honors. He received the Grand Prize for Graphic Work at the Venice Biennale in 1954. In 1974, he and fellow Catalan artist Joseph Royo created a tapestry for inside the New York City World Trade Center. It would be destroyed during the September 11, 2001 attack.

He stressed his Catalan nationality and pride throughout his life. He died at his home on the island of Palma de Mallorca on Christmas Day, 1983 of heart failure. He would be buried at the Montjuic Cemetery in Barcelona.

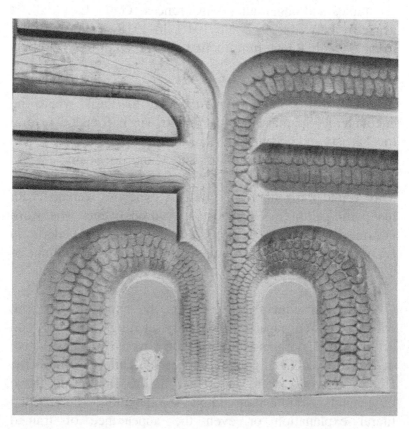

A Rebel Within The Surrealist Ranks
Andre Masson's Residence:
42 rue Blomet 75015 Paris

Andre Masson became known as an integral member of the Surrealism movement, best known for his automatic drawing works in pen and ink. Many abstract expressionists including Jackson Pollack credited him as an important influence. His erotic drawings often elicited adverse criticism by critics and governmental authorities. The Nazis classified his works as *degenerate* art.

He fought for France during World War I and was seriously injured. He evaded the German occupation of Paris by escaping by ship to the island of Martinique. He continued on to the United States. He had departed France hurriedly taking few possessions. Customs officials inspecting his luggage however found a cache of his erotic drawings.

Masson experimented with a variety of styles including throwing sand and glue onto canvas and making oil paintings based on the shapes that resulted. Many of his works were created under altered states of consciousness. After finding his automatic drawing technique too restricting, he abandoned the Surrealist movement opting for a more structured style. The results were compositions laced with violent and erotic themes.

Upon returning to France following World War II, he settled in Aix-en-Provence where he focused on the pastoral landscapes. He receded from public recognition and art world limelight. He passed away in Paris on October 28, 1987 at the age of 91.

Originality And Monopolizing Cobalt Blue
Yves Klein's Residence/Studio:
14 rue Campagne-Premiere, 75014 Paris

Visual artist Yves Klein attempted to monopolize the color cobalt blue during a creative stage between 1949 and 1962. He petitioned to have the color renamed *International Klein Blue*. He would be commissioned to design interiors of theatre and performance venues employing his signature monochrome color.

His 1960 staging of an art exhibition at the Paris Galerie Internationale d'Art Contemporain became legendary. Dressed in a black tuxedo, he escorted nude female models swathed in cobalt blue paint to press their bodies on a blank canvas. The remaining impression would become the artwork. He personally made no direct contact with the models, instead conducted a background orchestra in a sustained D-Major chord performance.

Klein formed a *Nouveau Realisme* clique that included many of the most renowned names in French Pop Art. Arman, Jean Tinguely, Niki de Saint Phalle and Christo followed his lead along with other popular conceptual artists.

Klein was distinctive with another passion. During his formative years at the Ecole Nationale des Langues Orientales, he began practicing judo. He attained a 4th degree black belt by the age of 25 and even wrote a book on the subject.

His internationally renowned photograph *Le Saut* (The Void) became his best-known work. The remarkable picture displays Klein fearlessly leaping off a wall, arm outstretched, towards the open pavement. The image was originally published in his 1960 art book *Dimanche*. The print was obviously retouched in the darkroom to eliminate his padded landing below.

As bold and daring as Klein's art became, he also shared vulnerability and sensitivity towards ridicule. In 1962, an Italian documentary called *Mondo Cane*, considered shocking, showcased numerous absurd, sometimes staged and excessive global cultural practices.

A recreation of Klein's female blue model paintings was displayed restaged during five minutes of the cinematographic freak show. Klein became upset viewing the final cut of the movie at the Cannes Film Festival on May 11, 1962. He felt that the directors had purposely misled and humiliated him towards their intentions. Afterwards, Klein suffered the first stages of a heart attack. Two more cardiac arrests would follow resulting in his death on June 6 at the age of 34.

Ironically, he was immersed during that period with creating artwork out of coffins and tombs. He was also extending his female tracing theme with gas flames creating a scorched silhouette impression around his models.

An Obsessive Recreation Of The Human Malaise
Albert Giacometti's Studio Location:
46 rue Hippolyte-Maindron, 75014 Paris

Inside his spare and spartan studio, Alberto Giacometti obsessively labored on his emaciated figures of humanity. He became best known for these tall, thin human figures that he fashioned between postwar 1945 until 1960. Observers sensed an isolation, fear and loneliness behind each work. Many concluded that they represented the sadness and detachment of the Cold War era.

Giacometti was a relentless perfectionist that routinely acknowledged that he had failed to capture the human depiction that he pursued. As his sculptures became larger in height, their thinnest created an unsettling appearance. His principle female model was his wife Annette Arm, a former secretary for the Red Cross. They met in 1946 and married four years later.

Another series of walking men sculptures expressed his interpretation of individuals austerely striding through the pace and emptiness of contemporary society.

Giacometti was born in Borgonovo. Switzerland, the eldest of four children to a well-known post-Impressionist painter Giovanni Giacometti. Two of his brothers, Diego and Bruno would become renowned artists and architects. Alberto attended the Geneva School of Fine Arts before relocating to Paris to study under sculptor Antoine Bourdelle, an associate of Auguste Rodin. His early professional associations included Joan Miro, Max Ernst, Pablo Picasso and Balthasar Rola (Balthus).

Giacometti experimented with the prevalent styles of Cubism and Surrealism. From the outset, his works were clearly distinctive. He began sculpting the human head and then expanded with figuratives featuring elongated limbs. The finished and often tortured outcomes epitomized his imperfect concept of perspective reality. During World War II, he took refuge in Switzerland and concentrated on constructing sculptures as thin as nails reduced to fit neatly into a cigarette package. When he returned to Paris following the war, he enlarged the miniature prototypes into his full-scale works.

His hand drawn portraits and oil paintings consistently employed neutral and sparsely colored backgrounds. Any torso outline became generally insignificant with light sketching. The intense gaze of his models emerged through precision strokes using paint, pencil or charcoal. These repeated strokes added layers of surface depth ultimately resulting in a head and face with distinctive features emerging. Many of his finished works created the appearance of deep-set, contoured eye-sockets and hollowed out cheeks. The effect became mesmerizing to the viewer as through the portrait sitter was staring through them.

In 1958, Giacometti was asked to create a monumental sculpture for the Chase Manhattan Bank building in New York City. The projected large-scale installation terrified him. He became dissatisfied by the relationship with the sculpture and the structural site. The commission was never begun.

He was awarded the grand prize for sculpture at the 1962 Venice Biennale resulting in further worldwide acclaim. His success never altered his grand objective towards portraying the human figure. He could never concede that he had been successful.

The year following his triumph, he was diagnosed with stomach cancer and would undergo surgery in February. He made his only American visit in 1965 for an exhibition of his works at the Museum of Modern Art in New York. His career had peaked, but not reached any level of plateau. He doubtlessly envisioned substantially more to contribute. As his health steadily declined, he reconciled himself to his impending demise. In 1966, he would die of heart disease in the canton hospital in Chur, Switzerland. He was buried close to his parents in his hometown.

His sole heir was his wife Annette who labored to compile a full listing of his authenticated works. Although his sculptures, drawings and paintings were distinctively unique, they were frequently counterfeited due to their escalating value. When she died in 1993, the French government established the Fondation Giacometti.

In May 2007, the executor of Annette Giacometti's estate, former French foreign minister Roland Dumas was convicted of illegally consigning some of Alberto's works to Jacques Tajan, a premium level auctioneer.

A Triumphant 1971 Painting Retrospective Darkened By Suicide
Francis Bacon's Early Residence:
Hotel des Ecoles, 35 rue Delambre, 75004 Paris
Grand Palais Art Exhibition:
3 avenue du General Eisenhower, 75008 Paris

Irish painter Francis Bacon first traveled to France in 1927 at the age of eighteen. He had lived the previous two months in Berlin indulging in the gay underworld and drifting professionally.

Paris offered him an intimate glimpse of the modern art universe for a year and a half via gallery and museum exhibitions. For three months during his stay, he lived with Yvonne Bocquentin and her family. She was a pianist and art collector. Her family lived in the suburbs near Chantilly. His inability to master French prompted him to return to London in late 1928 to begin work as an interior designer.

When Bacon returned to Paris in October 1971, his gripping figurative paintings had made him a celebrity. His much-anticipated Grand Palais retrospective would become darkened by a real life tragedy. Two days before the opening, the artist's lover George Dyer's corpse was discovered slumped over the toilet inside his room at the Hotel des Saint Peres.

His death was due to a deliberate drug overdose. Bacon's handlers and associates managed to collaborate with the hotel and police to remain silent about the suicide until the day following the opening ceremony.

Dyer and Bacon had shared a troubled and turbulent past. Dyer had originally met Bacon in 1963 when he reportedly crashed through his studio skylight during a burglary attempt. Others sources have claimed they simply met at a pub. East

End Londoner Dyer was a petty criminal that Bacon often acknowledged was *too nice* to become a successful criminal.

There were numerous theories speculated as to why Dyer had consumed an overdose of barbiturates. The accepted conclusion was that that his role in Bacon's life was rapidly diminishing. The suicide was viewed as his attempt at attention and to tarnish or sabotage the importance of the exhibition. Dyer had served as the model for numerous Bacon paintings.

Bacon was already acknowledged as Britain's *greatest living* painter. His ultimate ambition was to ascend to the highest level of European art occupied by visionary Pablo Picasso.

Bacon's overall subject matter navigated within the realm of shock and sleaze. His novelty integrated perfectly into the Parisian artistic palette. His most renowned works, the screaming Pope series, animalistic figuratives and disturbing triptychs had vaulted him into international recognition. The brutality portrayed by his images often attracted vicious criticism. Bacon, whether admired or loathed, was not an artist to be simply overlooked.

The man himself was accessible, articulate and irreverent. In London, he spent his time painting, dining, drinking and gambling in modest Soho establishments.

He freely distained religion and confessed that humans were *bodies without souls*. He would remain deeply affected by Dyer's death. He spent the balance of his stay in Paris attending to promotional activities and funeral arrangements. He did not publicly express his pain, but remained stoic throughout the dark aftermath and Dyer's funeral.

Over the subsequent two years, he would return to paint the image of Dyer as a form of therapy and inspiration. One of his grimmest paintings was entitled *Black Triptych*, depicting Dyer sitting on the toilet moments before and after his suicide. In typical Bacon style, he often painted clearest amongst bleak depression while suffering from emotional and physical breakdowns.

The 1971 Paris exhibition would result in triumph and anticipated recognition. Bacon's work would continue themes stressing a preoccupation with blood, morbidity and death. Many spectators found his works too graphic and disturbing to appreciate. His supporters felt that he'd frozen the proper repulsion and horror mirroring contemporary angst.

While on holiday in Madrid during 1992, he was admitted to a private health clinic. His chronic asthma had developed into a more severe respiratory condition inhibiting his breathing. He died of a heart attack on April 28, 1992. His estate subsequently became entangled and complicated, particularly involving his gallery representation. In 1998, the contents and haphazard arrangement of his London studio were surveyed, moved and reconstructed into the Hugh Lane Gallery in Dublin.

Grand Palais

revolutionaies

The Posthumously Disgraced Leader of the French Revolution
Count Mirabeau Residence:
42 rue de la Chaussee d'Antin (Death Site), 75009 Paris

Honore Gabriel Riqueti, the Count of Mirabeau died at the peak of his acclaim and involvement with the French Revolution. As a previous nobleman, he had been involved with various scandals that had compromised his reputation. His previous gambling debts, violent disposition and rash behavior landed him in prison at the Chateau de Vincennes.

His oration skills at the beginning of the Revolution sanitized his past and vaulted him into a top leadership role in the political hierarchy between 1789-1791.

He was considered a *voice of the people* and known for his politics of moderation in an increasing radical Revolutionary Council. He was one of the few voices advocating the continuance of the French throne. He envisioned a constitutional monarchy structured similarly to Great Britain.

His health ultimately betrayed him from the excesses of his youth and the strenuous toll from political activity. In 1791, he contracted pericarditis, an inflammation of the sac surrounding the heart. He continued his duties as President of the National Assembly until his death on April 2, 1791 at the age of 42. He was feted with an extravagant funeral and buried in the Pantheon. His legacy at that moment elevated him into a national hero and one of the esteemed early leaders of the revolution.

The following year, that perception changed radically. During the trial of Louis XVI, it was unveiled that Mirabeau had secretly acted as an intermediary of the monarchy for payment by the nation's Austrian enemies. His duplicity reversed his status to national traitor. His remains were removed from the Pantheon and replaced with those of Jean-Paul Marat. He was buried anonymously in a Clamart graveyard.

Numerous historians have advocated that Mirabeau, had he lived longer, might have spared France from the notorious *Reign of Terror* following his death. They are mistaken. His moderate views were already receding in popularity at the time of his death. Compromise between the king and revolutionaries would have been impossible. The ultimate disclosure of his clandestine payments would have sealed his demise. Instead of a celebrated natural death, he would have faced the guillotine following their disclosure.

42 rue de la Chaussee

A Nearly Discarded Revolutionary Voice Becomes A Martyr
Jean-Paul Marat's Residence (Demolished)
18 Rue de l'Ecole de Medicine, 75006 Paris
Marat's Bathtub (Musee Grevin)
10 Boulevard Montmartre, 75009 Paris

Jean-Paul Marat was described as *a man short in stature, deformed in person, and hideous in face*. The fifty-year-old Marat had a debilitating skin disease that some observers suggested was syphilis. Others have claimed that is was a rare condition called dermatitis herpetiformis. His skin itched continuously with extensive blistering. He spent most of his last three years in his bathtub. He soaked in various minerals and medicines to reduce his discomfort and had a bandana soaked with vinegar wrapped around his head.

He became a radical journalist and politician during the French Revolution. His writings were fierce and uncompromising towards the leaders and institutions. His publication *L'Ami du Peuple* (Friend of the People) was unsparing in its venom and wrath. He was blamed for inciting the *September Massacres* that occurred during September 2-6, 1792 when approximately 1,500 prisoners were slain by radical law enforcement groups.

Forced to retire from the Revolutionary Convention due to his worsening skin condition, he continued to work and write from home where he soaked in his medicinal bath. His role in the government had waned and most of the Convention members began ignoring his letters.

On July 13, 1793, twenty-four-year old Charlotte Corday from Caen appeared at his apartment door. She claimed to have important information on escaped Girondin Party members who'd relocated to Normandy. Marat asked her to enter his bath chamber despite his wife's protests against. For fifteen minutes they conversed. He wrote out a list of names to investigate that she had verbally provided him with. He promised her their that each would be guillotined despite no longer having the authority to do so.

Marat did not realize that Corday was a Girondin sympathizer from a ruined royalist family. She rose from her chair after their talk and withdrew a five-inch kitchen knife from her corset. She thrust the knife into his chest. The massive bleeding from the stabbing proved fatal almost instantly. His last feeble words were directed towards his wife asking for assistance.

Corday would be arrested and charged with murder. Expressing no remorse, she testified at her trial that she carried out the murder alone adding *I killed one man to save 100,000*. She would be convicted and guillotined on July 17. Jean-Jacques Hauer completed a haunting and pensive portrait of her a few hours before her execution. Writer Alphonse de Lamartine would later call her the *Angel of Assassination*.

The Revolution had added a fresh martyr to its cause partially due to a heroic painting entitled *The Death of Marat* by Jacques-Louis David.

His fabled bathtub would follow its own provenance journey. Marat's wife sold it to her journalist neighbor. It was then purchased and relocated to Morbihan in Brittany. A journalist for *Le Figaro* tracked down the tub in 1885. The Musee Carnavalet refused to purchase it due to concerns regarding its ownership. The Musee Grevin had no such reservations. They acquired the tub where it remains on display.

18 rue de l'Ecole de Medicine

10 boulevard Montmartre

The Silenced Voice of the French Revolution
Georges Danton's Residence:
1 cour du Commerce Saint-Andre, 75006 Paris

Every uprising requires a charismatic spokesperson. The French Revolution elevated Georges Danton to that role until he tired of the role.

He was born in October 1759 in the Champagne region of northeastern France. His father Jacques was a respectable attorney. As a baby, he was attacked by a bull and trampled by pigs. Smallpox disfigured and scarred his face. What he lacked in aesthetics, he compensated by charisma and persuasion.

In 1780, he settled in Paris and began law studies becoming a clerk. By June 1787, he became a member of the king's council. He married and settled in a six-room apartment in the Left Bank. He would have three sons, one who died in infancy. His wife Antoinette would die in February 1793 while giving birth to their fourth son as he was traveling on a mission in Belgium.

Upon his return to Paris one week later, the grief stricken Danton would open her coffin and kiss her face repeatedly. He implored her pardon for his numerous sexual indiscretions. He had her death mask created. He would marry sixteen-year-old Louise Geley in July. She had been a friend of the family and took care of their children.

Danton was a man who pursued his passions vigorously. Once the Revolution ignited, he became intimately involved. He first became a deputy to the Paris Commune presiding in the Cordeliers district. In August 1792, he became the Minister of Justice and was blamed for inciting a series of September massacres. In Spring 1793, he supported the foundation of a Revolutionary Tribunal and became the initial president of the Committee of Public Safety.

Throughout the bloody summer of 1793, Danton recoiled at the excesses authorized by the Tribunal. He lost his seat on the committee and developed a fatal rivalry with Maximilien Robespierre. He had shifted towards a moderation viewpoint contrary to the momentum of the *Reign of Terror* movement that he would condemn. He made speeches denouncing the killing crusade, but he was far too late.

In early April 1794 he became entangled in a scandal involving the bankruptcy of the French East India Company. His growing number of adversaries particularly Robespierre used the opportunity to indict him. He was charged with conspiracy, bribery and leniency towards enemies of the Revolution.

At his trial on April 3-5, Danton displayed a forceful oration and rebuttal to the charges. The spectator crowd cheered him on. He openly recognized that his fate had already been decided. No advocates dared defend him for fear of the resulting consequences. He was condemned to death and promptly executed with fifteen others on April 5. Fellow revolutionary Camille Desmoulins was beheaded third and Danton last. They were buried in the Errancis Cemetery. In the mid-19th century, their skeletal remains were transferred to the Catacombs of Paris.

He earned a measure of revenge on his rival when Robespierre was later arrested and unable to speak at his trial due to a fractured jaw. One spectator shouted to Robespierre as he attempted vainly to respond to charges, *the blood of Danton chokes him!*

It is difficult to measure and evaluated the life of Georges Danton. Like the majority of revolutionaries, he perished young at thirty-four. Historians have acknowledged him as the primary force in the overthrow of the French monarchy and establishment of the First French Republic.

Once the existing leadership and social structure was demolished, the extremes committed during the Revolution appeared far worse. Danton was described as *towering, athletic, coarse, and his voice shook the domes of the halls.* Would he have been capable of ultimately subjugating his energies to govern with moderation, forgiveness and mercy?

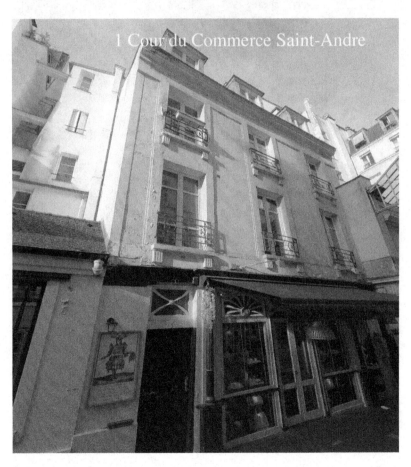

1 Cour du Commerce Saint-Andre

Public Sculpture of Georges Danton

Drowning Out The Press Urging Moderation
Camille Desmoulins' Residence:
22 rue du Theatre Francaise, 75006 Paris

Camille Desmoulins required a momentous event such as the storming of the Bastille to elevate his writings into exposure. He was an unsuccessful Parisian lawyer and regularly on the cusp of poverty.

His stutter inhibited his public speaking. Upon the sudden dismissal of popular finance minister Jacques Necker by King Louis XVI, he discovered his eloquence. On July 12, 1789, he reportedly leapt upon a table at the Café du Foy located in the gardens of the Palais Royale. He gave a passionate speech without stammering urging patriots to *take up arms*. He was convinced that a large number of soldiers massed in the city were preparing an imminent massacre of dissidents.

His audience shared his alarm and armed themselves with rifles, knives, pitchforks and pistols. Two days later, mobs streamed towards the Bastille prison and destroyed it.

Un until his fiery speech, Desmoulins was scarcely known. He had written a radical pamphlet the month before entitled *La France Libre* (The Free France). Parisian publishers refused to print it. His association with the Bastille raid elevated his public profile. His work would finally be published in September cementing his reputation as an ardent revolutionary.

His hard-edged text stressed the necessity to rid France of King Louis XVI. Desmoulins' own fate became intertwined amidst the surging currents of the Revolution. No lapse of moderation was tolerated. Desmoulins passionate printed accusations were blamed for the condemnation of several political figures including former friends. His own life would soon be heaved into the cauldron.

In December 1793, Desmoulins began publishing *Le Vieux Cordelier* that espoused slowing the momentum of the *Reign of Terror*. His timing was premature. The fervor to implicate and prosecute was still raw. Blood saturated the public squares and incited hysteria with each guillotine execution.

The Revolutionary leadership was splintering. Desmoulins' boyhood friend and fanatical classmate Maximilien Robespierre could not muzzle or control commanding orator George Danton. Danton was wearied by the daily carnage. Desmoulins sided with Danton's position and faction.

He published six editions of *Le Vieux Cordelier* before he was arrested along with Danton and brought before the Revolutionary Tribunal. The two men would share an identical fate. Both would be condemned for treason and sentenced to death on April 5, 1794. They were executed amongst a contingent of fifteen prisoners at the Place de la Revolution. Desmoulins was beheaded third and Danton last.

For Robespierre, the trauma of his condemnation pricked his conscience. He had served as a witness to Desmoulins' marriage with his wife Lucille in 1782. Within his rigid and purist code, he could not conceive of a crevice for sentimentality. One week following Desmoulins' death, his wife would also be executed. Robespierre realized that the deaths of Danton and Desmoulins were preludes to the end of the Revolutionary ideals and movement.

Barely three months later, Robespierre would be stripped of his authority, arrested and guillotined at the identical location as his former friends and allies.

Desmoulins Residence

TWISTED TOUR GUIDES.com

The Bloodied Hands of A Pure Ideologue
Maximilien Robespierre Residence:
20 rue de Saintonge (formerly 30), 75003 Paris
Rights of Man and Supreme Being Memorial (Champs de Mars):
2 allee Adrienne Lecouvreur, 75007 Paris

Maximilien Robespierre obsession with forming the ideal French Republic regardless of human cost ultimately sacrificed him his own life. He was one of the most complex and conflictive figures emerging from the French Revolution. He ultimately inspired the *Reign of Terror* that targeted royalists, aristocrats and even moderate reformists.

Under Robespierre ideology, there could exist no compromise. His rise from being a practicing lawyer to Member of the Committee of Public Safety during the Revolution was rapid. He campaigned for universal manhood suffrage offering the right to vote for people of color, Jews, actors and domestic staffs. Predictably, he omitted women from these rights.

He advocated the abolition of slavery and clerical celibacy. Many considered him an advocate for male citizens without a political voice. Throughout an estimated 900 public speeches, he urged unrestricted admission to the National Guard, public offices, commissioned ranks of the army, the right to petition and right to bear arms in self-defense. He stressed an obsession towards public morality absent a deity.

Many of his reforms resonated soundly, but the practicality of his envisioned overhaul became catastrophic. During his *Reign of Terror*, an estimated 300,000 suspects were arrested, 17,000 were officially executed and 10,000 died in prison without receiving a trial.

The pinnacle of his influence arrived on June 8, 1794 when the Festival of the Supreme Being was staged on an elevated platform at the Champs de Mars. The event was scheduled for the same day as traditional Pentecost. Robespierre would deliver two speeches emphasizing the concept of a Supreme Being and denounce the existence of Jesus Christ and Mohammed.

His fanaticism and radicalism alarmed members of the Revolutionary Convention and general public. He and his allies were arrested in the Paris town hall on 9 Thermidor, Year II (July 27, 1794). He was wounded in his jaw during his capture that many have speculated was self-inflicted. A doctor would remove some of his teeth and fragments of his broken jaw. A bandage held his jaw intact that would be torn off later by his executioner.

He would be executed with approximately 90 other radicals the following day in the blood drenched Place de la Revolution. He was 36-years-old. The sequence of his arrest and death would become known as the Thermidorian Reaction.

Measuring his legacy has proved problematic. His idealism that stressed creating virtue and sovereignty for individuals was admirable. His monstrous approach to pursing this goal and subsequent terror was unpardonable. He has been aligned as a staunch defender of democracy, yet his version could never be sustained.

20 rue de Saintonge

Rights of Man Memorial

TWISTED TOUR GUIDES.com

The Father Of A Movement Without A Patriarch
Pierre-Joseph Proudhon's Residence:
18 rue de Passy, 75016 Paris

Pierre-Joseph Proudhon was the first acknowledged person to declare himself an *anarchist*. Many consider him the father of a movement that had no patriarch. Proudhon described the liberty he pursued as the *synthesis of community and property*. He coined the term *property is theft!* in his 1840 publication.

He began a correspondence with Karl Marx afterwards, but the two ended their friendship when Proudhon defended his translator Karl Grun who Marx detested. The pair shared several common ideological beliefs, but differed on their means of implementation.

Proudhon was more theorist than activist. He was born in Besancon on January 15, 1809 and rigorously pursued a path of education despite his family's poverty. His father was a brewer and cooper and had great difficulty providing resources for his five sons. Pierre-Jacques would be ridiculed at school by classmates for his weathered shoes and shoddy clothing.

He supplemented his instruction by reading extensively from the school library during his free time outside of class. His father was unable to afford his full tuition, but the assistance from one of his employers enabled Pierre-Joseph to attend the local city college.

In 1827, Proudhon began an apprenticeship at a regional printing house. Over the next decade, he began examining his own religious beliefs. He taught himself Latin and Hebrew in order to understand the texts (frequently religious) that he was printing.

456

He relocated to Paris in 1838 living modestly, soberly and reportedly dressing as a peasant. He wrote exhaustively for bare compensation, but remained readily available to anyone seeking his advice or guidance on his writings. His work was neither popular nor widely accepted by Parisian authorities. His scholarly compositions would consume his daylight hours on a variety of political and philosophical concepts. He would be put on trial in 1842. His jury would acquit him because they determined that they could not condemn him for a philosophy that they could not understand.

He was considered a solitary thinker who varied little from his daily routine of writing about the legitimacy and activities of the French government. He resisted the temptation to socialize by regimentally sleeping by 9:00 p.m.

His life focused obsessively around a newspaper that he operated. Local authorities would shut it down and condemned him to pay a hefty fine. He married while incarcerated at the St. Pelagie Prison.

Proudhon had very pronounced complaints against authority that remain relevant today. He defined the burden of living under a government as *being watched, inspected, spied upon, directed, numbered, regulated, censured, preached at, hoaxed, deported* and beset by other restrictive chains. He summarized the entire institution as immoral defined by a warped sense of justice and control.

He proposed a society without authority stressing a decentralized federal government. He opposed dictatorship, militarism, nationalism and war. He defined anarchy *as the absence of a master or sovereign.*

Whether Proudhon's philosophy could have ever been truly implemented remains an unresolved issue. Anarchy remained a topic of discussion throughout the late nineteenth century.

The movement expanded during the era and into the early twentieth century. The practical application was usually manifested in civil unrest and political assassinations.

Proudhon would modify many of his rigid ideological beliefs as he aged. He would die in January 1865 at the age of 56 never having witnessed Marx's writings take root within Europe. He would also miss a version of his doctrine employed by the 1871 Paris Commune uprising.

Proudhon opposed both capitalism and rejected the excesses of centralized control espoused by communism. His writings would fade from public scrutiny. He became a figure relegated as a *thinker without a cause* lacking a violent popular force to install his purest theories into practice.

The Refinement of Communist Philosophy
Early Meeting of Karl Marx and Friedrich Engels (Café de la Regence):
155 rue St. Honore, 75001 Paris
Chess Matches Between Vladimir Lenin, Leon Trotsky and French Poet Guillaume Apollinaire (La Closerie des Lilas):
171 boulevard du Montparnasse, 75006 Paris

Karl Marx's Residences:
23 rue Vaneau, 75007 Paris
38 rue Vaneau, 75007 Paris
Daniel Stern's Salons:
29 quai Voltaire, 75007 Paris
38 boulevard Malesherbes, 75008 Paris

Vladimir Lenin's Residences:
3 rue de l'Estrapade, 75005 Paris
24 rue Beaunier, 75014 Paris
4 rue Marie-Rose, 75014 Paris
110 avenue General Lederc, 75014 Paris
Vladimir Lenin's Mistress Ines Armaud Residence:
2 rue Marie-Rose, 75014 Paris

Leon Trotsky's Residences:
Hotel d'Odessa: 28 rue d'Odessa, 75014 Paris
27 rue Oudry, 7513 Paris
23 rue de l'Amiral Mouchez, 75014 Paris
46 rue Gassendi, 75014 Paris

Ho Chi Minh Residence:
9 Villa Compoint, 75017 Paris

Paris has historically been the vortex for philosophical thought, dissent and writings no matter how unpopular. *The Manifesto of the Communist Party* was a collaboration between Karl Marx and Friedrich Engels published in 1848.

The work identified the party leadership as the guiding force and educating body of the working class, termed the *proletariat*.

Karl Marx and Friedrich Engels

Numerous sources have acknowledged Marx and Engels initial or second meeting at the Café de la Regence during August 1844. The then popular cafe no longer exists, but was located in the vicinity of where Joan of Arc and her armies attempted to breach the fortified walls of Paris in September 1429. Marx and Engels had previously established a written correspondence, but their backgrounds were significantly different. Engels was a journalist and activist, but also a businessman. His father owned large textile factories in Lancashire, England and Barmen, Prussia. His writings regarding the abuses of the working class were derived from direct management exposure and observation. He was a fierce opponent of child labor and his perspective often contradicted his more conservative father.

Engels lived near Manchester, England until 1844 espousing radical politics in his writings. His primary visit(s) to Paris involved sessions with Marx while traveling to Germany. They forged a close friendship and Marx assimilated Engel's views on the working class into his own evolving philosophy.

During his English residence, Engels met Mary Burns, a fierce young Irish woman that was employed in his factory. They established a romantic relationship that extended twenty years until her death. Both rejected marriage as an archaic institution. Engels developed a reputation for cultivating numerous sexual liaisons, many with French prostitutes.

Engels became a critical financial benefactor to Marx during his French residency. Marx was an impoverished intellectual.

His Jewish father, Heinrich had studied law at the French University in Mainz and had converted to Protestantism when Russia annexed the Rhineland territory to preserve his position. Karl Marx studied in Trier along the Moselle River. Political opposition in Prussia to his published writings prompted he and his fiancé Jenny von Westphalen to relocate to Paris from October 1843 until January 1845. The couple would later marry.

They would reside in two different addresses on the rue Vaneau. The first at 23 rue Vaneau was also the home of German political leader German Maurer, who headed a group called *Leader of the Just*. The second residence at 38 rue Vaneau accommodated their space requirements for their first child named Jenny. The three-bedroom apartment became an important hosting and political debate center for guests including Engles and Pierre-Joseph Proudhon.

During Marx's residence on rue Vaneau, there were fields and ponds located on the eastern side belonging to the ruling Orleans branch of the Bourbon family. Marx was a frequent guest to Daniel Stern's (Marie d'Agoult) salon on the Quai Voltaire. Agoult had formerly lived with her lover Hungarian composer and pianist Franz Liszt prior to establishing her cultural gathering.

Marx's writings in the journal *Vorwarts* put him at odds with the Prussian
king resulting in pressure exerted on Guizot, the French Prime Minister. He was expelled from Paris on February 3, 1845 and relocated to Brussels. Three years later he would return briefly in March viewing firsthand the revolution toppling the French government of Louis-Philippe. His observations convinced him that the world could only change through actual, physical and material activity.

While in Paris, he spoke to a Citizens Group located on the rue St. Martin and spent several nights at the Hotel Manchester before leaving for Cologne. He would periodically return to Paris under assumed names and stay with his eldest daughter. Towards the end of 1881, both his wife and daughter died abruptly leaving him distraught. He would die on March 14, 1883 at the age of 64. He was buried in London's Highgate Cemetery in a section reserved for agnostics and atheists.

Vladimir Lenin and Leon Trotsky

Vladimir Lenin and Leon Trotsky would crystallize the communist philosophy into the Bolshevik party of the Soviet Union. Lenin arrived in Paris originally in 1908 following his initial attempt at revolution against the Tsar failed three years earlier. He initially lived in the Pantheon district, but inhabited several locations throughout the city with his wife, mother-in-law and sister.

Lenin enjoyed repose, cultivated Russian friendships and devoted hours of study at the National Library. He devoured materials regarding the Paris Commune uprising of 1871 that would prove influential to his own organizational political designs.

Amidst his Parisian exile, Lenin cultivated a profoundly intimate relationship with French communist activist Ines Armand. She became his mistress, ideological comrade and neighbor. She was already married to Alexander Armand from one of Russia's wealthiest families. Her devotion towards Lenin remained constant until her own death in 1920. Although her role was downplayed in the Soviet press, Lenin considered her *the love of his life*. She was given the honor of a national funeral and buried in the Necropolis of the Kremlin wall.

Lenin would return to his beloved Russia following the 1917 February Revolution that ousted the Tsar. The October Revolution ascended the Bolsheviks to power. Communism would evolve into one of the greatest experimental travesties in western culture during the twentieth century. The government of Josef Stalin accentuated the abuses and failure.

Stalin's chief ideological rival was Lev Davidovtich Bronstein, better known as Leon Trotsky. He arrived into Paris alone during November 1914 lodging at the Hotel d'Odessa. Several addresses have been attributed to his local stay, but his designation as an *undesirable enemy alien* made his welcome abbreviated.

During his stint in Paris, he regularly played chess with Lenin and French poet Guillaume Apollinaire at La Closerie des Lilas on Montparnasse Boulevard. The club no longer exists. The French police would escort and deport Trotsky to the Spanish border on March 31, 1916.

He would become a key participant in the October 1917 Revolution and initial Politburo leadership group. Upon Lenin's death from a stroke on January 21, 1924, Stalin and Trotsky battled for leadership control. Stalin outmaneuvered Trotsky and the Politburo expelled him from the Soviet Union in February 1929.

He spent the rest of his life in exile aware that Stalin maintained an active vendetta against him. In August 1940, he was assassinated by his daughter's fiancé inside his home in Mexico City. The assassin, Ramon Mercader was an agent of the Soviet secret police. Trotsky's name would not be officially *rehabilitated* in Russian history until 2001 by the Russian Federation.

Ho Chi Minh

Ho Chi Minh would become a reviled western villain while governing the communist regime in North Vietnam. He had completed his formative studies in Vietnam before relocating to Paris in 1919. He worked in the Ritz Carlton Hotel restaurant scraping by and blunted with his ambitions for higher education. His father was a Confucian scholar and minor colonial administrator.

Minh cultivated an intense belief in Vietnamese identity and independence from colonial rule. The evolution of his Marxist beliefs remains vague, but his conclusion towards the aim of self-government became crystalline. Despite the cost in lives, he determined that assistance from the People's Republic of China, not western powers offered the most pragmatic path towards self-government. The Vietnam War escalated into an international travesty and for the United States, an unwinnable conflict.

Was the war ultimately preventable?

Site of Former Cafe Regence

Former Site La Closerie des Lilas

23 rue Vaneau

38 rue Vaneau

3 rue de l'Estrapade

TWISTED TOUR GUIDES.com

Author, photographer and visual artist Marques Vickers was born in 1957 in Vallejo, California. He graduated from Azusa Pacific University in Los Angeles and became the Public Relations and Executive Director for the Burbank, California Chamber of Commerce between 1979-84.

Professionally, he has operated travel, apparel, wine, rare book and publishing businesses. His paintings and sculptures have been exhibited in art galleries, private collections and museums in the United States and Europe. He has previously lived in the Burgundy and Languedoc regions of France and currently lives in the South Puget Sound region of Western Washington.

He has written and published over one hundred and forty books spanning a diverse variety of subjects including true crime, international travel, social satire, wine production, architecture, history, fiction, auctions, fine art, poetry and photojournalism.

He has two daughters, Charline and Caroline who reside in Europe.

Made in United States
North Haven, CT
31 December 2024

63773818R00261